IMAGES
of America

THE MISSISSIPPI RIVER: FATHER OF WATERS

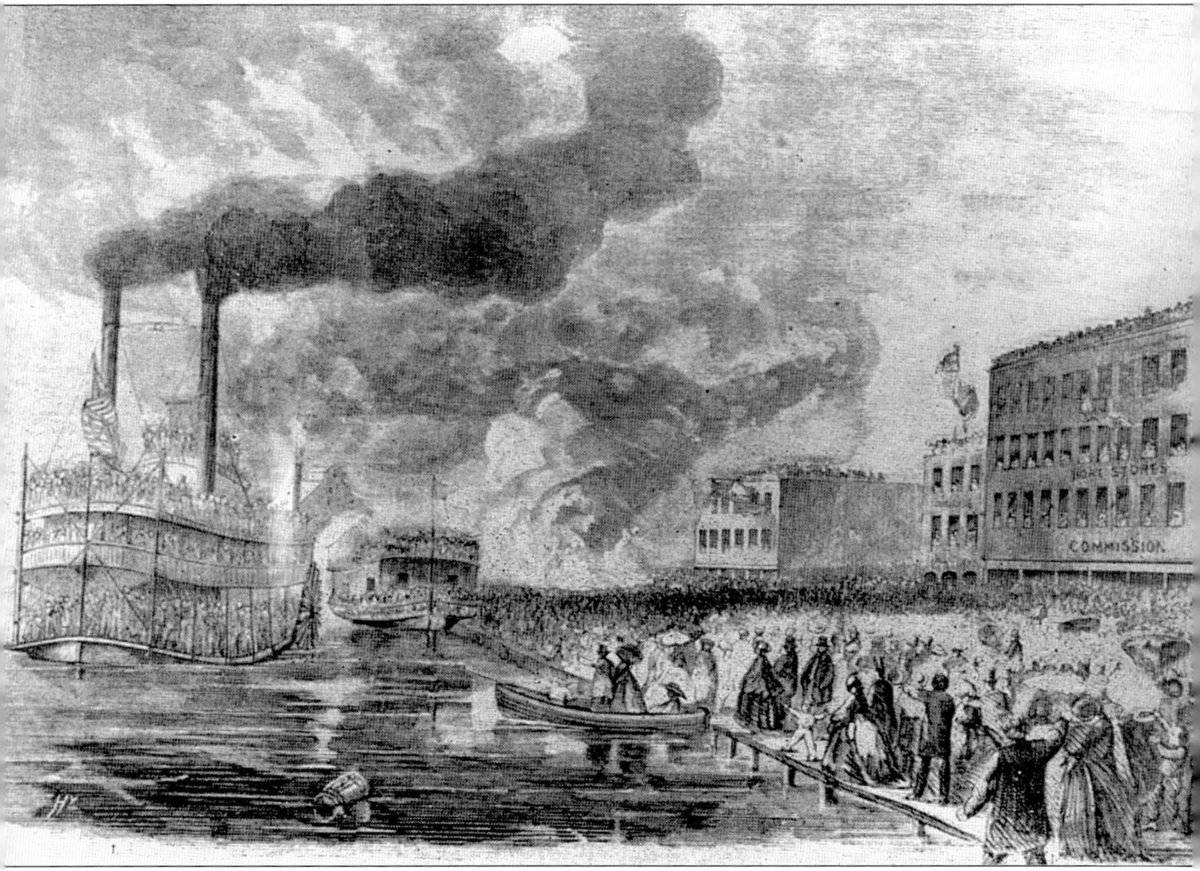

The steamboat *Alhambra* pulls away from the dock in 1861 at Dubuque, Iowa in this steel engraving. Aboard are the Governors' Greys and Jackson's Guards. Organized in 1859, the Governors' Greys' services were pledged by Governor Samuel Kirkwood in 1861 to President James Buchanan, Lincoln's predecessor. The Iowa unit was the first in the nation to tender its services to their country and is pictured here, leaving to fight in the Civil War.

IMAGES
of America

THE MISSISSIPPI RIVER: FATHER OF WATERS

James L. Shaffer and John T. Tigges

ARCADIA
PUBLISHING

ISBN 978-0-7385-0745-3

Published by Arcadia Publishing
Charleston, South Carolina

Printed in the United States of America

Library of Congress Catalog Card Number: 00108690

For all general information contact Arcadia Publishing at:
Telephone 843-853-2070
Fax 843-853-0044
E-mail sales@arcadiapublishing.com
For customer service and orders:
Toll-Free 1-888-313-2665

Visit us on the Internet at www.arcadiapublishing.com

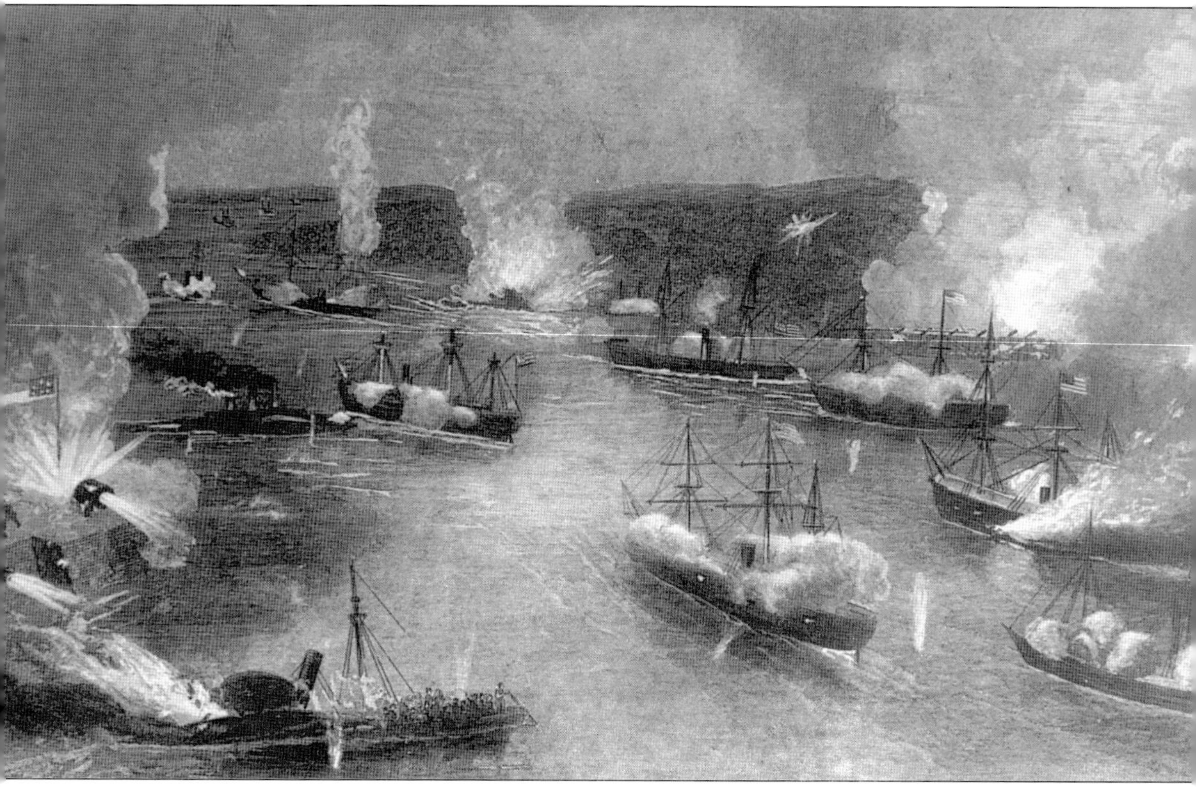

Pictured is a steel engraving of the great naval battle at New Orleans, Louisiana, which took place April 24, 1862, and during which Captain David Farragut captured Forts St. Philip and Jackson. His heroics at New Orleans opened the way for the Union boats to move upriver toward Vicksburg. In 1866, Farragut was made an admiral.

Contents

ACKNOWLEDGMENTS

Thanks to the Burlington, Iowa Convention and Tourism Bureau; the City of Dubuque, Iowa; Center for History, Loras College, Dubuque, Iowa; Clinton Area Convention and Visitors Bureau, Julie Allesee; The Delta Queen Steamboat Company; Dubuque Area Chamber of Commerce; Dubuque Dragon Boat Association, Sue Hamilton; the Greater Alton/Twin Rivers Convention and Visitors Bureau; Hannibal, Missouri Convention and Visitors Bureau; James L. Shaffer Collection; Jeanne Helling; Hickman Chamber of Commerce, Velva Yarbro; John T. and Kathryn E. Tigges Collection; Kathryn E. Tigges, typist/editor/proofreader; Mississippi Valley Division of the United States Corps of of Engineers, Karen Buehler; the People of Dubuque; Port of Dubuque Museum, Tacie Campbell; Quad Cities Convention and Visitors Bureau, Davenport, Iowa; Riverbend CVB, Fort Madison, Iowa; Shaffer Photography, Carla Hines; Vicksburg Convention and Visitors Bureau; Zebulon M. Pike Lock and Dam Number 11 Personnel, Dubuque, Iowa.

INTRODUCTION

In 1832, Henry Schoolcraft, an Indian agent and historian, asked the local Chippewas where the Mississippi River started. Where were the head waters? A guide led Schoolcraft to a Y-shaped pool, which the local people called Elk Lake. Being a well-educated man, Schoolcraft renamed it Itasca, a name he created from the Latin words *veritas* and *caput*: true and head. He used the last four letters of *veritas* and the first two of *caput* to indicate the lake was the true head of the Mississippi River. Actually, the river drains two provinces in Canada, and the head waters might be located there.

The Mississippi River is not the longest river in the world, ranking 15th overall. Nor does it have the largest drainage basin. It ranks third in that regard, behind the Amazon and the Congo. Even one of its tributaries is longer—the Missouri River is 2,714 miles long, while the Mississippi is measured as 2,350 miles in length.

Then what makes the Mississippi so great? Its productivity, that comes from part, if not all 31 states, and produces almost 75 percent of the United States' Gross National Product. Now that is something to shout about.

In truth, there are many Mississippi Rivers. The upper Mississippi, just below the Twin Cities in Minnesota, is a series of lakes backed up by 29 navigational locks and dams. Along the way it picks up silt, and the river is dark gray in color because of the rich black silt being eroded away from the land by ever-flowing water. Where the Missouri empties into the Mississippi, its color is a coffee-with-cream color—and the two refuse to mix for some reason, probably density. However, when the Ohio River enters just below Cairo, Illinois, it rushes in and mixes everything together. The Mississippi is called the world's muddiest river by many. It's too thick to drink and too thin to plow. Still, both the Colorado and the Missouri carry ten times more mud.

When the river is mixed with the waters of many states and flows southward, it is the river of the deep south, and songs and magnolia blossoms as well as earthen dikes keep the river within its banks.

The deepest part of the river lies between Baton Rouge and New Orleans, Louisiana, where depths of 40 to 200 feet exist at bends where the current plows away the soil. Considering that New Orleans is a seaport a few miles inland, it's not unusual to spot sea-going ships loading or unloading their cargo every day.

From the Ohio River, Mile 0, to the Twin Cities is 900 miles. Starting at 0 miles again at New Orleans, it is 953.8 miles from there to the mouth of the Ohio River.

When a quick thaw hits the upper valley and its tributaries, and the ground is still frozen, and rain pours down on the snow, the result inevitably is a flood. The last great one was in 1993. The engineers call them one hundred year floods, or a flood that happens every one hundred years. In the last half of the 20th century, there were at least five or more of these one hundred year floods. Well, the Mississippi River Valley is over five hundred years ahead. But, will there be more floods? Will the sun come up tomorrow?

Some cities, such as Dubuque, Iowa, have taken measures to keep from becoming a disaster area every few years. A flood wall was built the entire length of the city and has worked perfectly each time the water rises.

To show the Mississippi River and its complete history, beauty, and savagery in one book would be impossible. However, the authors have done their best to give the reader, in 128 pages and a couple hundred pictures, the story of the greatest river in the world.

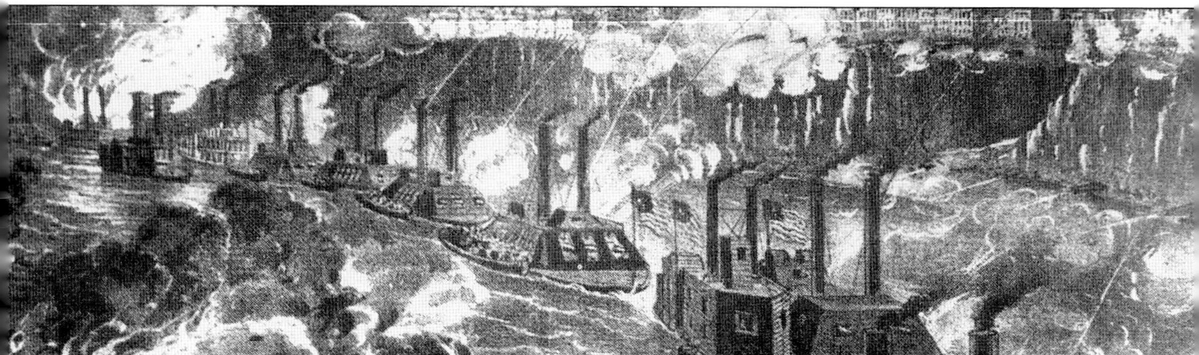

In October 1862, Ulysses S. Grant was appointed commander of the department of Tennessee and ordered to clear the Mississippi River of Confederate resistance. Every maneuver Grant made was resisted by the Southern forces during the winter of 1862–1863. Both sides understood that Vicksburg was the key to cutting off Louisiana, Texas, and Arkansas from the rest of the Confederacy. The Currier and Ives chromolithograph above shows Admiral Porter's fleet of ironclads and regular riverboats passing the Confederate batteries at Vicksburg on April 16, 1863. The soldiers of the Confederacy and the people of Vicksburg put up a stalwart fight, but on July 4, 1863, Vicksburg officially surrendered.

One

Mankind Comes to the River

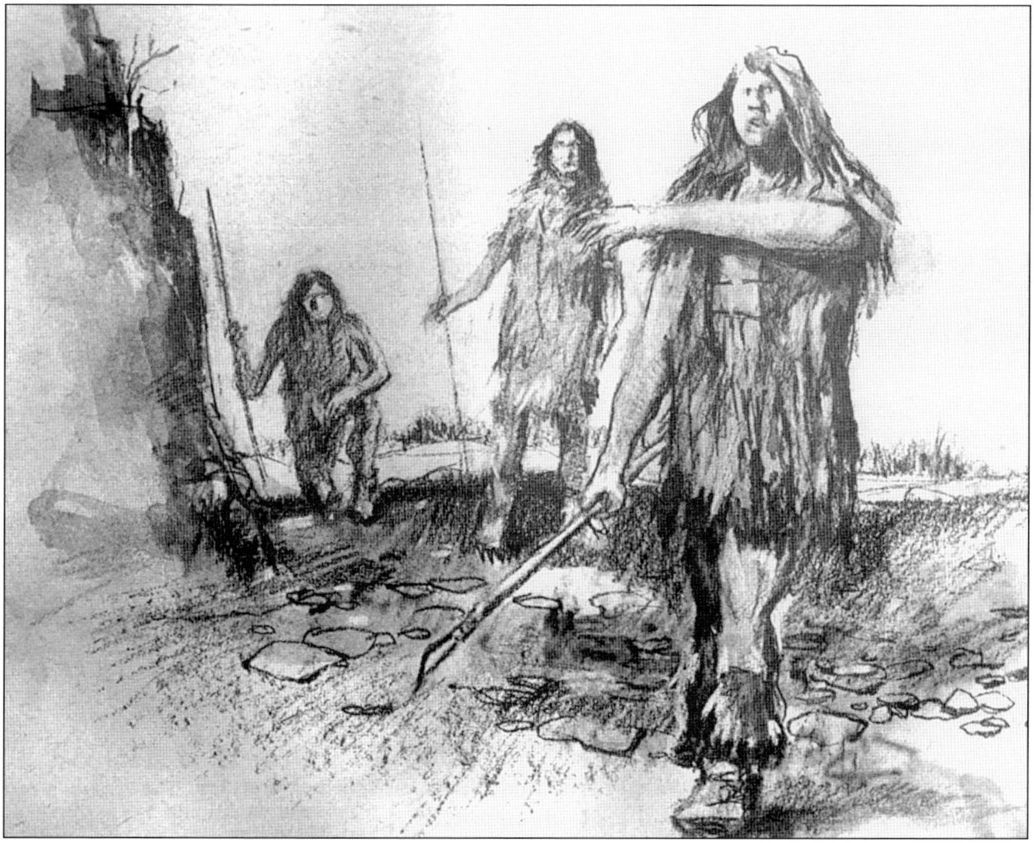

No one knows for certain when mankind first set foot on the North American continent. One indicator that some race of people was here about ten thousand years ago is the Clovis spear and arrow points that have been found in almost every part of North America. Did groups cross the Aleutian chain of islands when the oceans were low during one of the Ice Ages? No one knows when humans first entered the Mississippi River Valley. Probably, we'll never know.

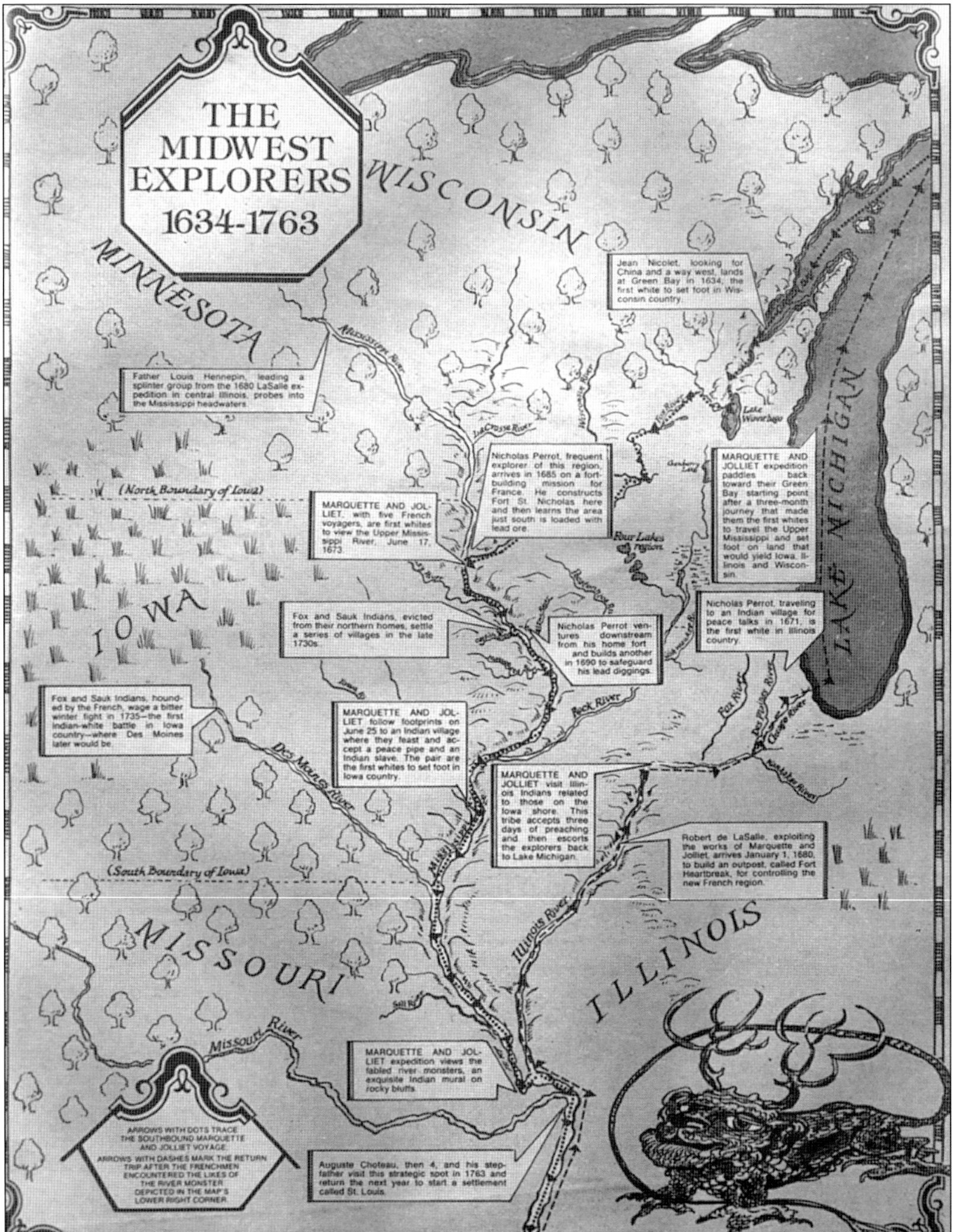

This map identifies the first Europeans who explored the upper Mississippi River and its tributaries, from 1634 to 1763. The river itself was discovered by Hernando DeSoto around May 1541 at Chickasaw Bluffs, which is in the state of Mississippi.

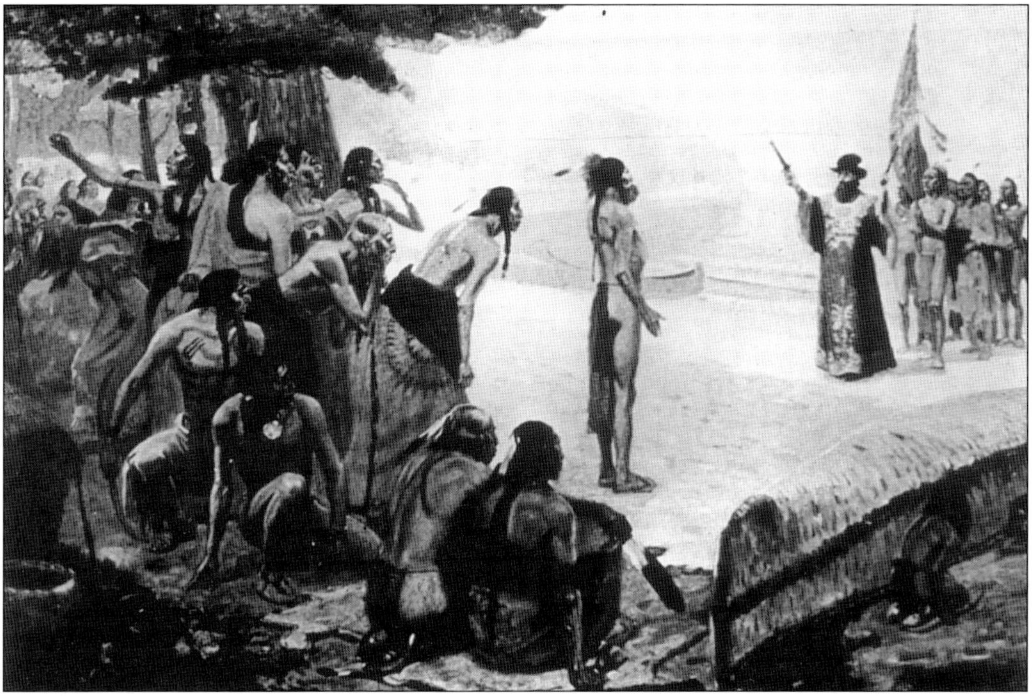

While Jean Nicolet was the first to explore the area in 1674, it was a Jesuit priest, Jacques Marquette, and Louis Jolliet, a French Canadian explorer, who first saw the Father of Waters on June 17, 1673. They were the first to encounter the valley's inhabitants.

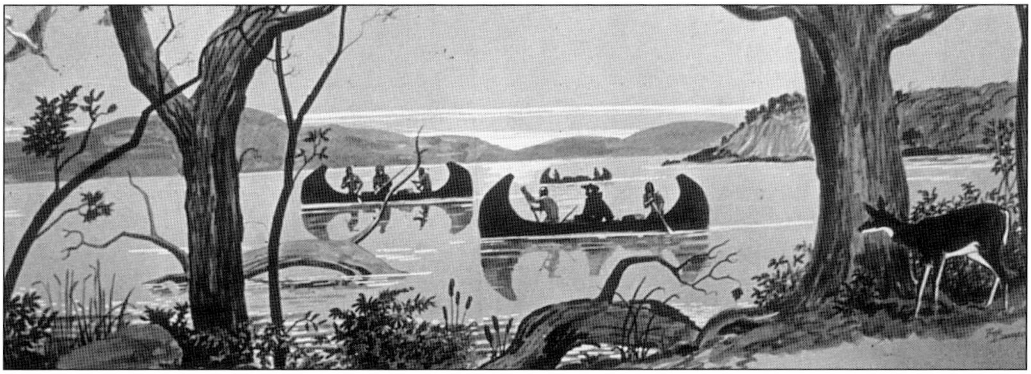

The priest and explorer made friends with the Mesquakie and Fox tribes, and Indians traveled with them to introduce the strangers to other tribes and camps.

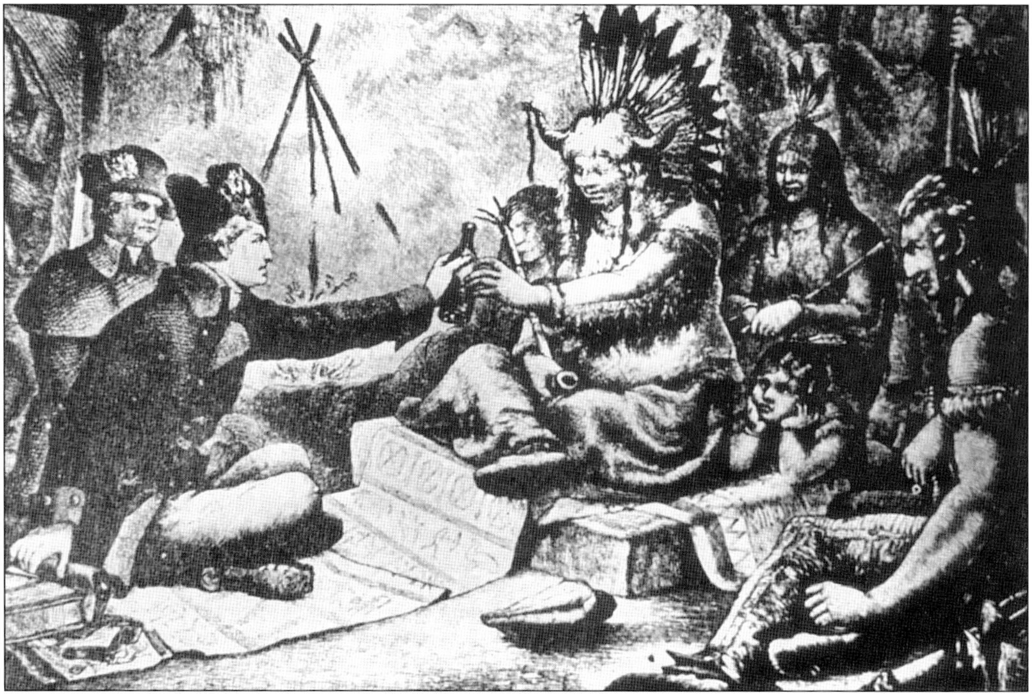

The French made friends with the Mesquakie, Fox, Chippewa, and other tribes to gain the trapping rights for beaver, which abounded in the upper valley.

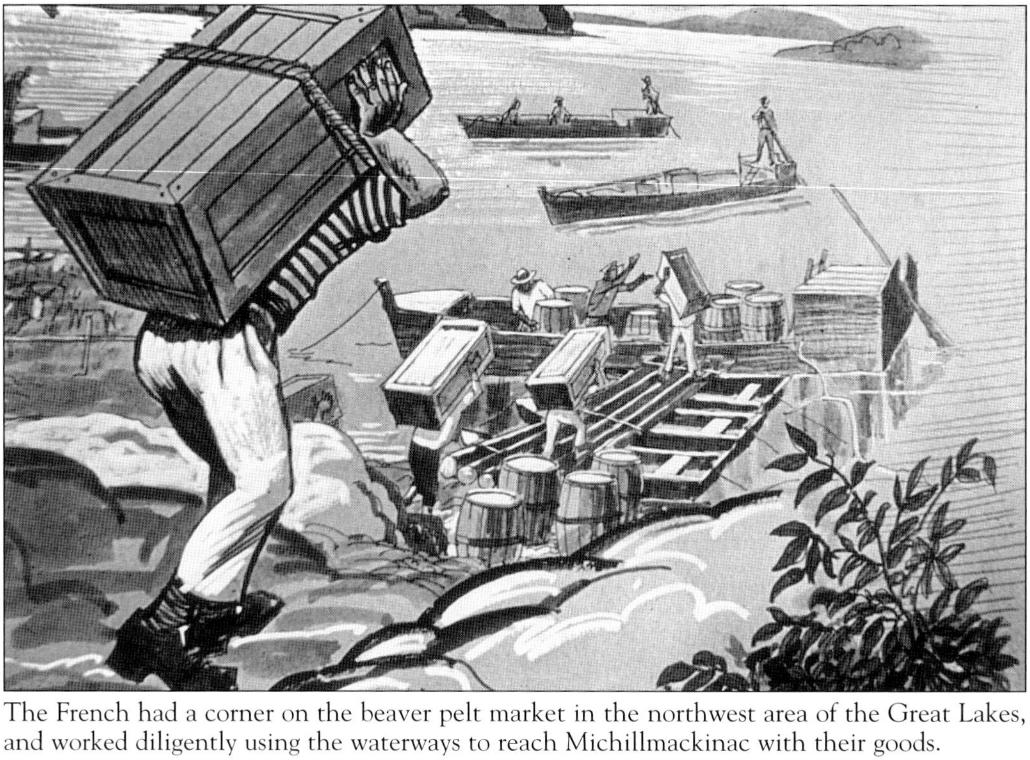

The French had a corner on the beaver pelt market in the northwest area of the Great Lakes, and worked diligently using the waterways to reach Michillmackinac with their goods.

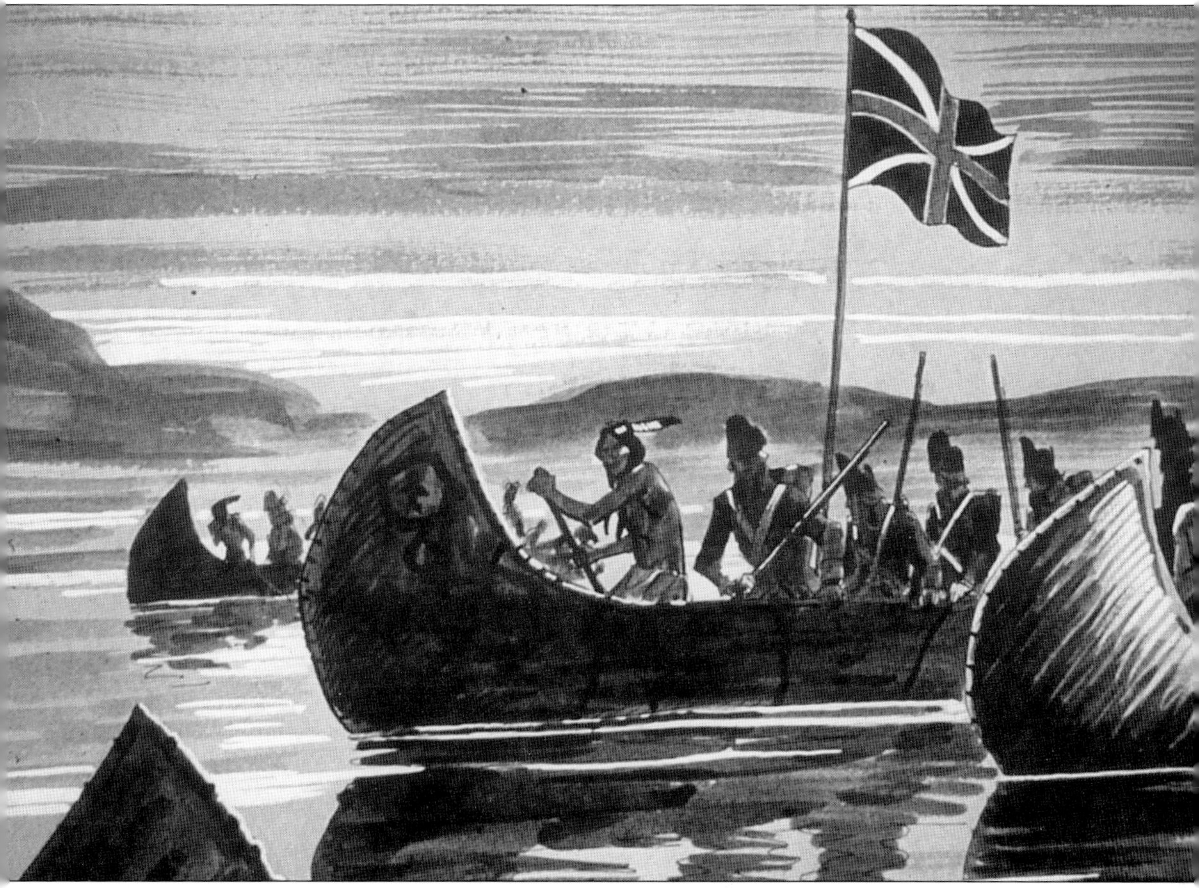

The English looked on the French Territory with envious eyes and began trading with the different tribes, while European coalitions fought, loosely linking with the British actions in America. The English began their campaign on the eastern shores of North America and moved inland. While four different wars raged in Europe between 1688 and 1748, the fifth and last war was fought in America—the French and Indian War of 1754–1760. The British utilized the waterways of the Mississippi and its tributaries to move quickly and silently, using their Indian allies' canoes.

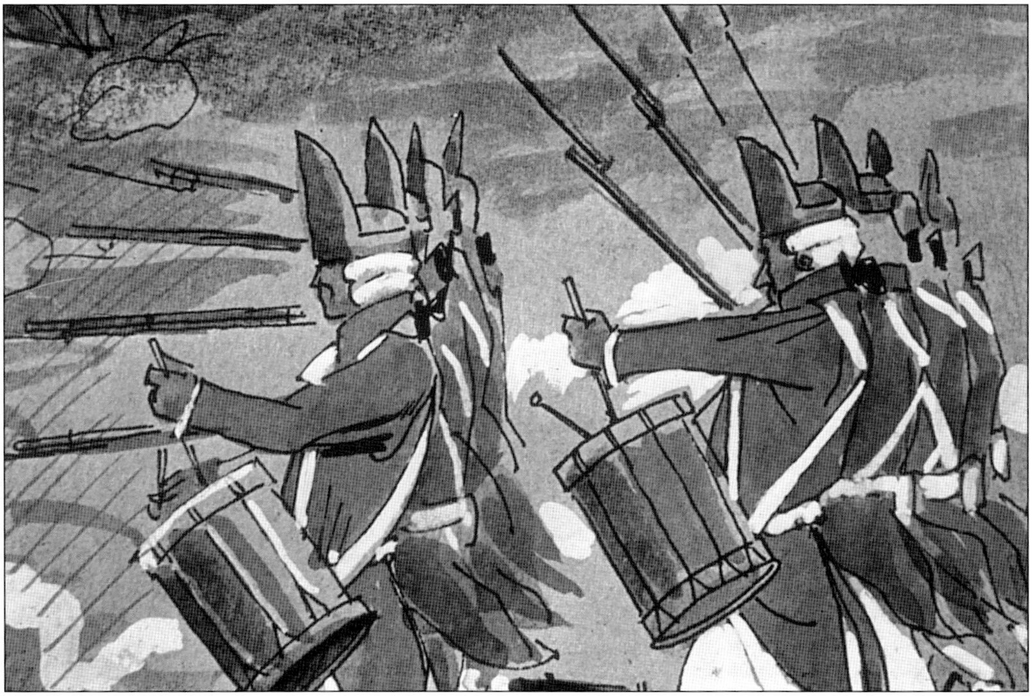

On land, the British formal style of warfare must have seemed strange to the Indians.

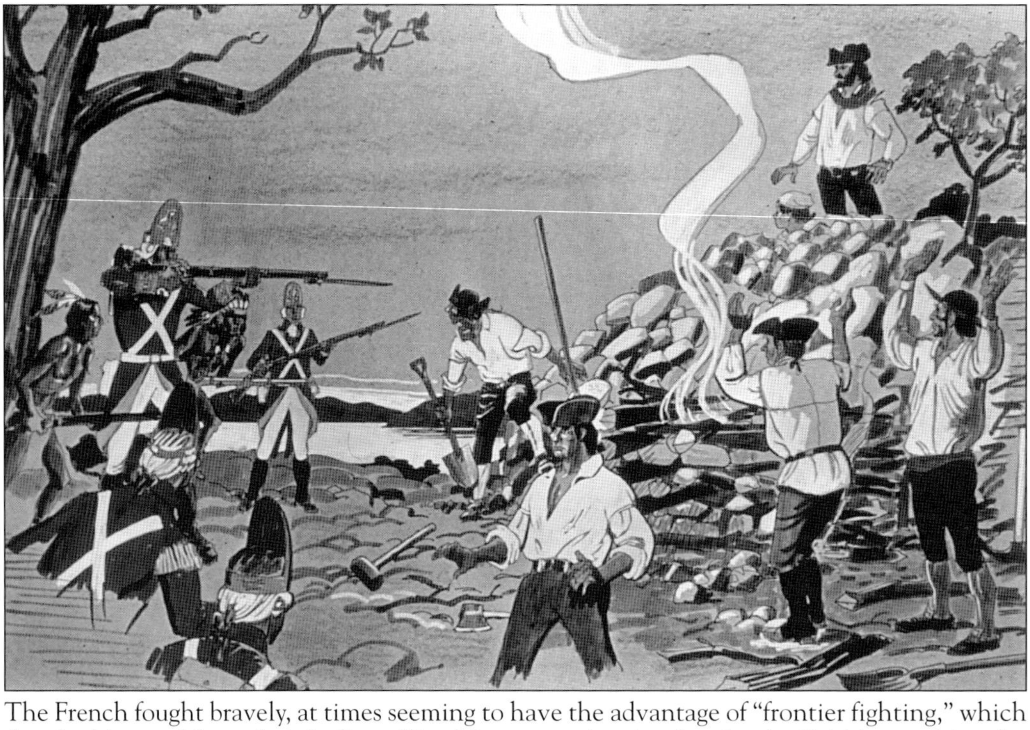

The French fought bravely, at times seeming to have the advantage of "frontier fighting," which they had learned from their Indian allies. Here, a smelter is taken by the British, catching the Frenchmen off guard.

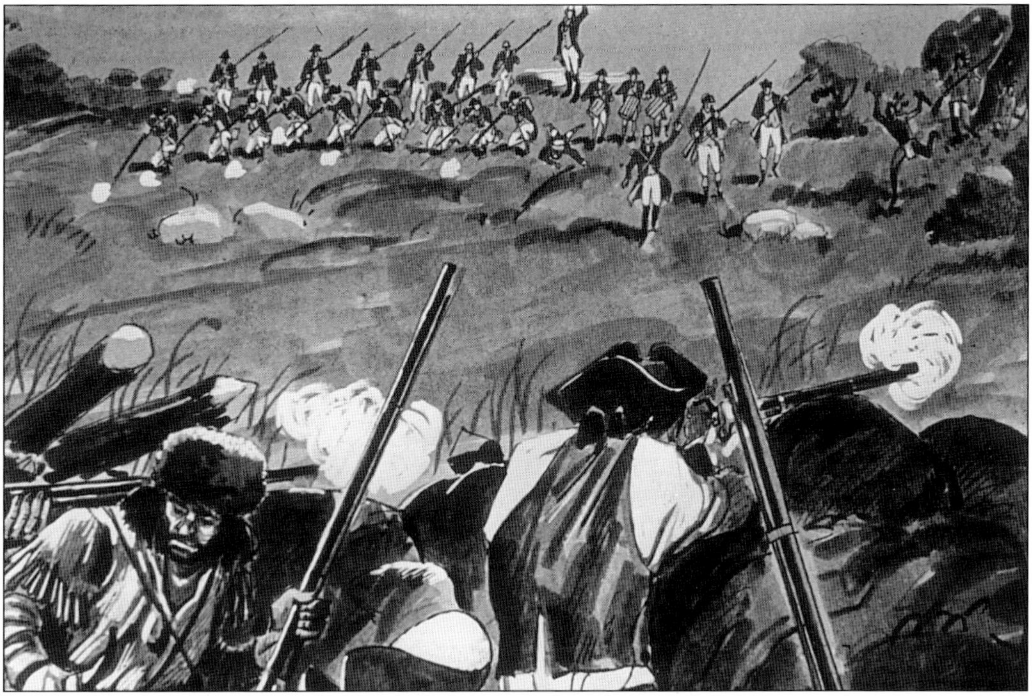

Superior numbers eventually won out, and the British defeated the French and their native allies in 1760.

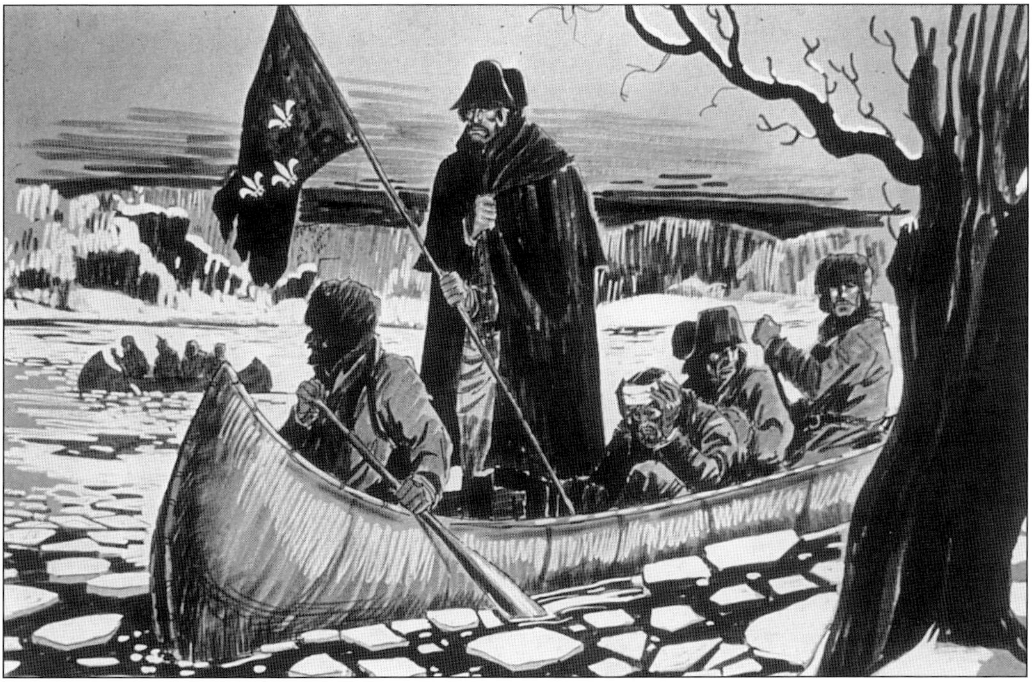

Defeated, the French were forced to quit the area and give up their profitable fur trade and lead mining, and the British moved into the territory. When the Treaty of Paris was signed in 1763, the French were finished in Canada and the known Northwest Territory.

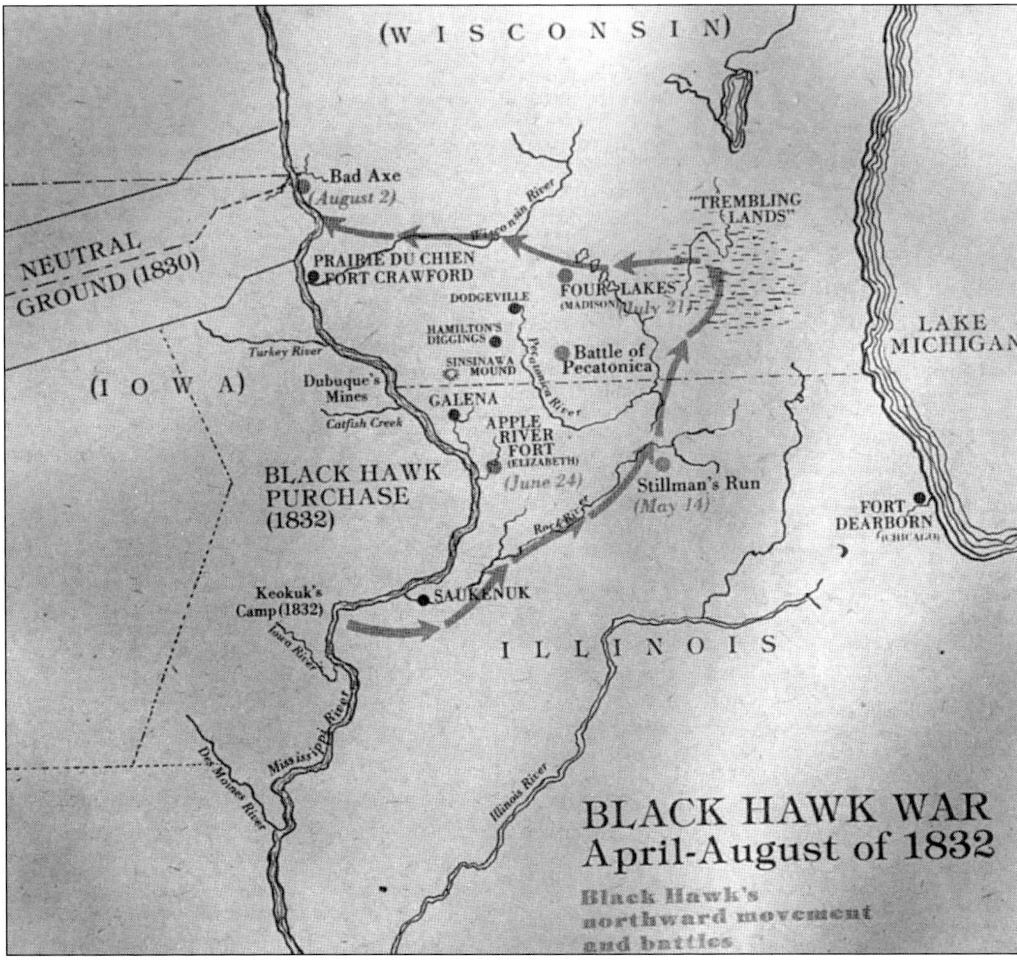

This map of the Black Hawk War shows the route Chief Black Hawk took from Chief Keokuk in 1832, leading his few warriors and families to find a home for themselves to allow them peace and good hunting.

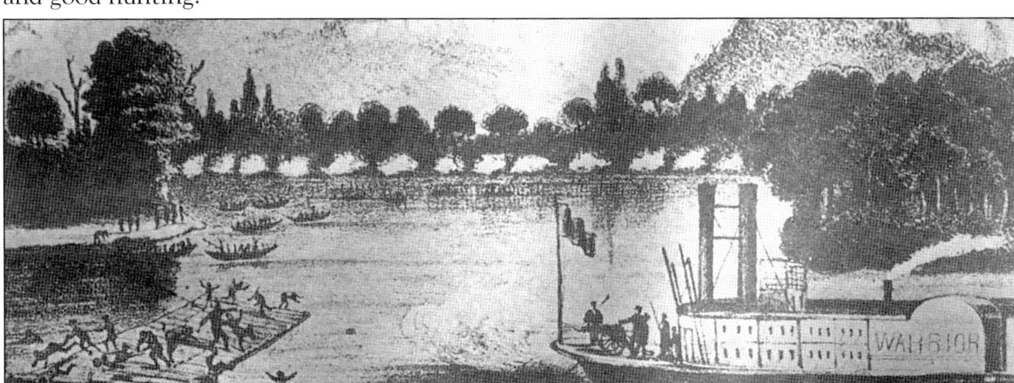

On August 2, 1832, the Americans caught up with Black Hawk's followers and defeated them at Bad Axe, Quisconsin (Wisconsin) Territory. The victory opened the land west of the Mississippi River for settlement once the Black Hawk Treaty was signed in 1833.

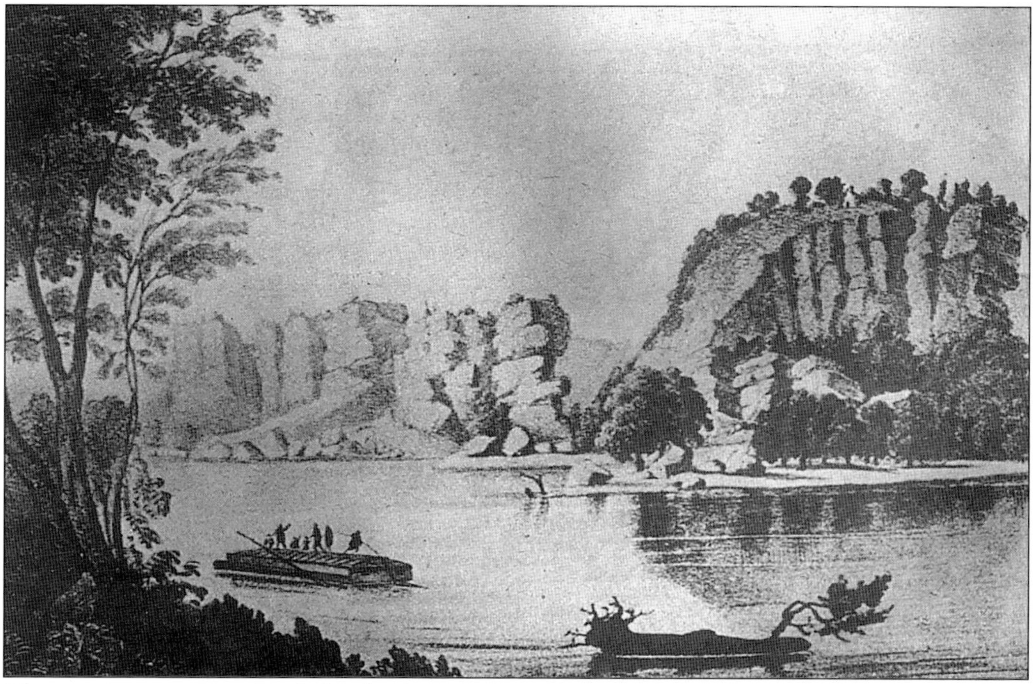

The river was open and safe for flat boats to carry miners' and trappers' produce downriver to Saint Louis.

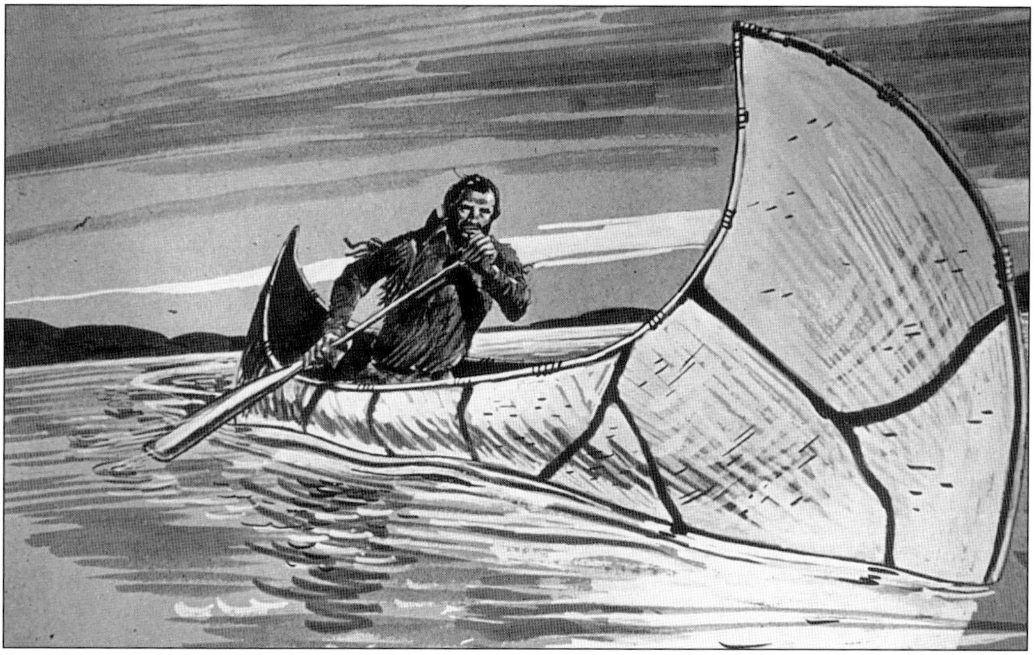

A popular legend of the Mississippi concerns a French-Canadian trapper and miner who allegedly warned St. Louis in 1783 that British forces, with their Sioux allies, were going to attack. Jean Marie Cardinal's alert was supposed to have given St. Louis time to prepare. Cardinal died in the abbreviated battle, which had the British won, the outcome of the Revolutionary War might have been different.

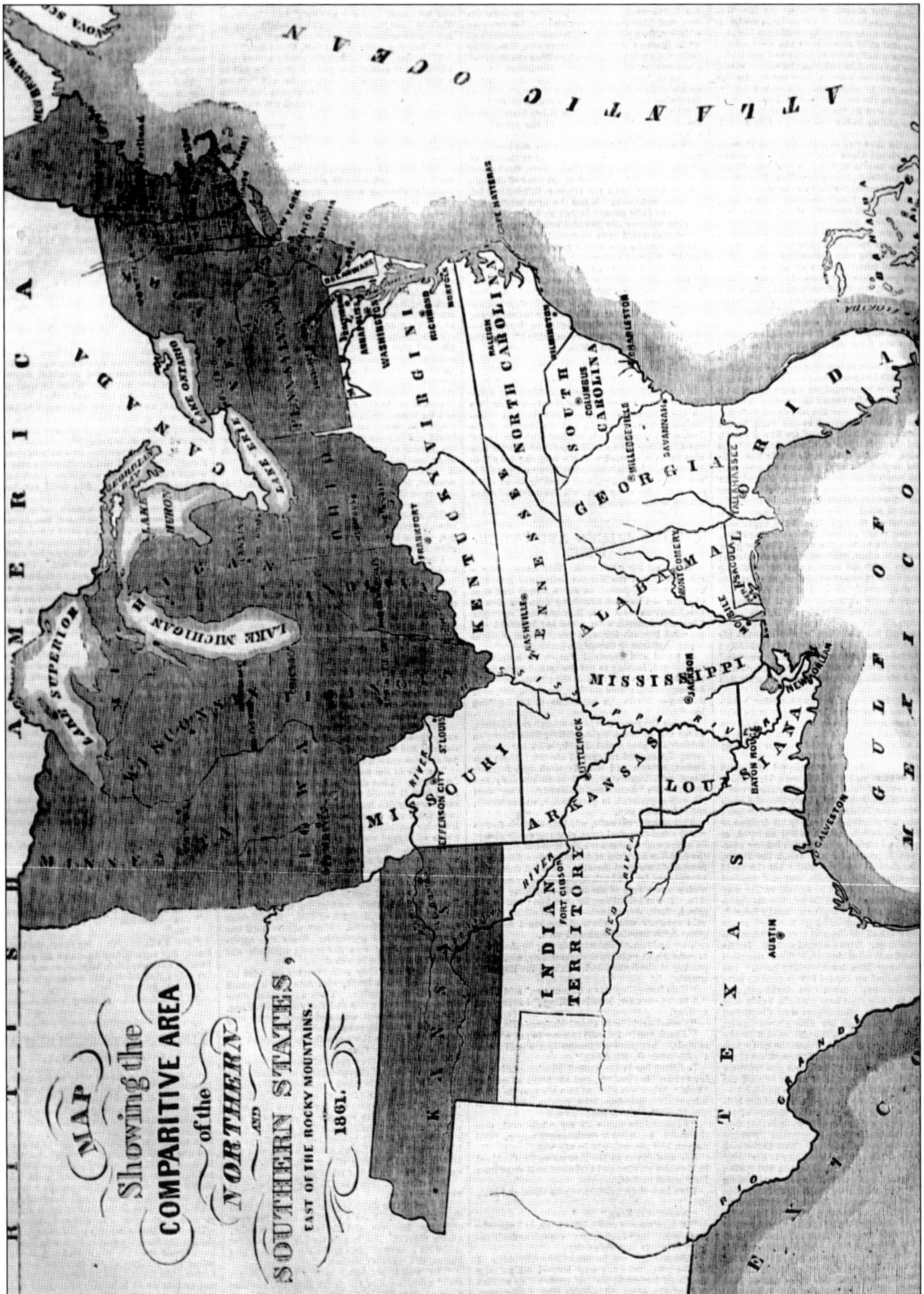

This map shows the United States in 1861 when the Civil War began. In both the Revolutionary War and the Civil War, whoever controlled the Mississippi River held a distinct advantage.

Two

The Golden Age of Steamboats

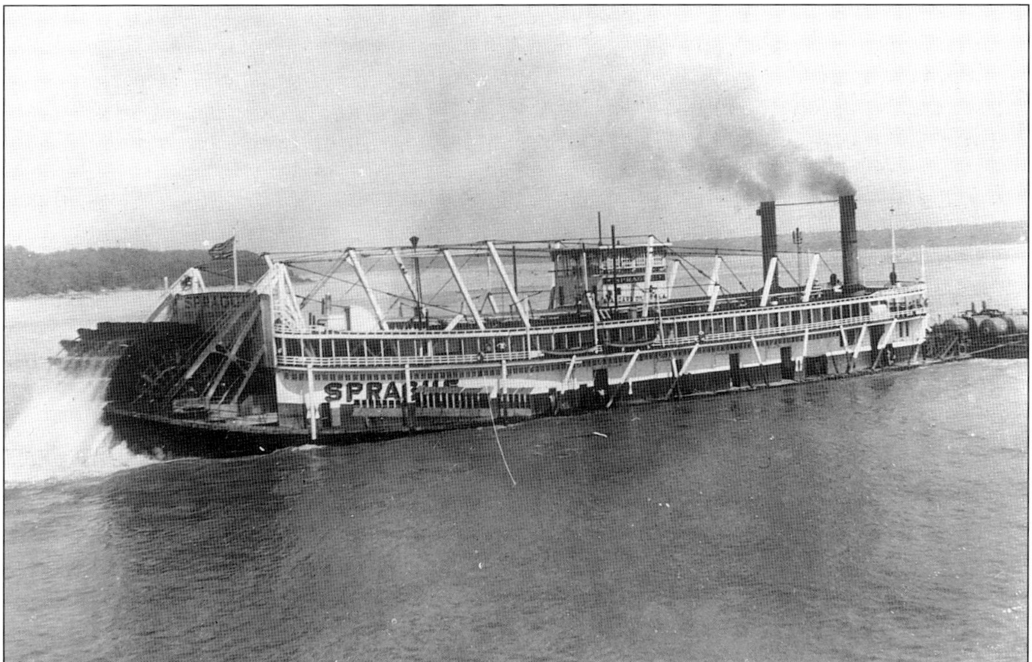

Not until 1976, when the *Mississippi Queen* was launched, had a riverboat larger than the *Sprague* ever operated on the Mississippi River. Built in 1901–1902 at the Dubuque Boat Works, she was 276 feet long with a beam of 63 feet and a 40-foot stern wheel. In 1907, she transported a tow of 56 coal boats and 4 barges of coal. The tow was 925 feet long, 312 feet wide, and covered 7 acres, a record that still stands in 2000. She was affectionately called "Big Mama."

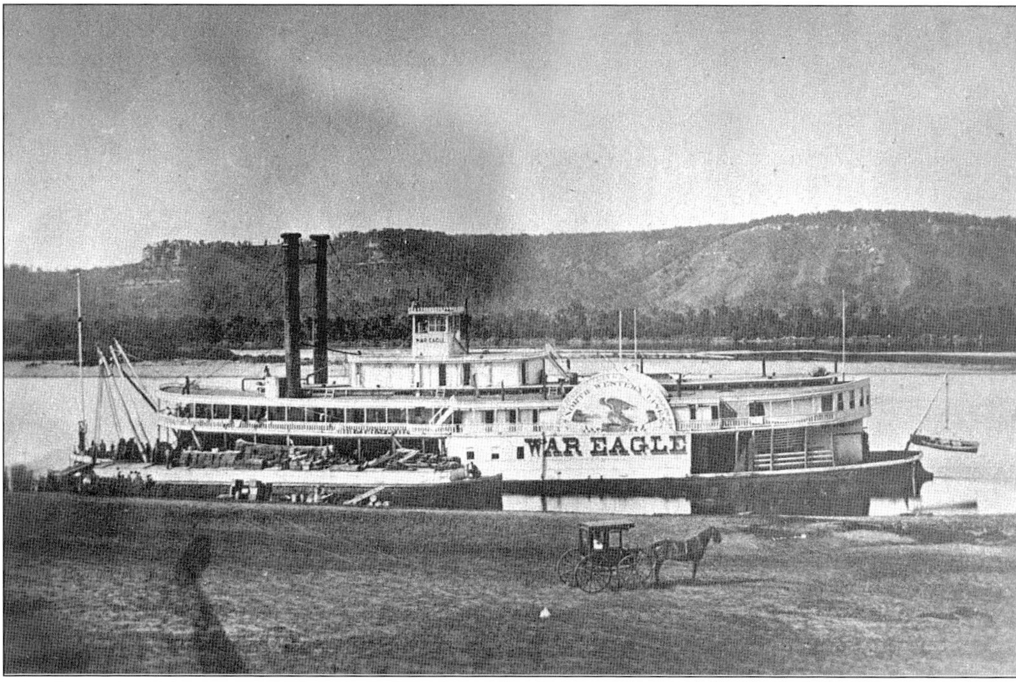

The *War Eagle* was one of four boats that made upriver trips to St. Paul, Minnesota, once the Civil War started. All four boats were owned by the Minnesota Company.

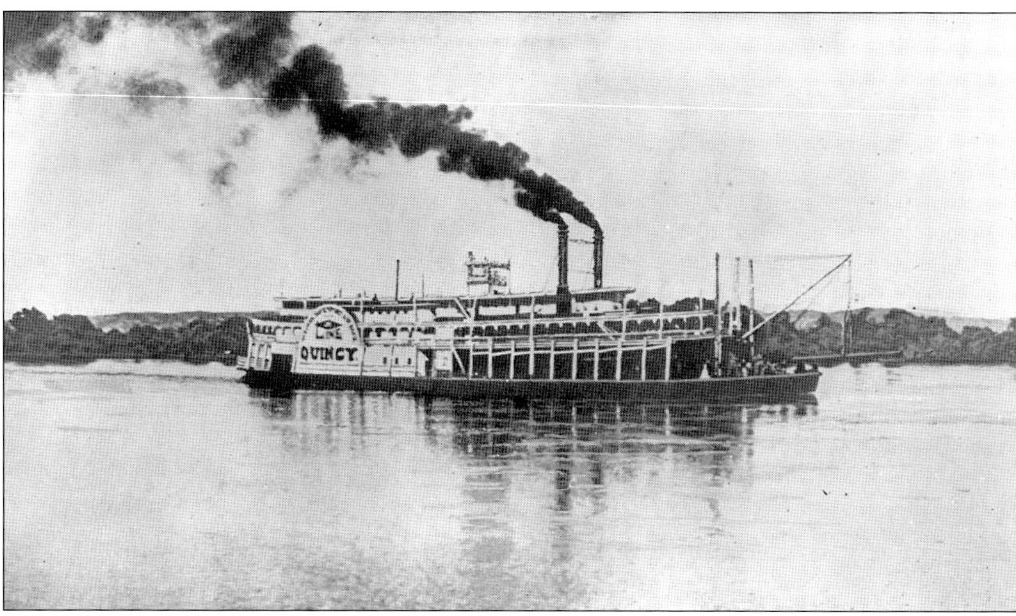

The side-wheeler *Quincy*, one of the Diamond Jo Lines' boats, heads downriver, her stacks belching black smoke.

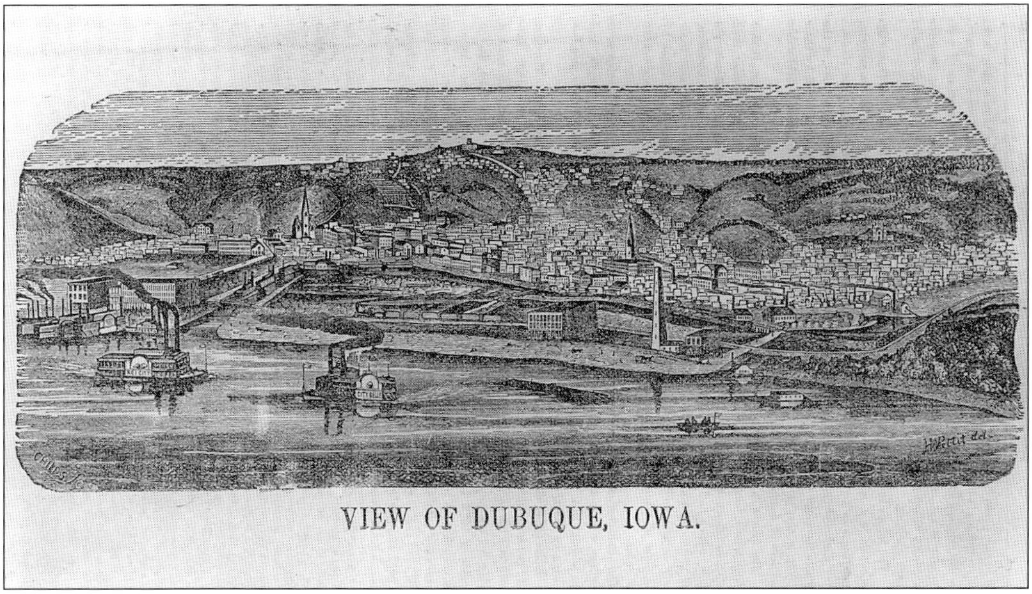

This early engraving by H.W. Pettit, of Dubuque, shows the city's noticeable shot tower. The boat on the left is the *Key City*, which was built in Cincinnati but called Dubuque its home port. At one point, she collided with a circus steamboat. The other boat, heading downriver, is the *City Belle*.

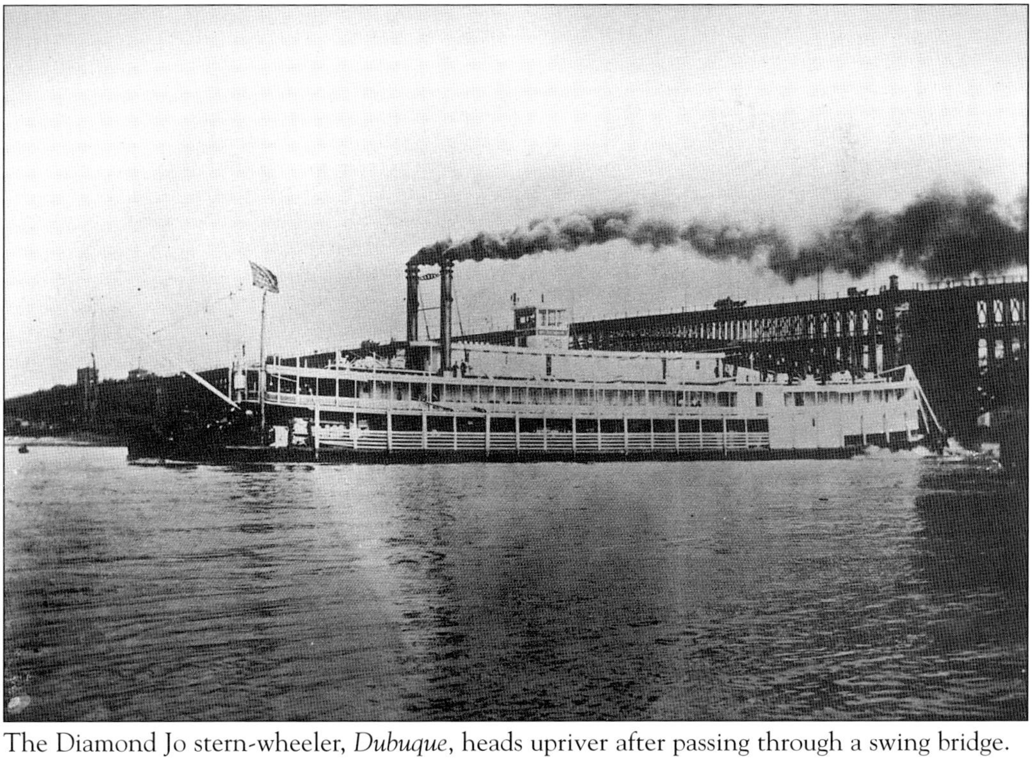

The Diamond Jo stern-wheeler, *Dubuque*, heads upriver after passing through a swing bridge.

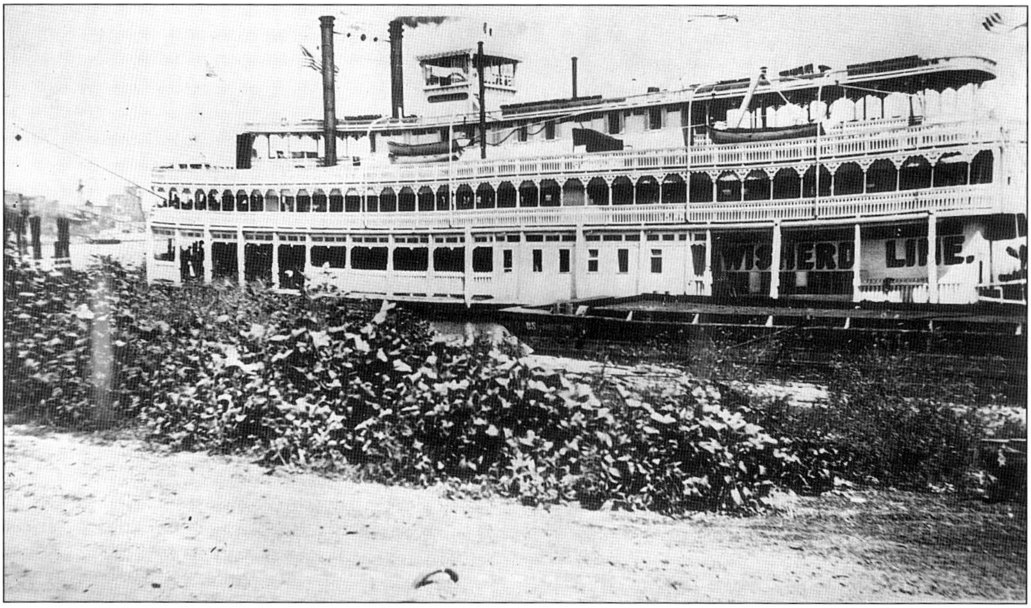

The Wishered Line's *Geo. Hill* stops for fuel at one of the many stops along the Mississippi River in the 19th century.

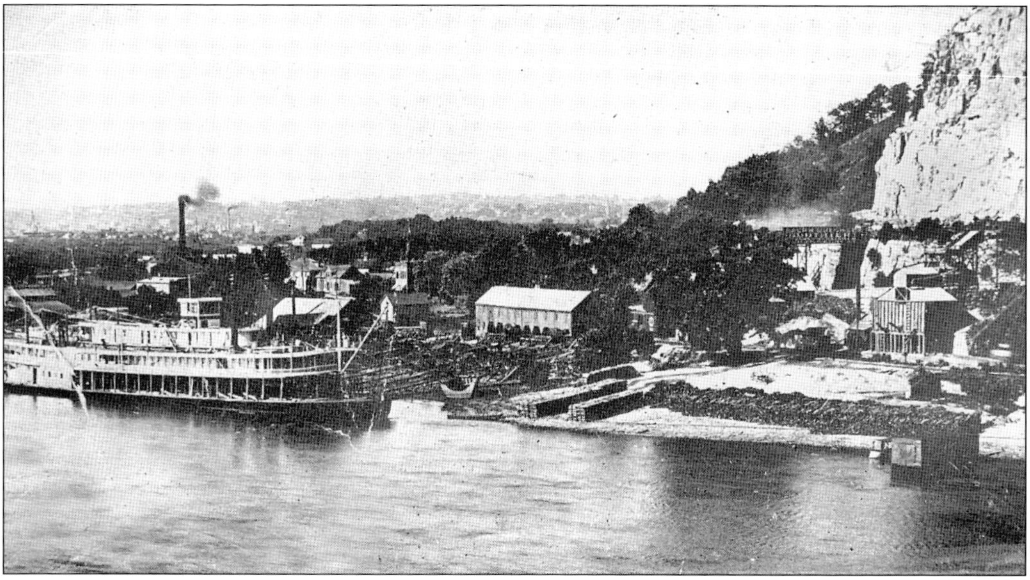

A boat, believed to be the Diamond Jo Lines' *Dubuque*, pulls up on the muddy and sandy shore to refuel, load, and unload cargo.

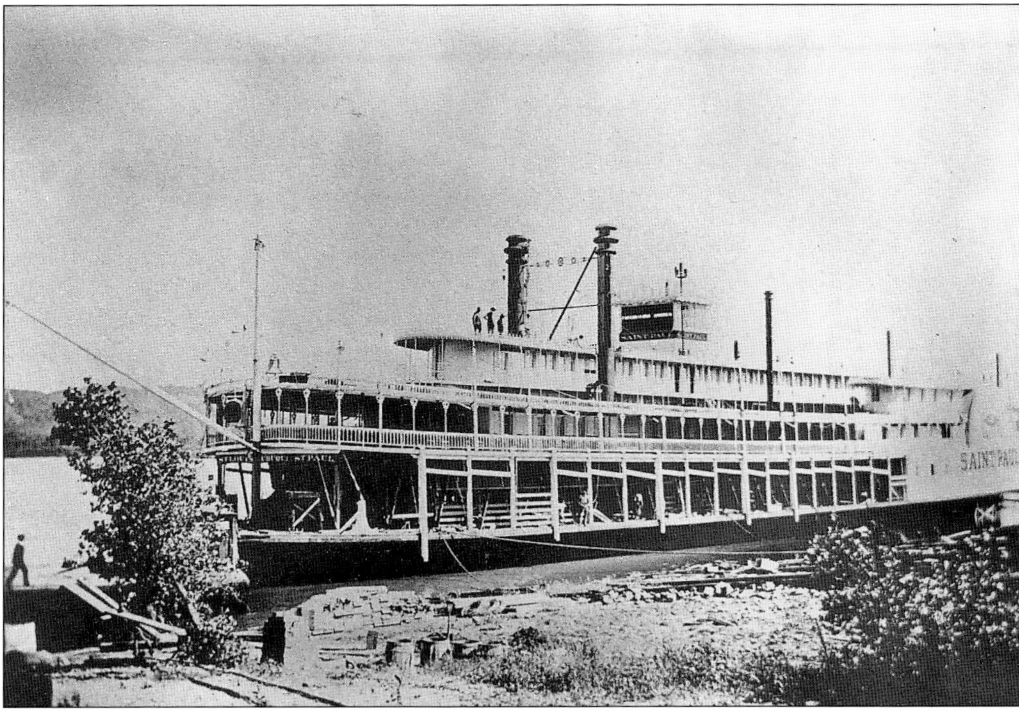

The Diamond Jo Lines' excursion steamboat *St. Paul* is shown here under construction at Eagle Point, the company's headquarters.

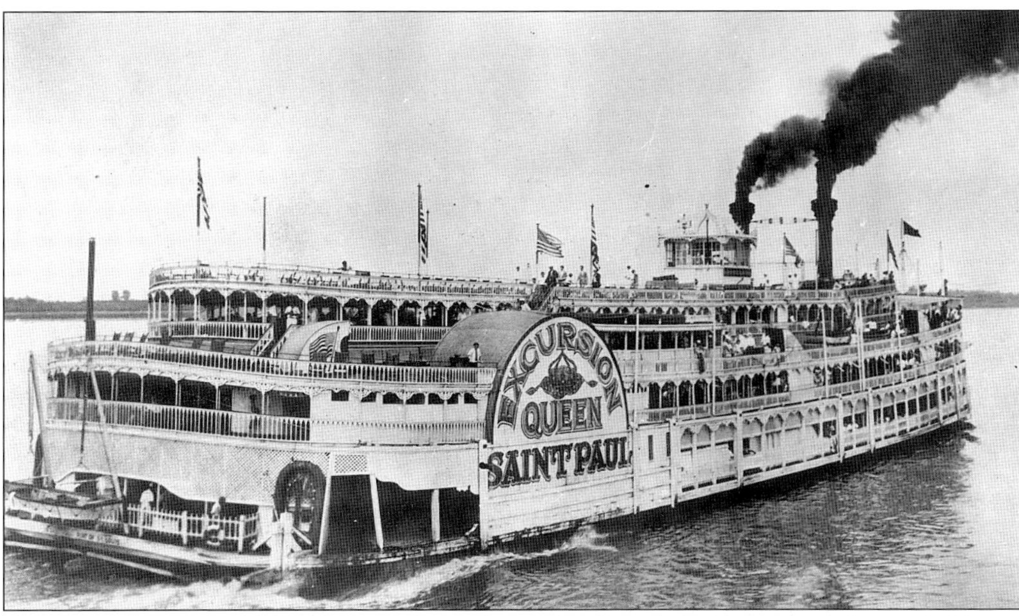

The *St. Paul*, completed, heads upriver on a day with only a slight breeze from the south. Notice the flags. Most are hanging, while three have caught a stronger gust of wind. The smoke is carried in front of the boat.

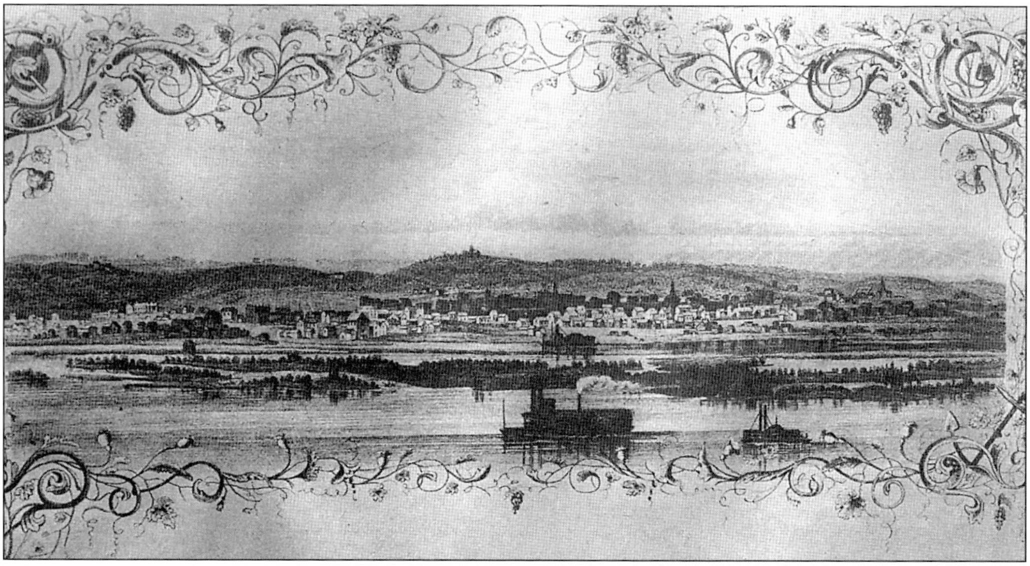

This engraving of two packet boats passing Dubuque, Iowa, is by an unknown artist. It was engraved around 1850 in New York.

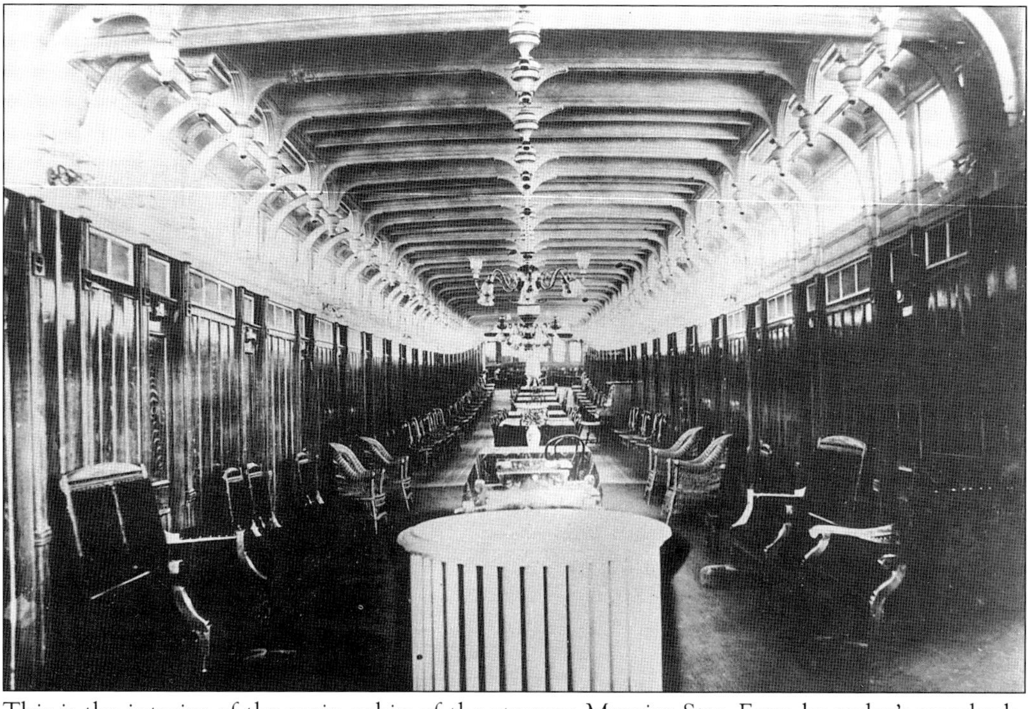

This is the interior of the main cabin of the steamer *Morning Star*. Even by today's standards, the cabin was plush in 1911.

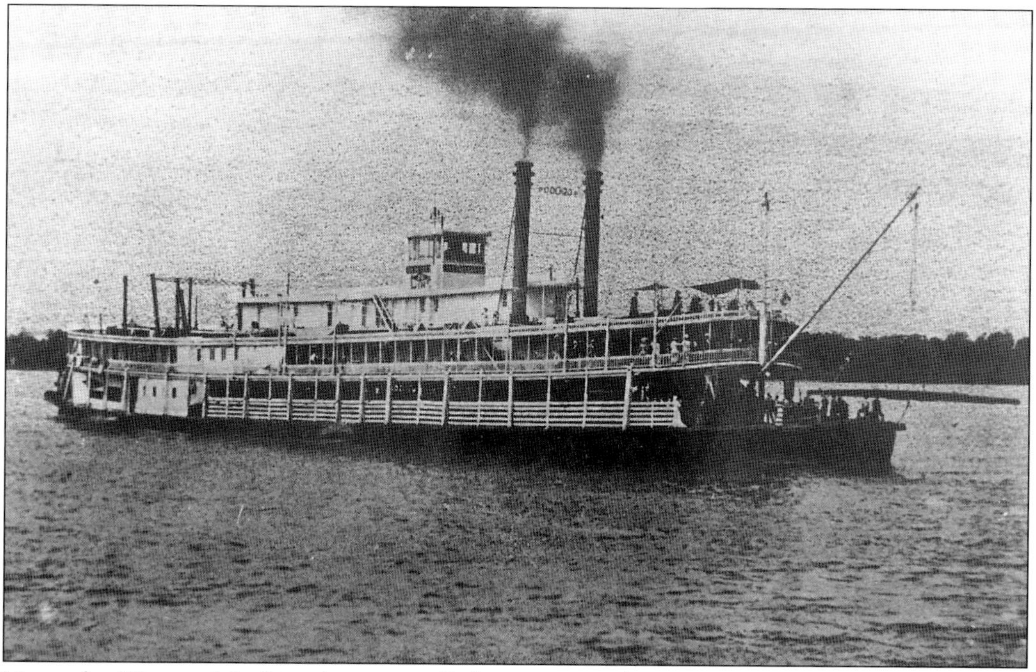

Here, the Diamond Jo Lines' steamer, *Dubuque*, is on the Mississippi River in 1912, out of Dubuque and bound for. . .

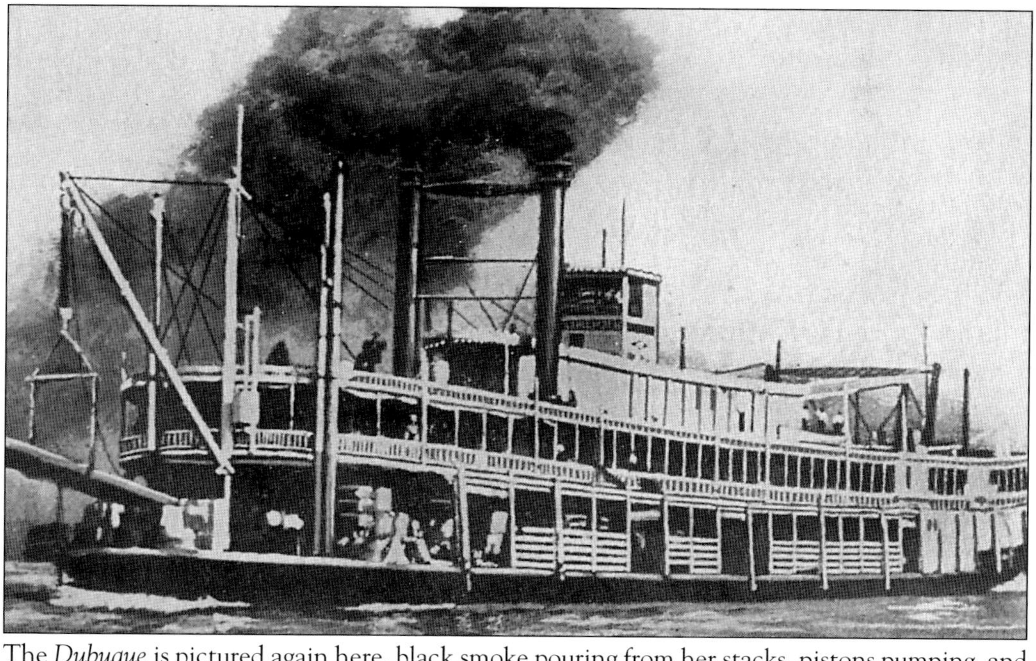

The *Dubuque* is pictured again here, black smoke pouring from her stacks, pistons pumping, and her deep-throated whistle announcing her presence.

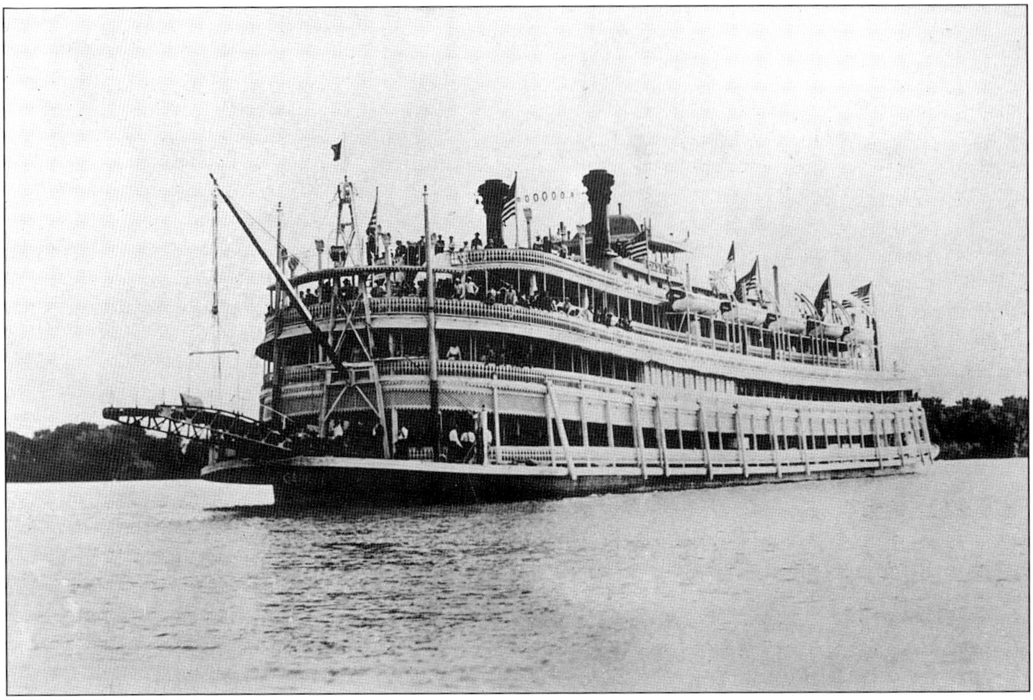

While her first name was *Dubuque*, she became the *Capitol* after the Diamond Jo Lines sold her. She was a beautiful example of the boat builders' art.

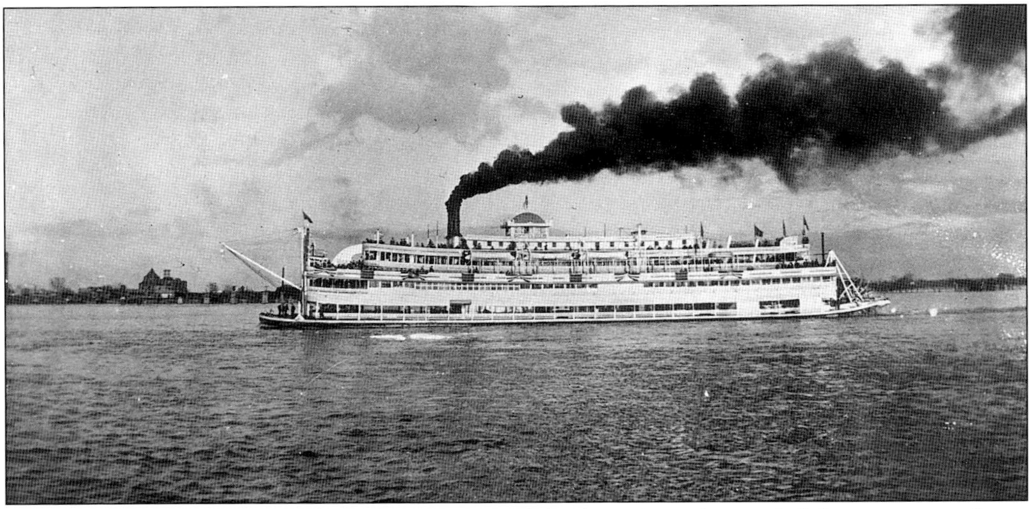

The *Capitol* shows her port side to the camera and displays classic lines of a Mississippi riverboat, while she passes an unidentified town.

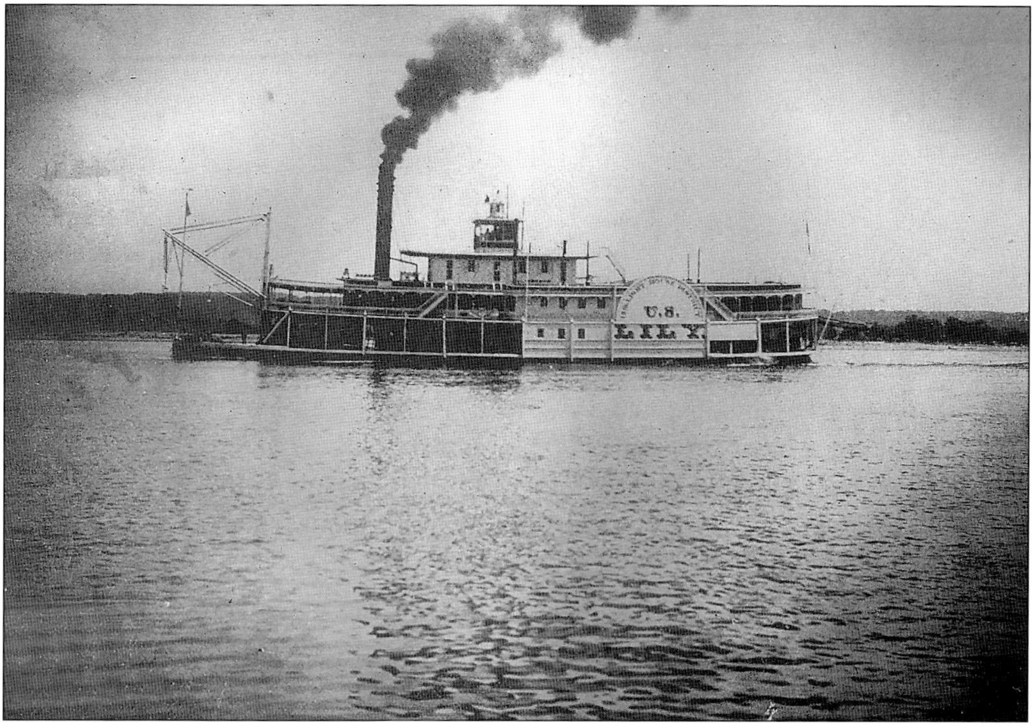

The government light boat *U.S. Lily* side-wheeler plies the river, making certain regulations are met by larger craft.

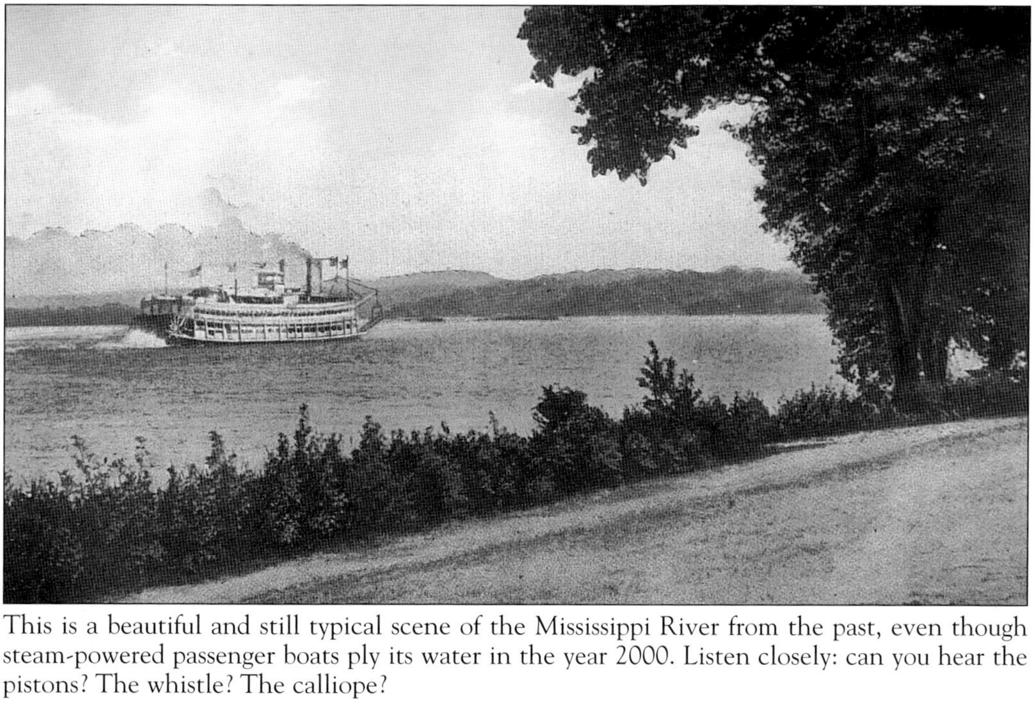
This is a beautiful and still typical scene of the Mississippi River from the past, even though steam-powered passenger boats ply its water in the year 2000. Listen closely: can you hear the pistons? The whistle? The calliope?

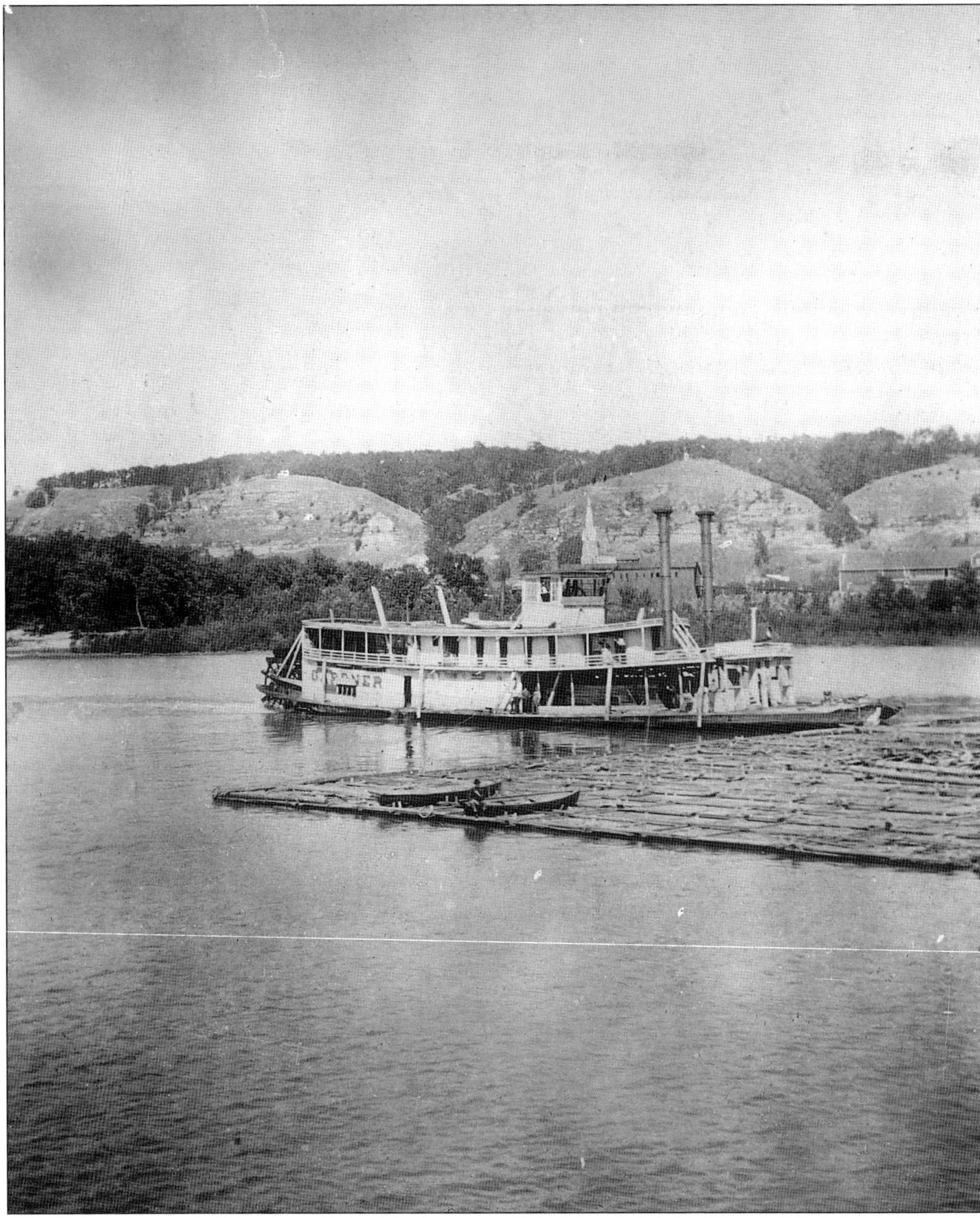

The G. *Boner* heads south toward one of the lumber mills along the Mississippi, with its raft of logs. Rafting logs to mills lasted into the 20th century. Notice the two rowboats on the raft and the man sitting in the one on the right.

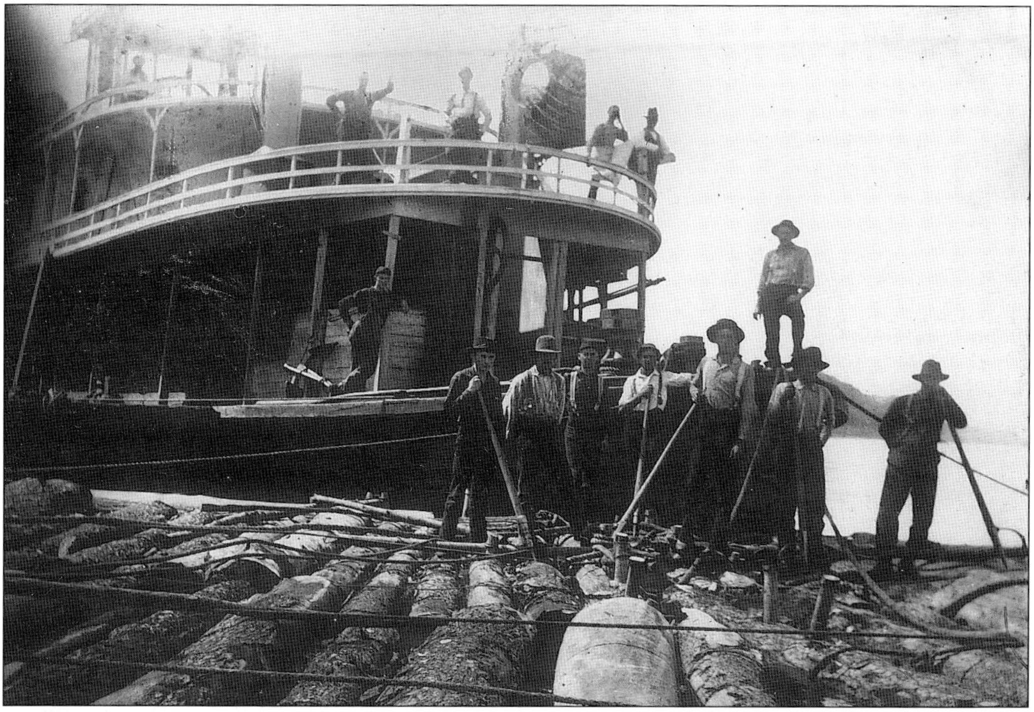

Lumbermen lean on their pike poles to have their picture taken. Pike poles were used to control floating logs.

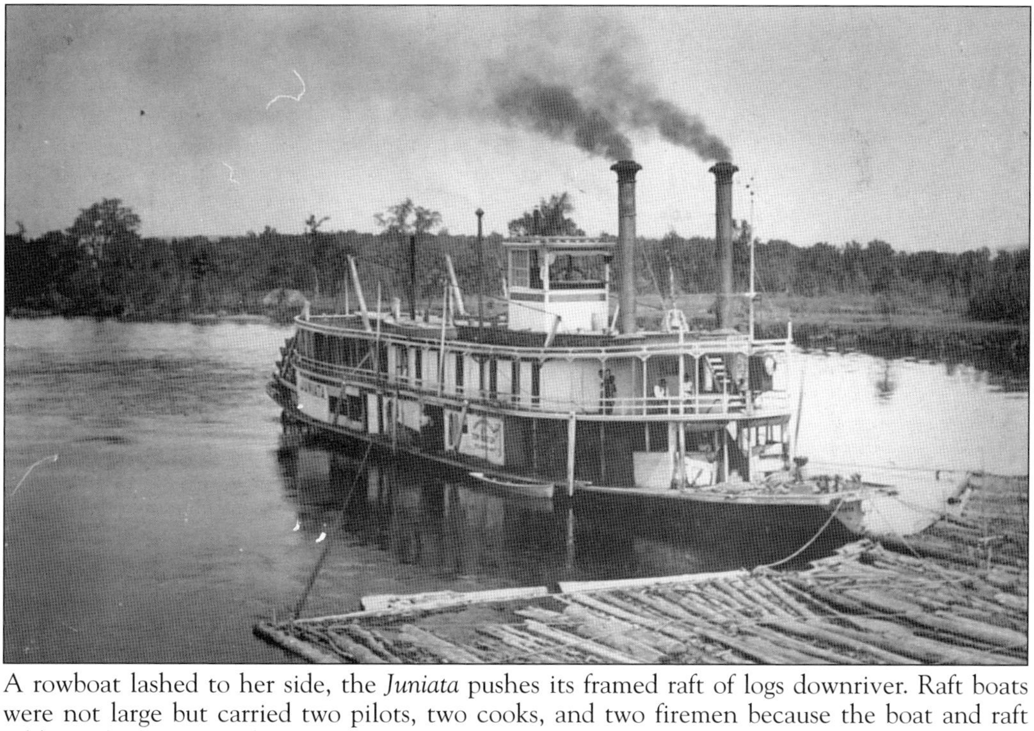

A rowboat lashed to her side, the *Juniata* pushes its framed raft of logs downriver. Raft boats were not large but carried two pilots, two cooks, and two firemen because the boat and raft seldom, if ever, stopped until the mill was reached.

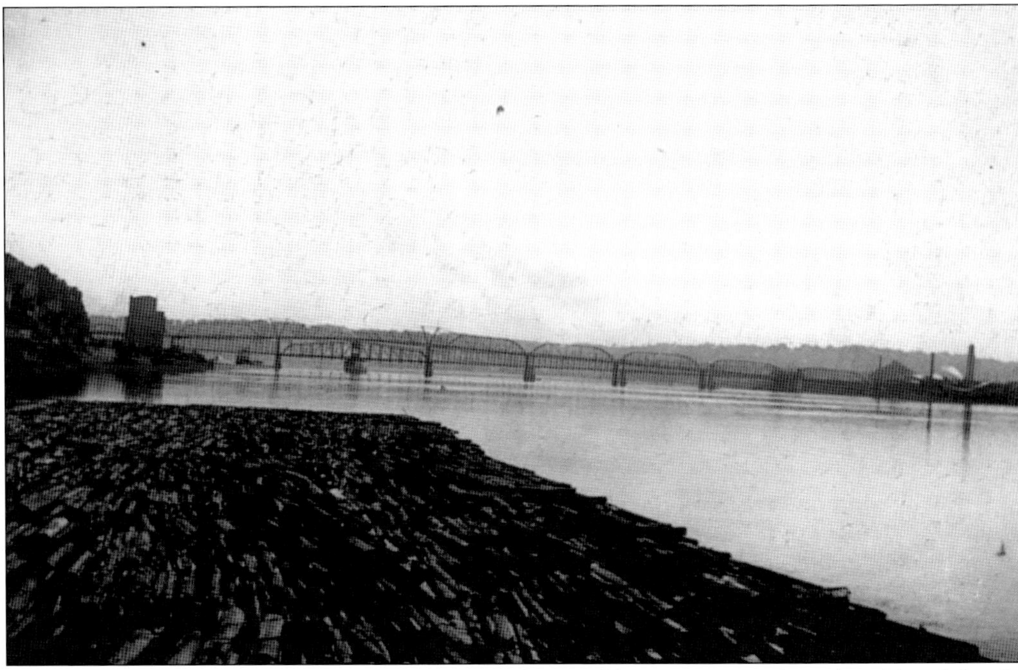

This pilot's-eye view catches a raft while it readies itself to turn to starboard and head for the Standard Lumber Mill at Dubuque, Iowa. If the boat and raft were heading past Dubuque to Clinton's W.J. Young's Mill, the world's largest by a small degree over the Standard Lumber Mill, the swing bridge would be open.

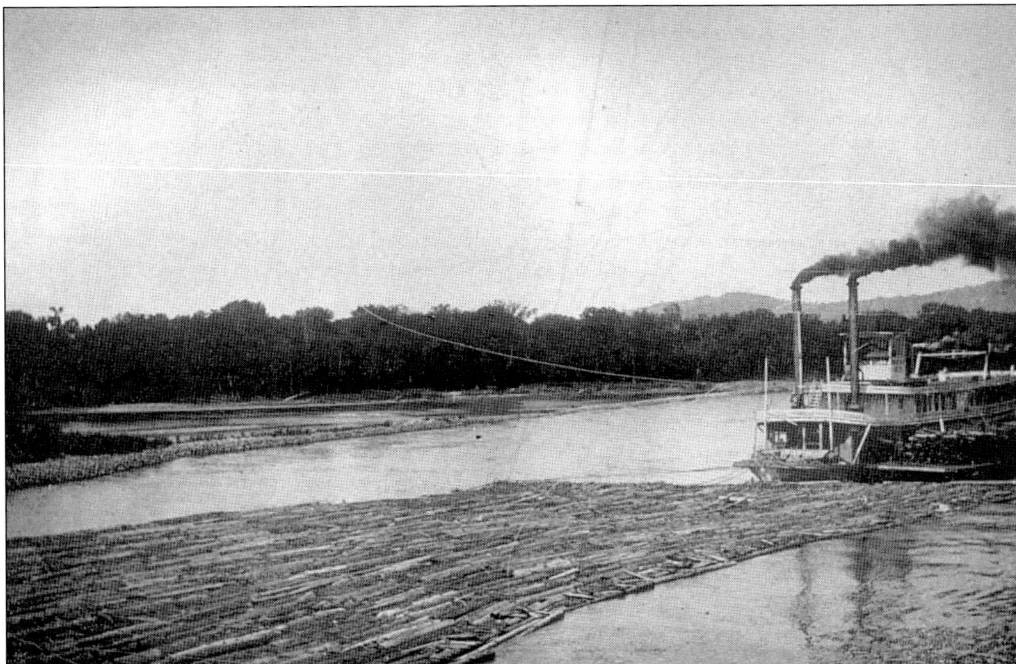

The *Mountain Belle* heads south with its log raft made up of one to three million board feet of lumber. A raft is lashed to the port side of the *Belle*, which carries fuel for the boiler.

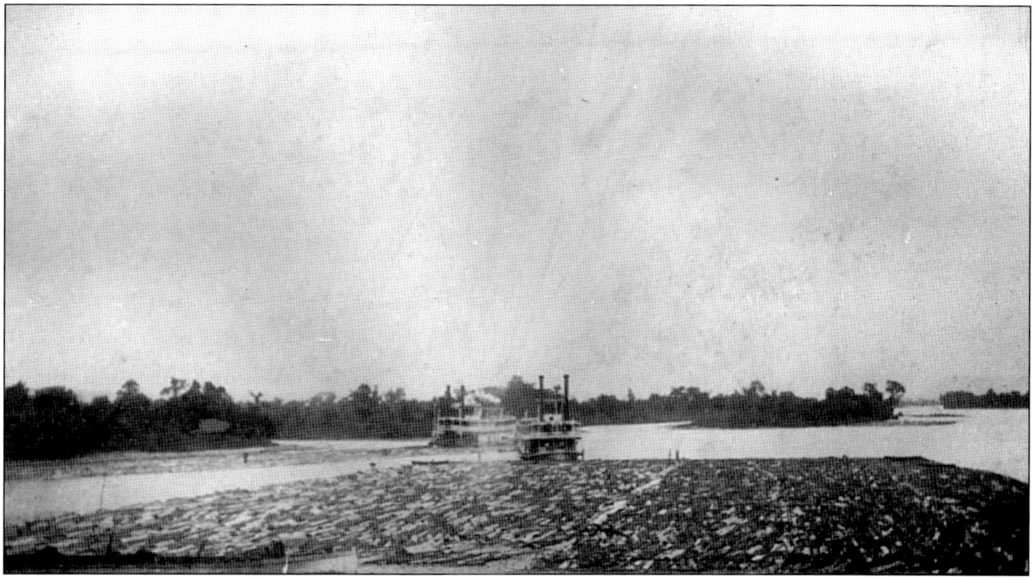

Two raft boats move downriver almost side by side. A canoe is lashed to the front of the raft on the right.

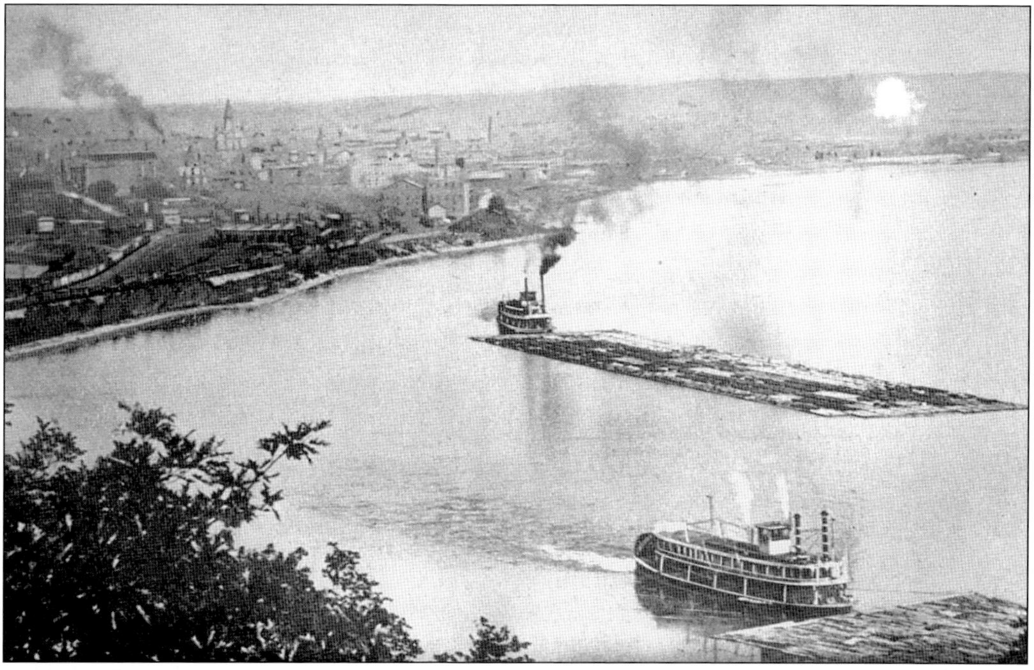

The Federal Rivers and Harbors Act of March 3, 1899, required forming a boom of logs around rafts and chaining them in place. Both rafts in the picture above are rectangular. Bypassing Dubuque, the boats' destination is probably Clinton. Still, there were few days when at least one raft was not being broken up at Dubuque.

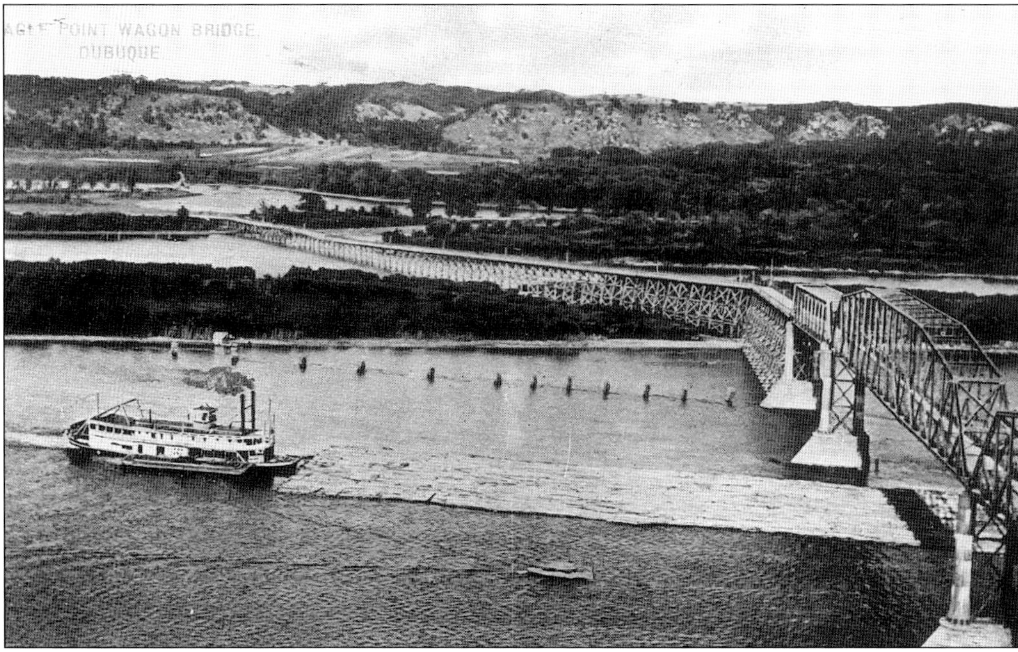

On August 9, 1915, the *Ottumwa Belle* pushed the last raft of logs to Clinton, Iowa. The Standard Lumber Company had been destroyed by two fires on May 26 and May 28, 1911.

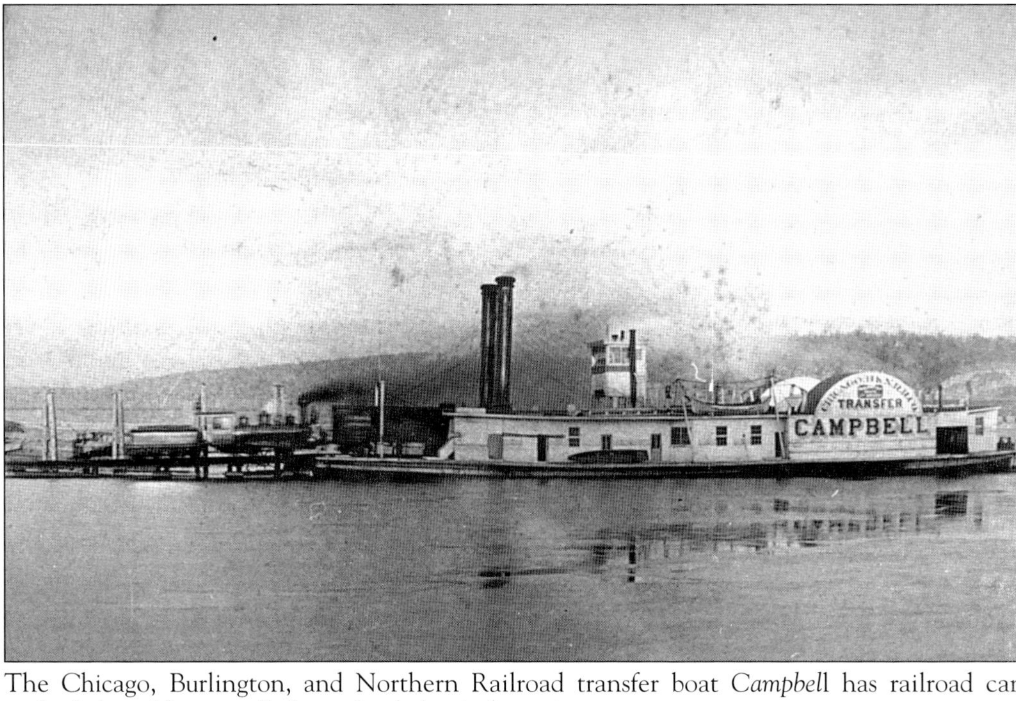

The Chicago, Burlington, and Northern Railroad transfer boat *Campbell* has railroad cars pushed aboard by a small, four-wheeled switch engine.

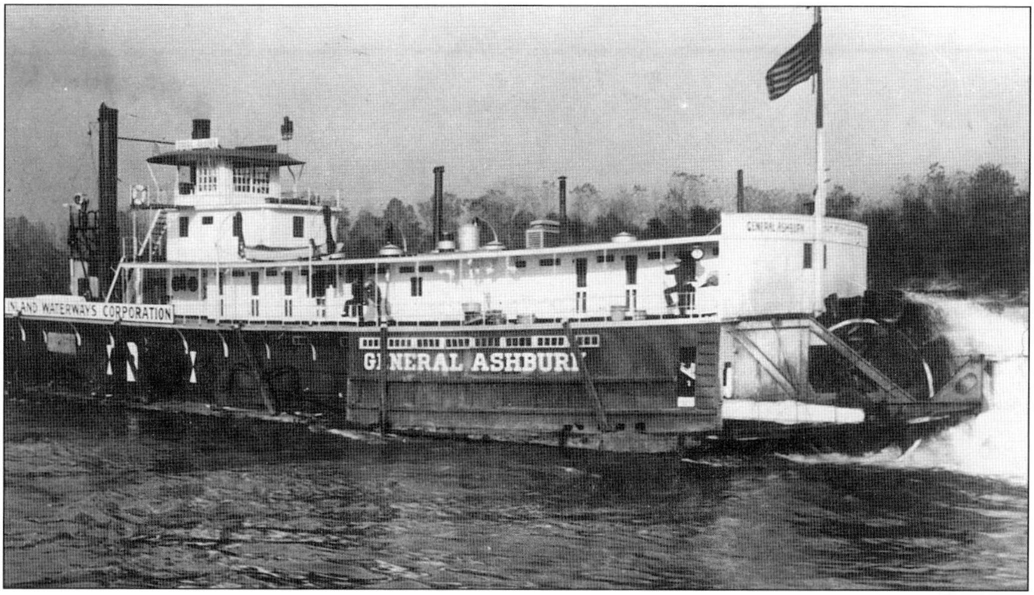

Inland Waterway Corporation's *General Ashburn* is apparently heading upriver, considering the stern-wheeler's white foam.

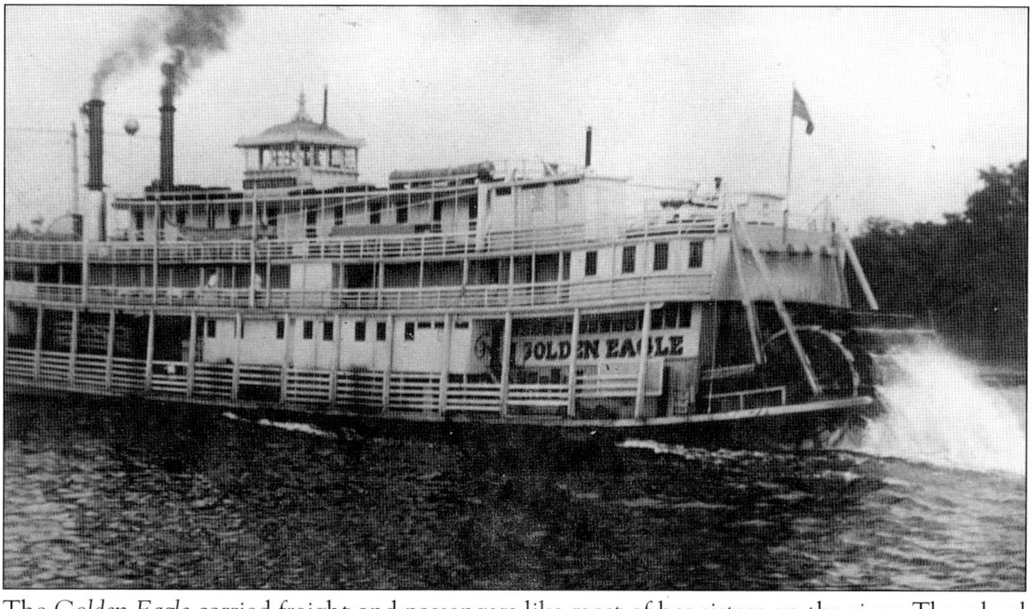
Golden Eagle
The *Golden Eagle* carried freight and passengers like most of her sisters on the river. The wheel is small compared to that of the *Sprague* (seen on page 17).

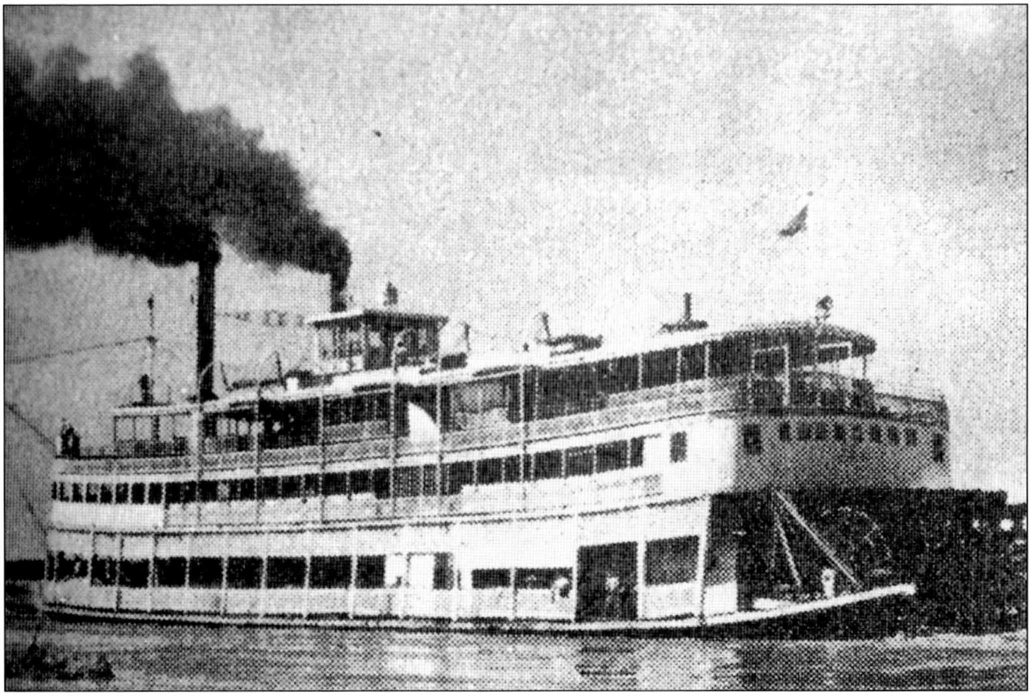

The *Avalon* must be stopped, when the lack of water activity at the stern wheel is taken into consideration.

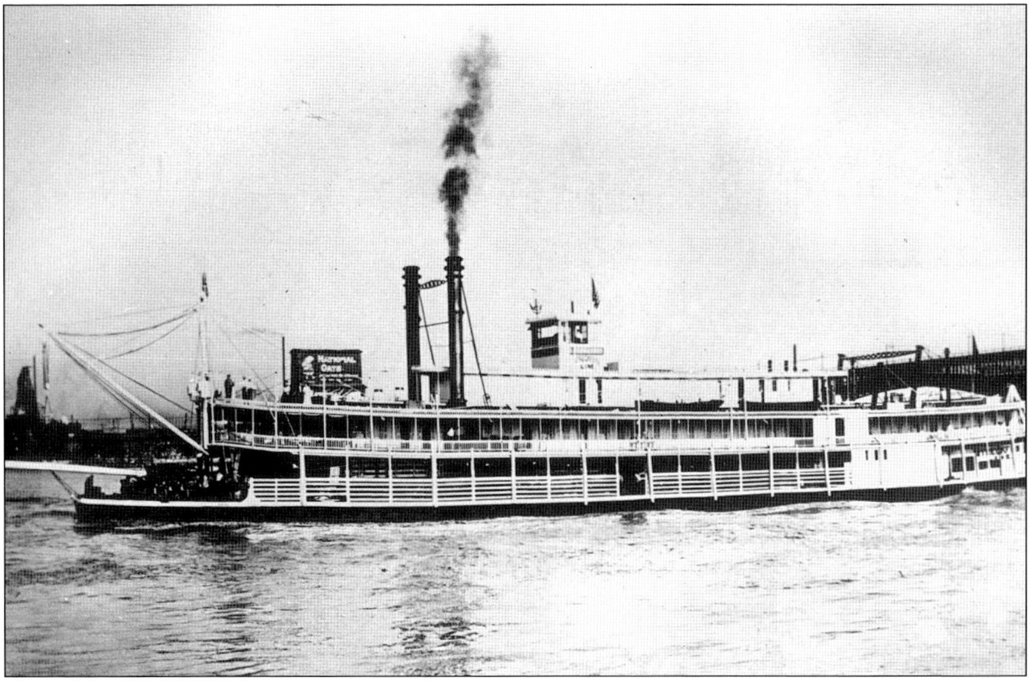

The *Pettigout*, a long, lean-appearing stern-wheeler, heads upriver with its load of freight and passengers.

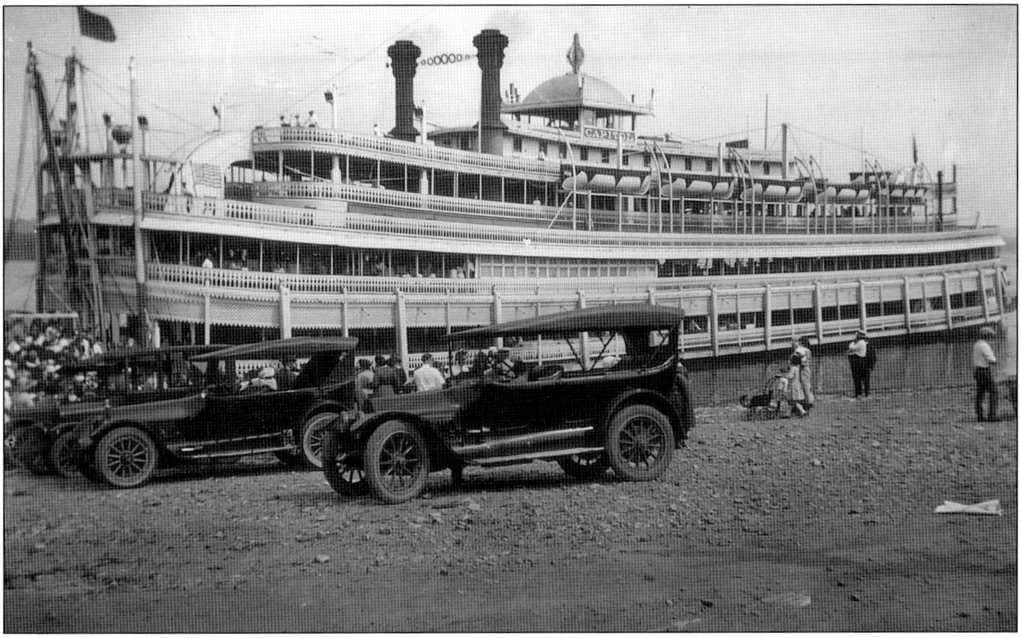

It is sometime in the 1920s, and excursionists crowd the gangplank four abreast to board the *Capitol*.

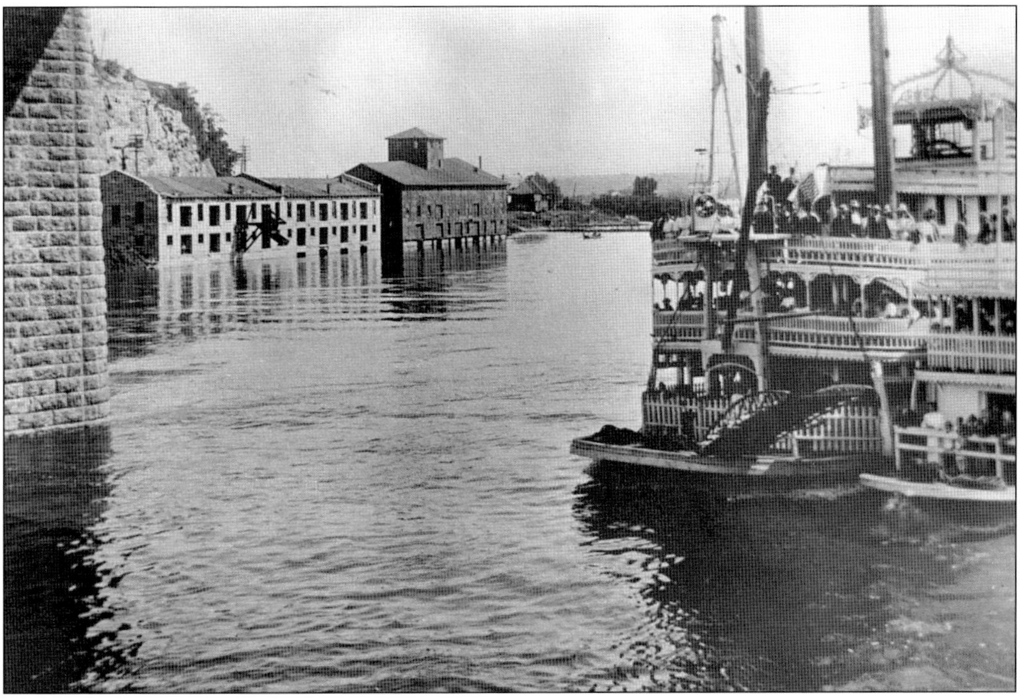

The excursion boat *W.W.* is about to pass beneath the Wagon Bridge that connected East Dubuque, Illinois, on the left, and Dubuque, Iowa.

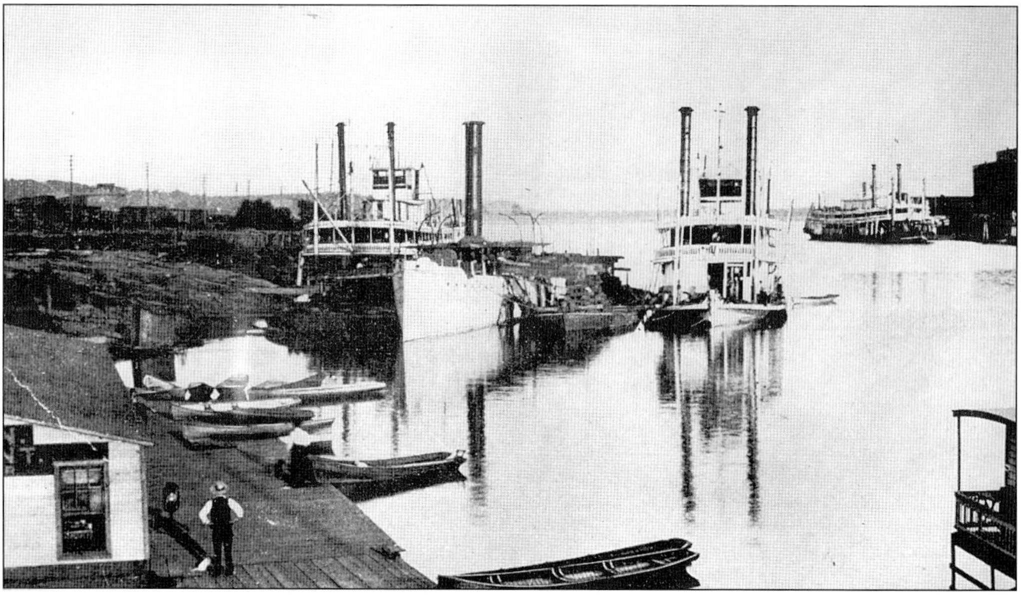

The Ice Harbor at Dubuque, Iowa, was considered one of the best on the Mississippi River. The harbor was home to the Iowa Iron Works that built hundreds of boats. Later, the company would become the Dubuque Boat and Boiler Works. The boat on the far left is the revenue cutter *Windom*.

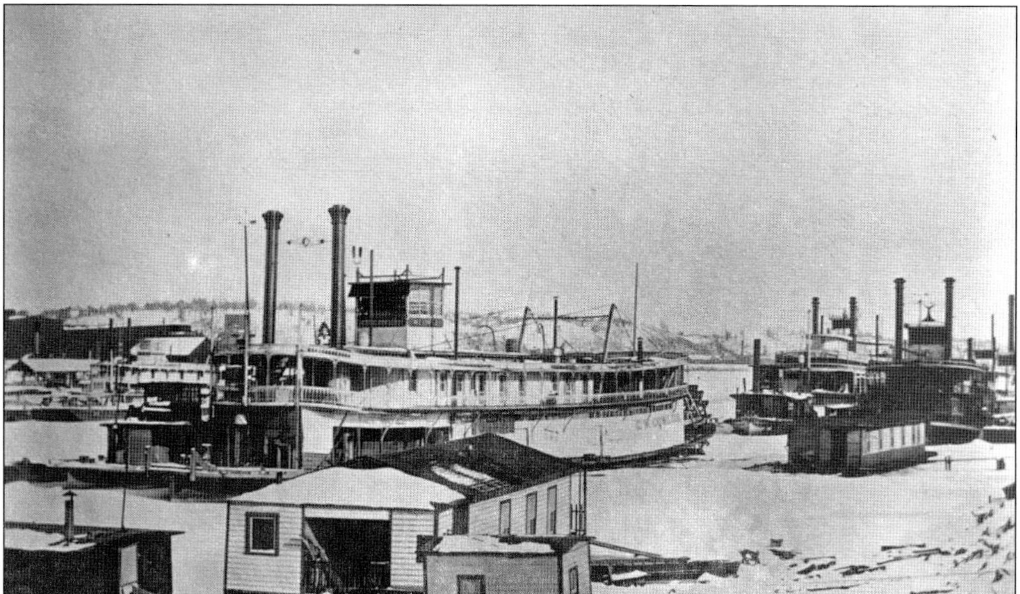

When the Mississippi froze, the Ice Harbor did, too. Boats would rush for a harbor to be near a town for supplies, and to be more protected from the weather. It appears the *C.W. Cowles* was in first this day.

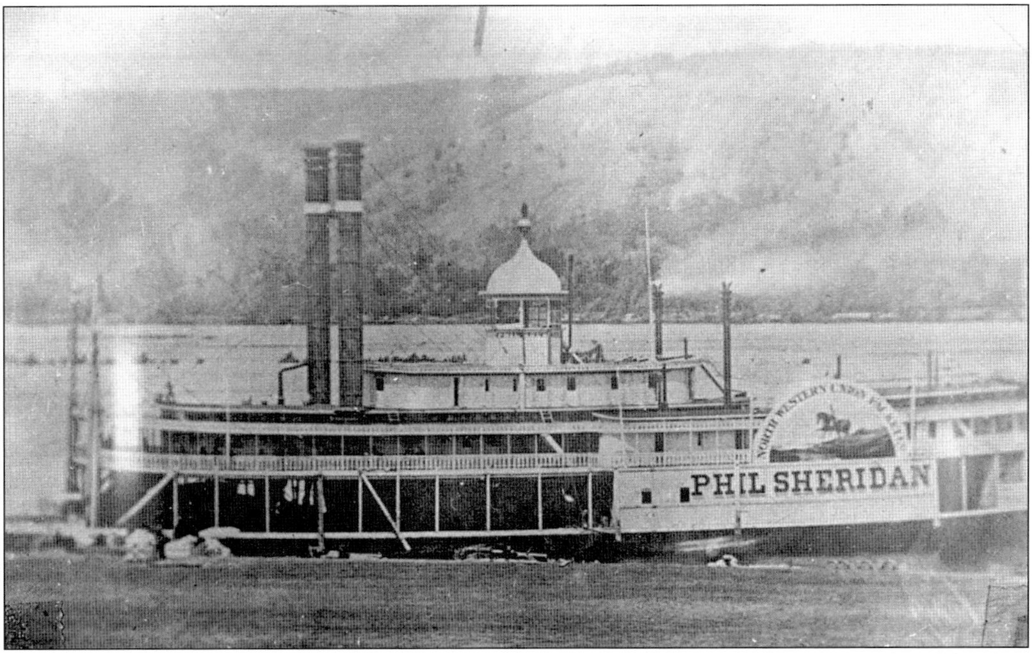

The *Phil Sheridan* is here tied up at a stop along the Mississippi River. Once railroad bridges spanned the Father of Waters, the tall stacks were hinged and could be lowered. Sometimes, the pilot house was also hinged for the same reason.

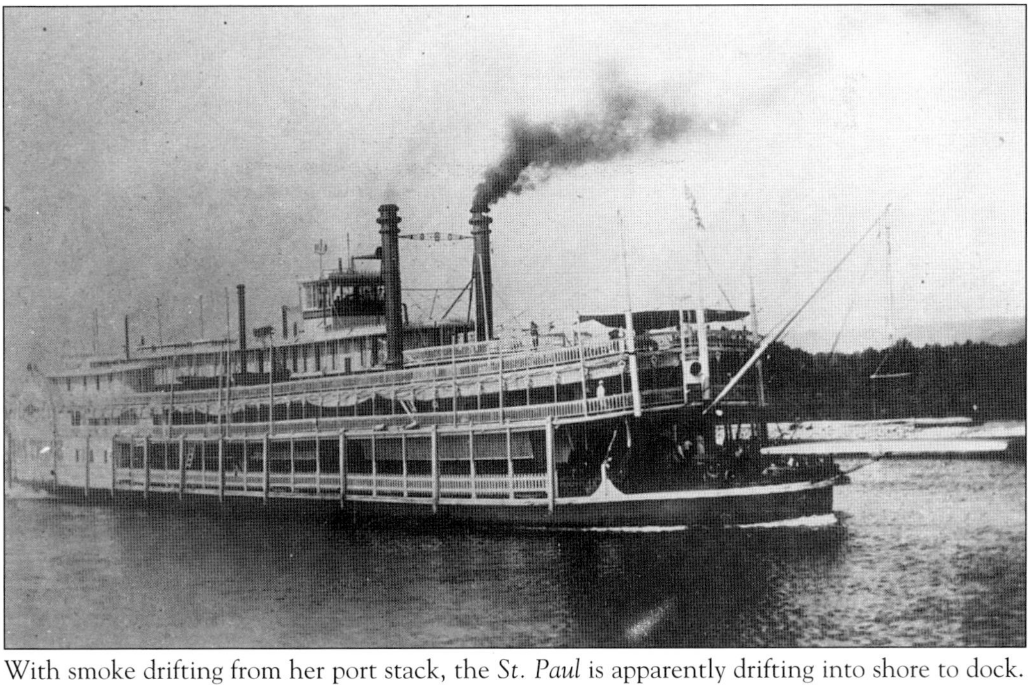

With smoke drifting from her port stack, the *St. Paul* is apparently drifting into shore to dock.

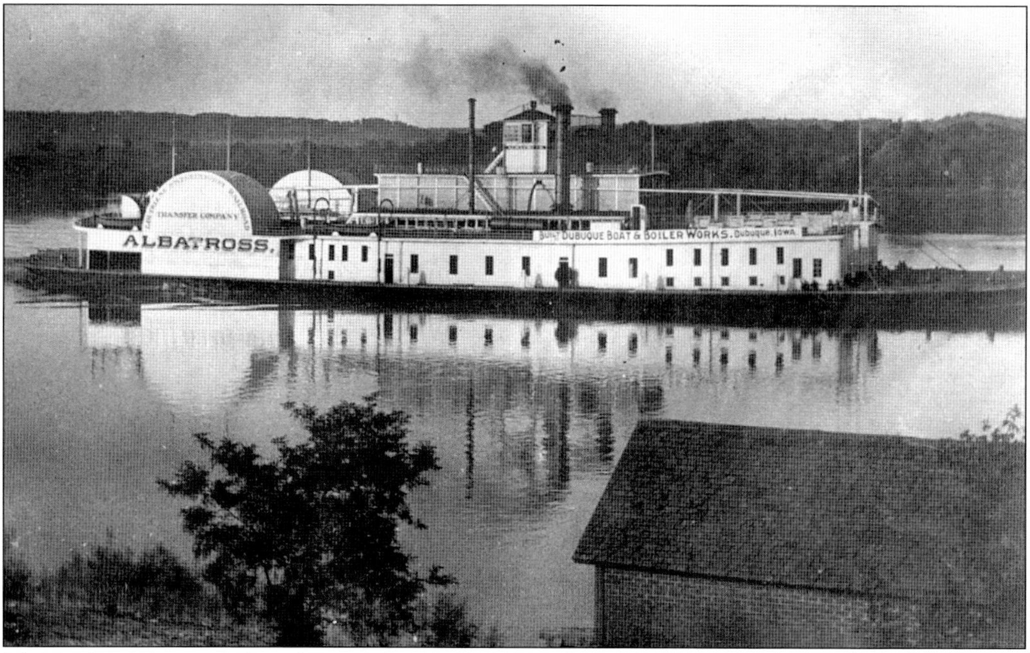

The Dubuque Boat and Boiler Works produced railroad car ferries such as the *Albatross*, shown here passing Bellevue, Iowa, for different railroads. The *Albatross* was built for the Louisiana and Mississippi Railroad.

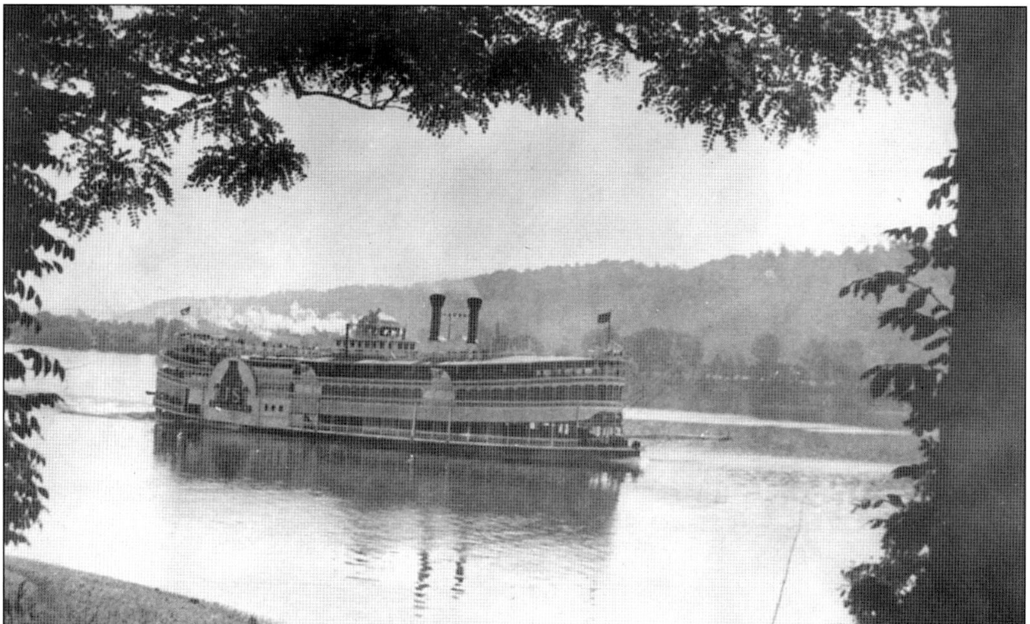

The side-wheeler *J.S.* makes its way along the Mississippi River, and is framed by the bole of a tree and foliage from others. It is a beautiful scene of a time long gone.

Three

The Upper Mississippi

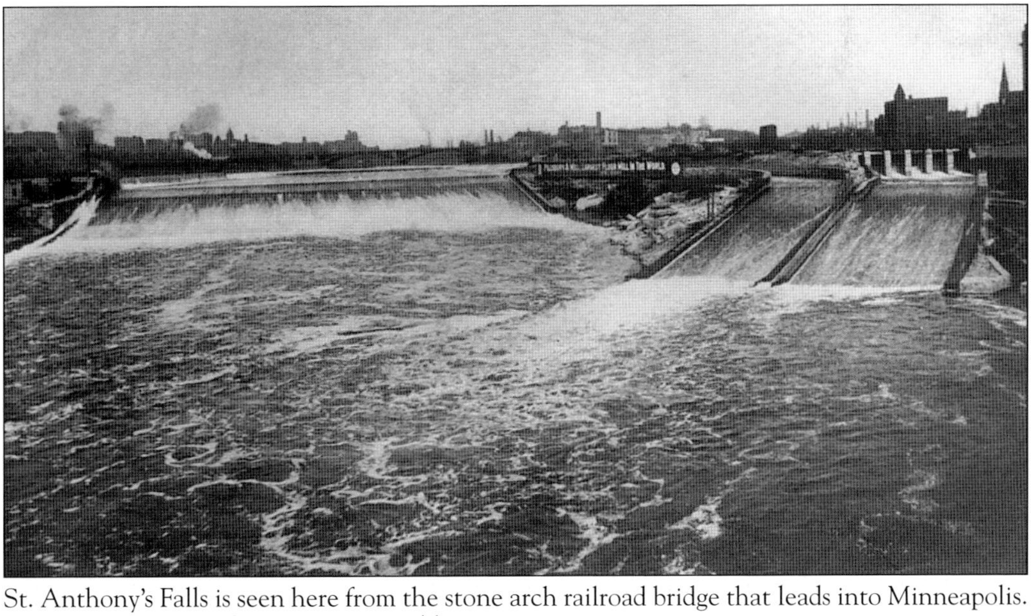

St. Anthony's Falls is seen here from the stone arch railroad bridge that leads into Minneapolis. From this point on, the river is navigable.

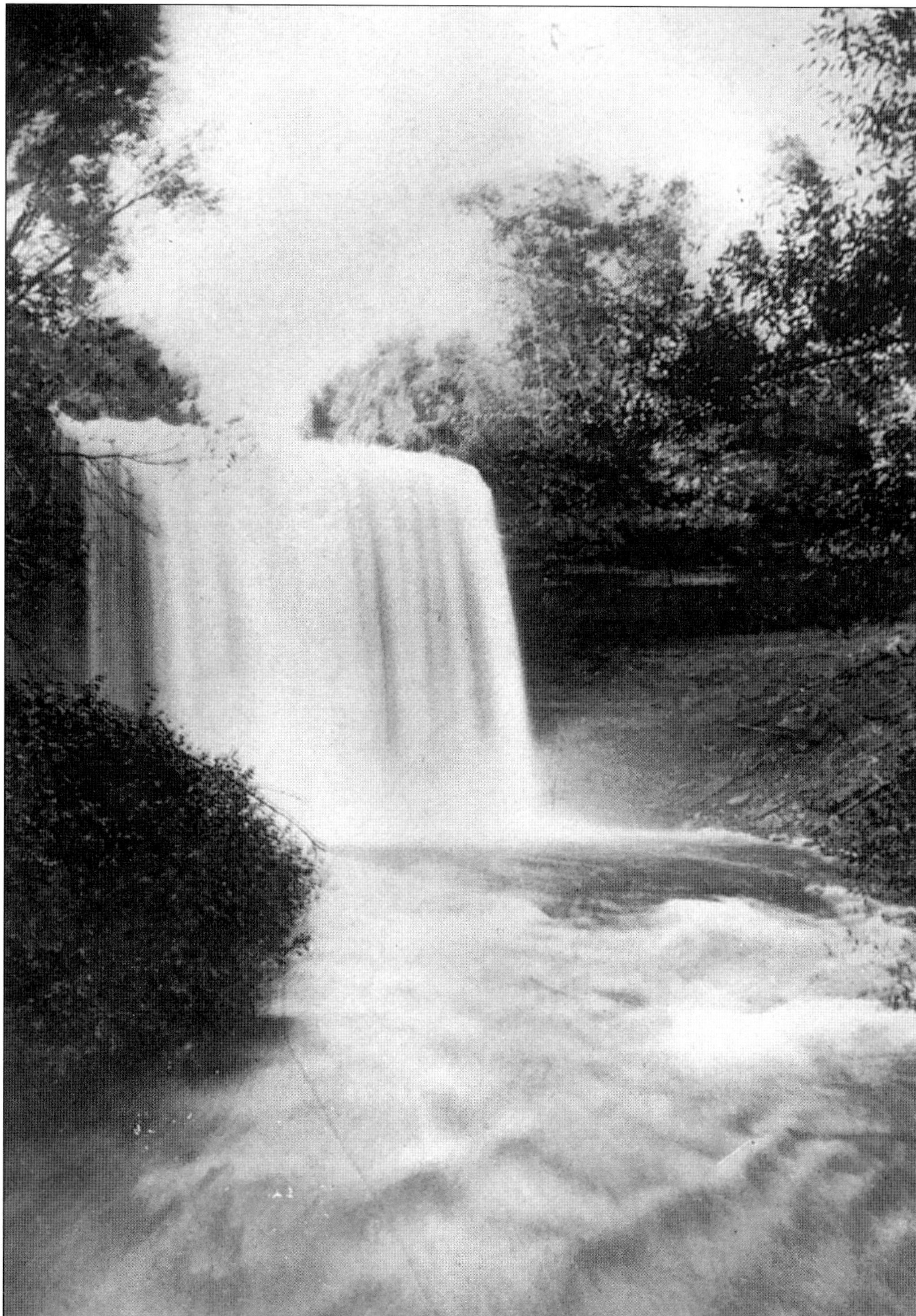

Minnehaha Falls, named for the Indian maiden made famous by Henry Wadsworth Longfellow's epic poem *Hiawatha*, is farther north than St. Anthony's Falls.

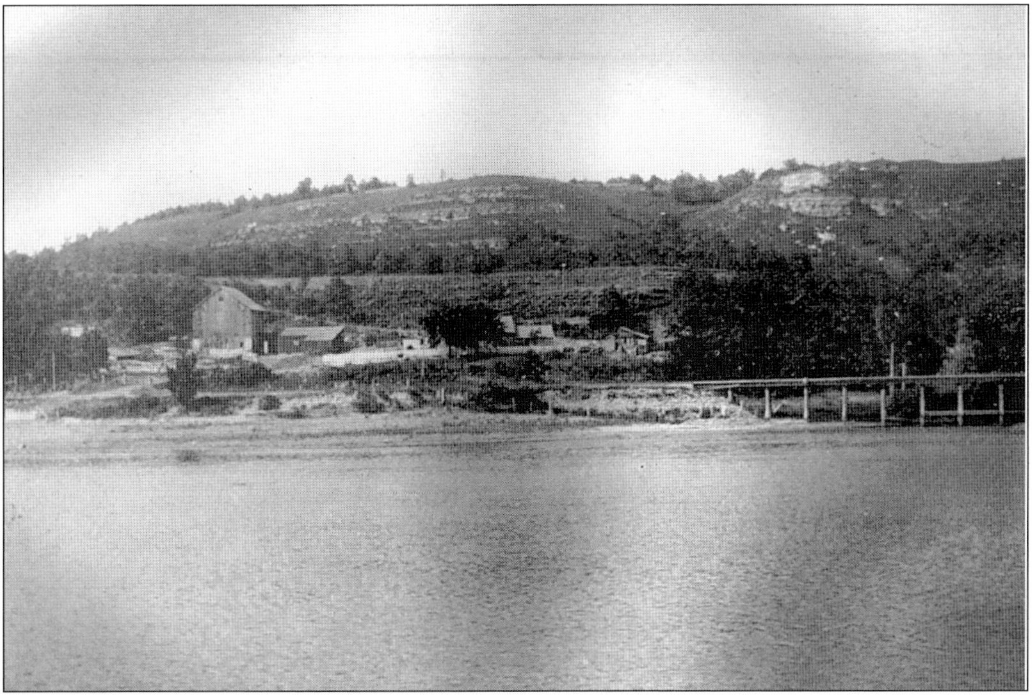

A farm spreads out beneath Diamond Bluff, which was near St. Paul to the south. Notice the railroad trestle of the Chicago, Milwaukee, and St. Paul Ry.

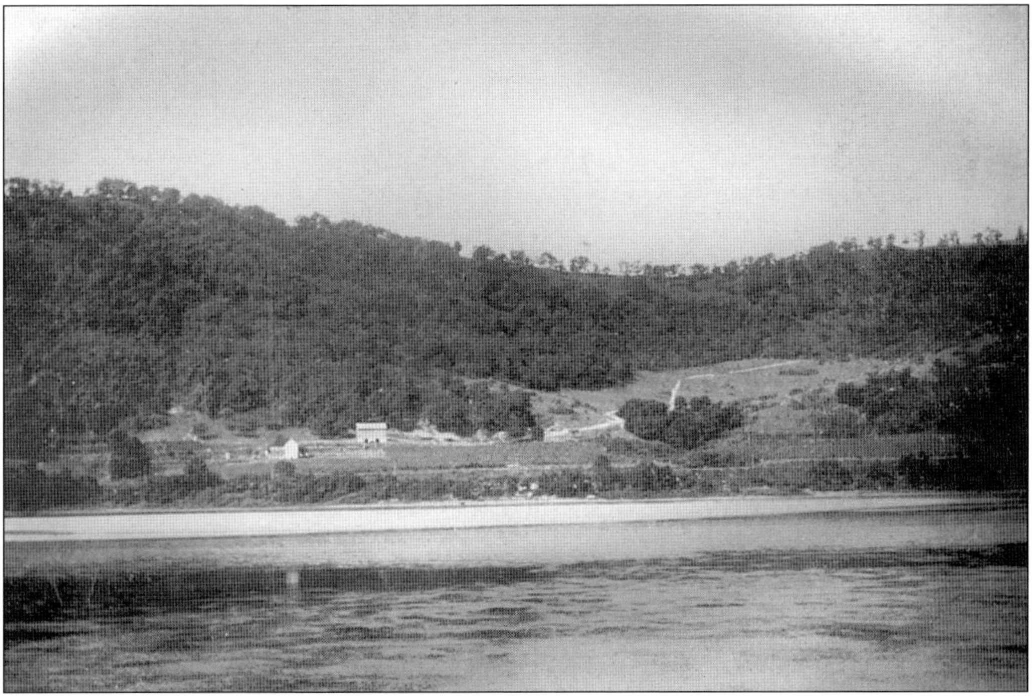

This view of Minnesota from the Wisconsin shore shows farmland, a farm, and timberland.

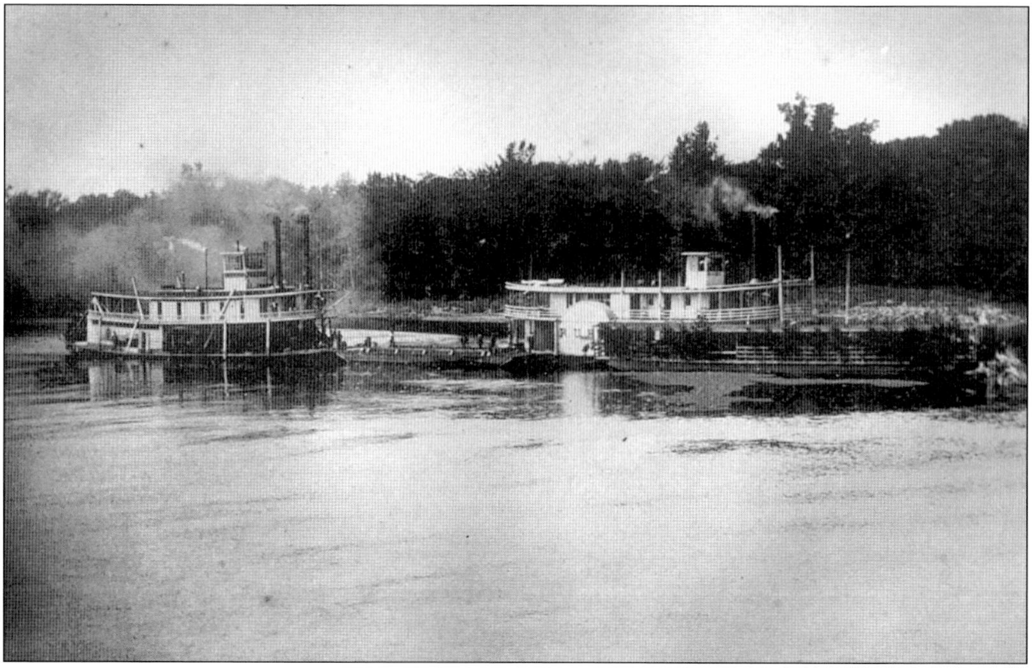

The side-wheeler *Ruby* and an unidentified stern-wheeler help move material around to assist the crew building wing dams in the Mississippi River above Hastings, Minnesota, sometime around 1900.

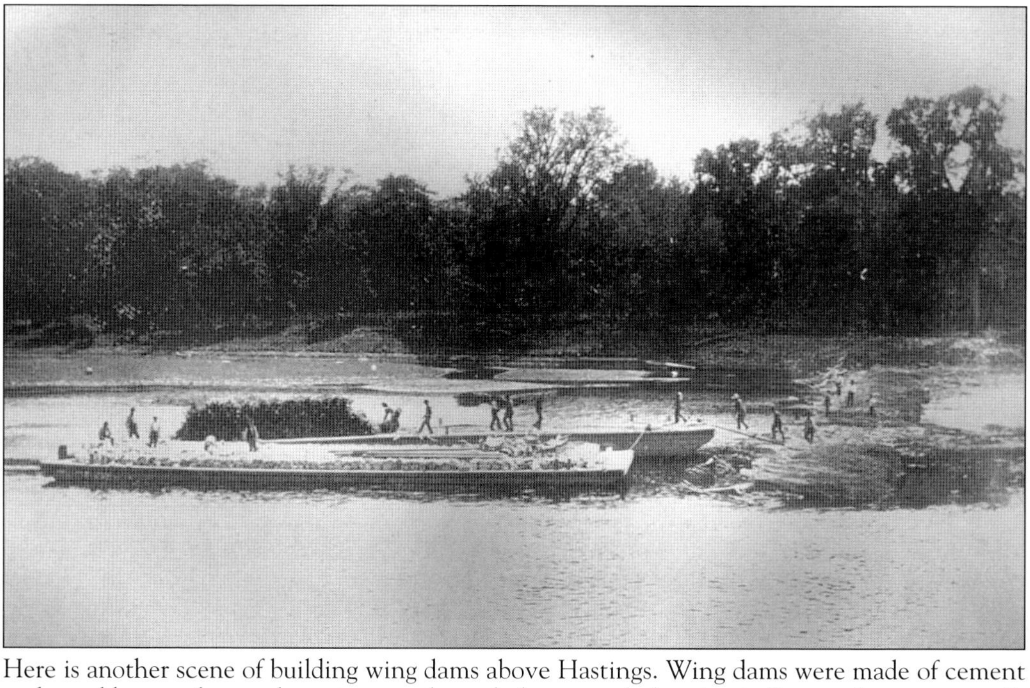

Here is another scene of building wing dams above Hastings. Wing dams were made of cement and would extend at a downriver angle to help control the river's flow and prevent a silt buildup. Dams were usually built in series of three. They were no longer needed once the locks and dams were built in the 1930s.

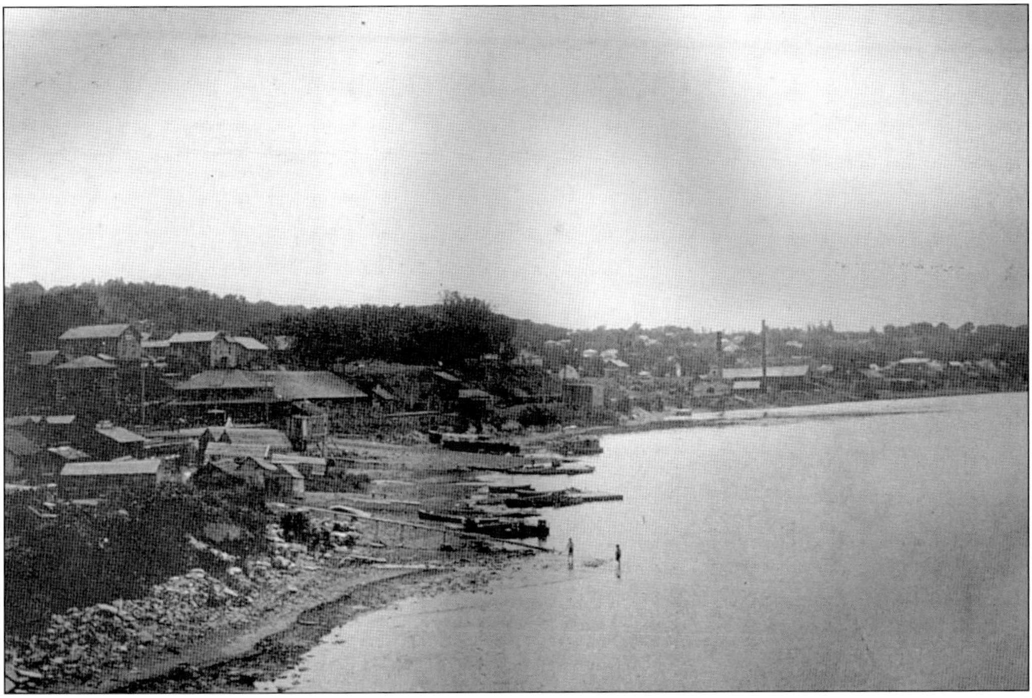

Red Wing, Minnesota, is shown here around the turn of the 20th century. The waterfront is suited to steamboats landing, taking on fuel, freight, and passengers, or discharging the last two.

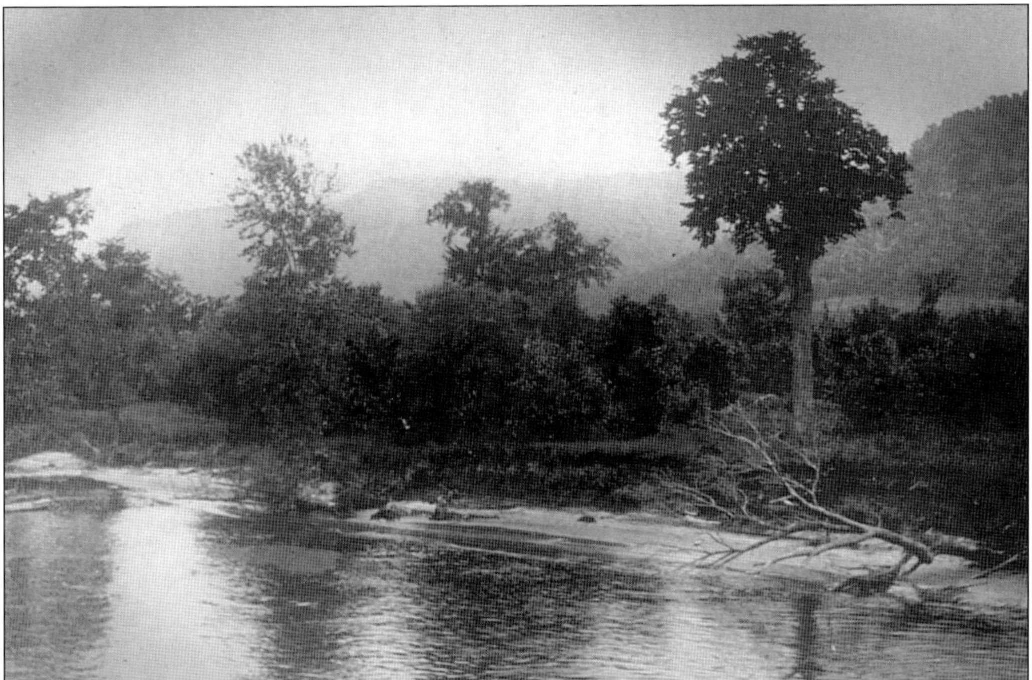

This photograph was taken along the Mississippi shores of Minnesota. The water was relatively low before the locks and dams were built, that in turn made the river more navigable.

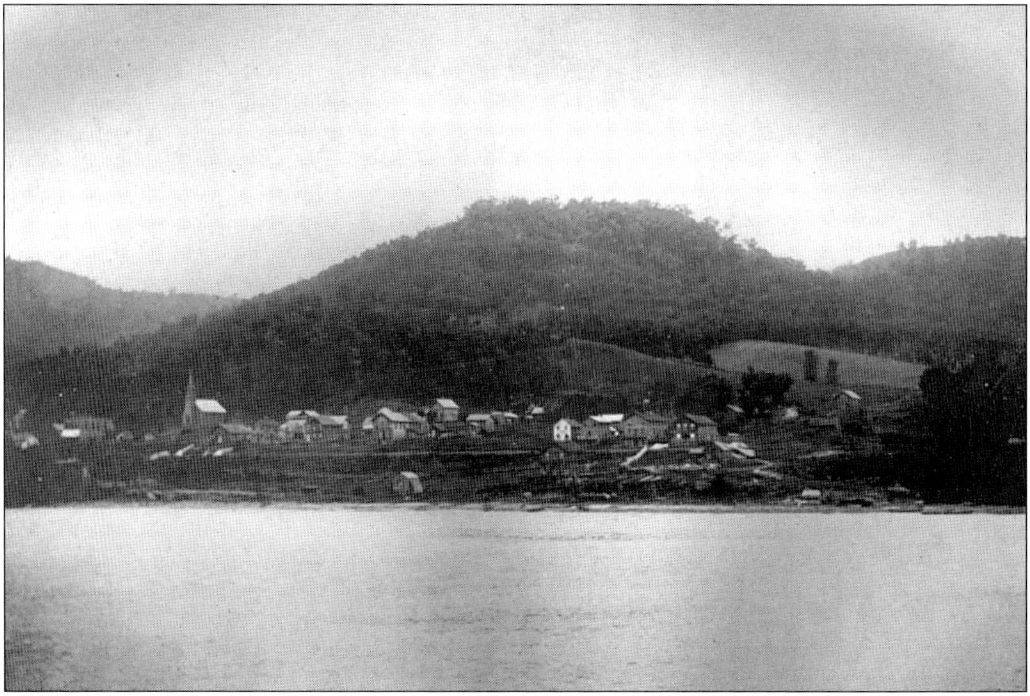

Like most river towns, Dresbach, Minnesota, clung to the shore and stretched along the river.

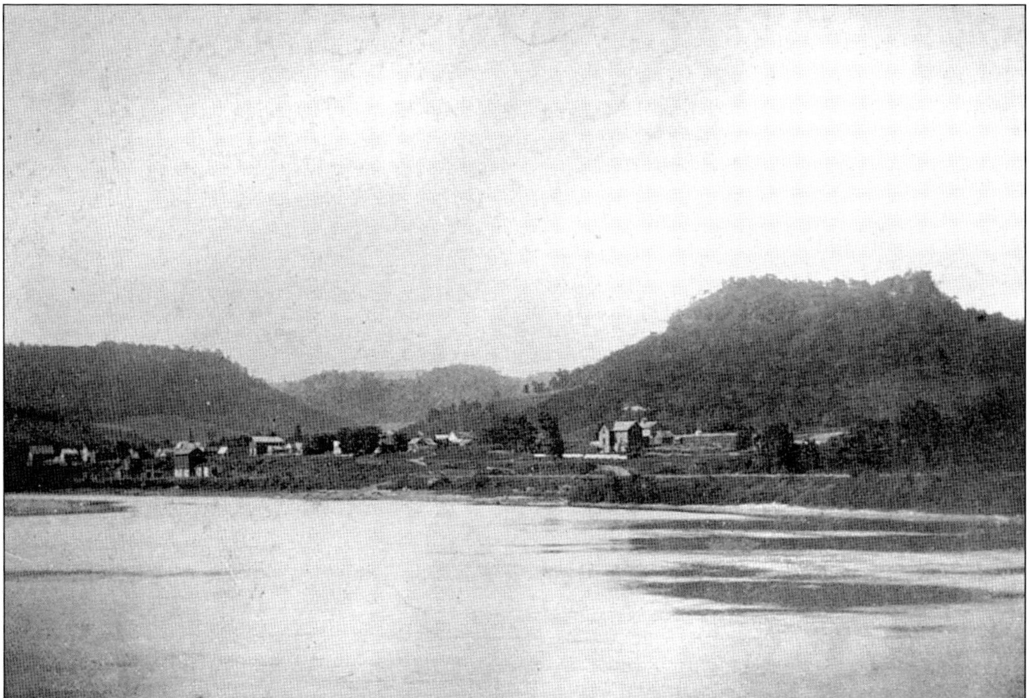

The lower half of Dresbach extended south and the small town was hemmed in by the hills.

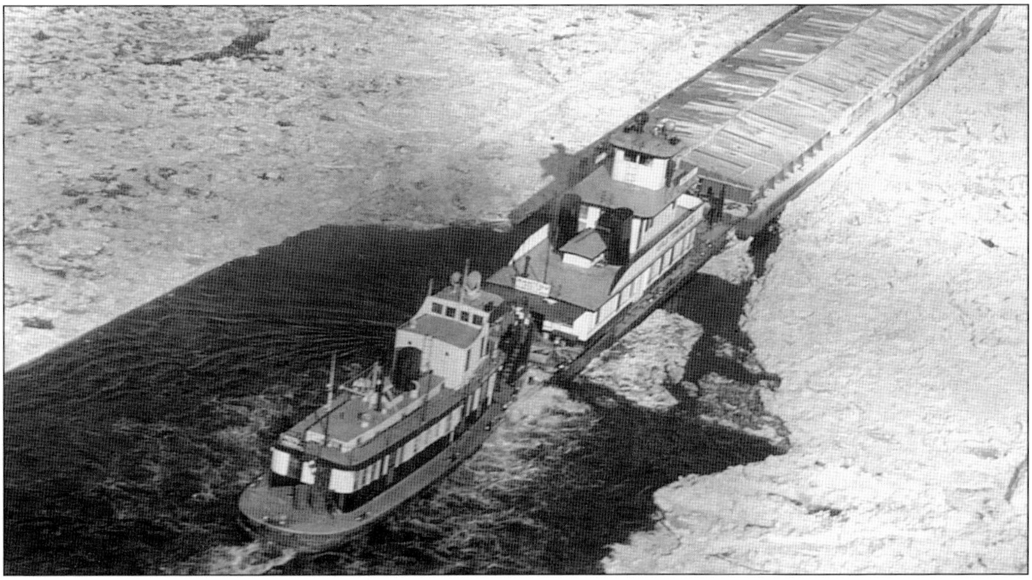

Winter usually closes the upper Mississippi for 90 to 120 days. In the above photograph, the first boat, *Manitou*, is pushing a loaded barge with the help of an unidentified boat, to open the channel. Such a practice was unheard of in steamboat days.

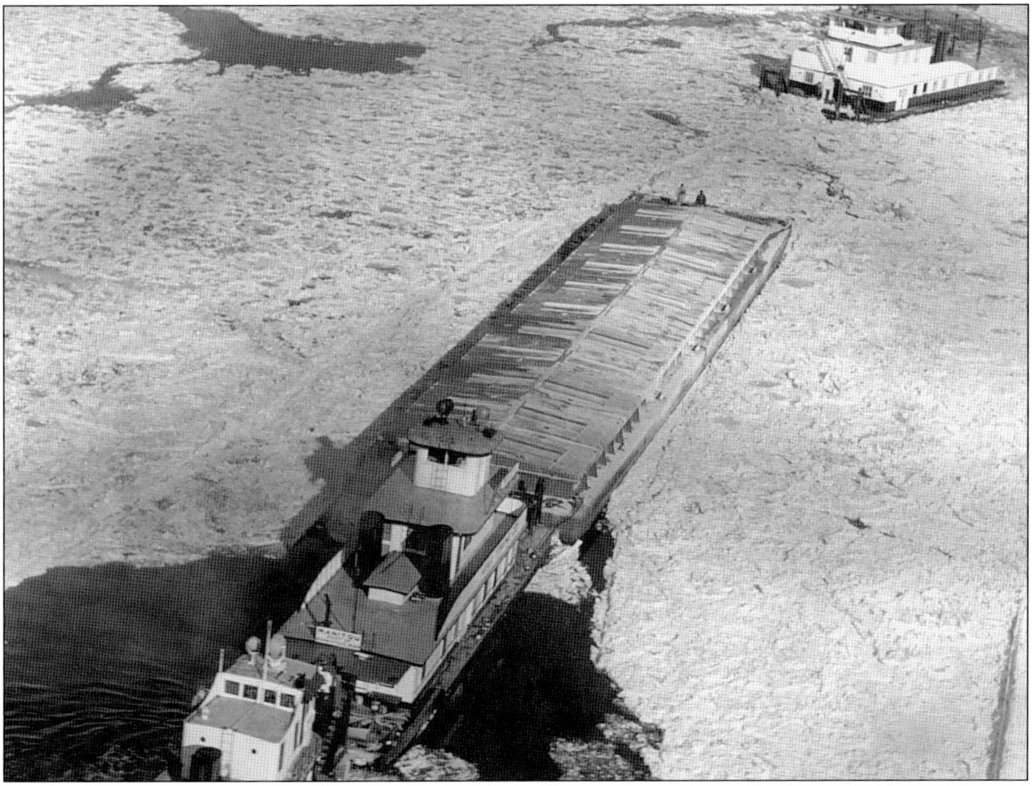

Coming downriver is a third diesel-powered boat that is about ready to meet with the *Manitou* and her entourage. When the ice breaks up of its own accord and floats downriver, the ice rubbing against other pieces sounds a great deal like crystal being softly struck.

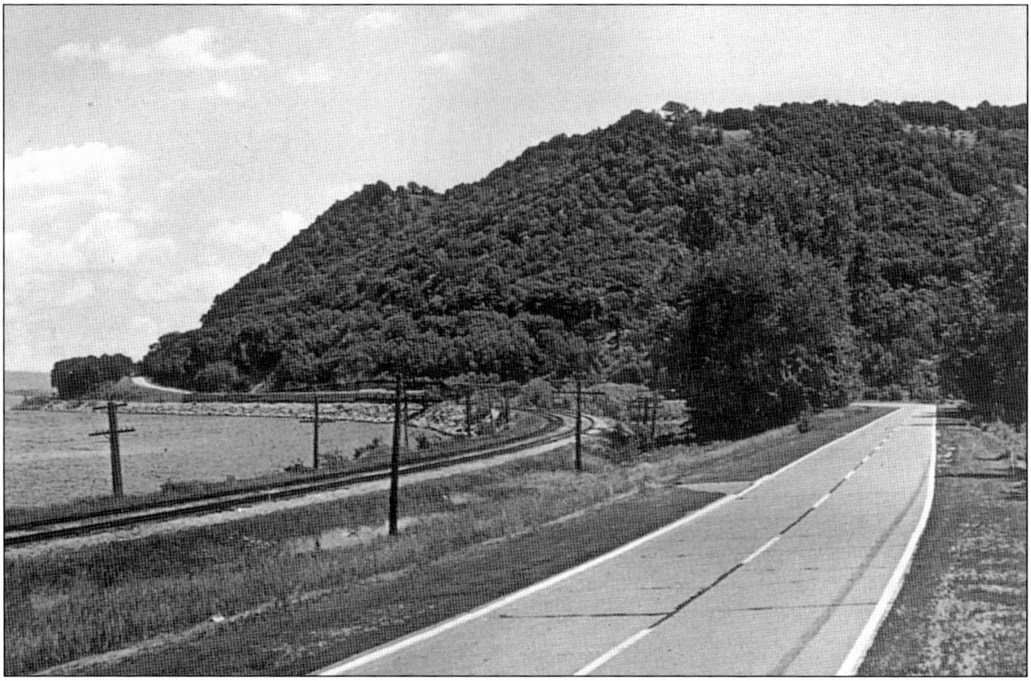

Minnesota in the summer is beautiful. This two-lane highway is four-lane in 2000, and the double mainline of the Chicago, Milwaukee, St. Paul, and Pacific Ry parallels it for some distance before crossing the Mississippi to LaCrosse, Wisconsin.

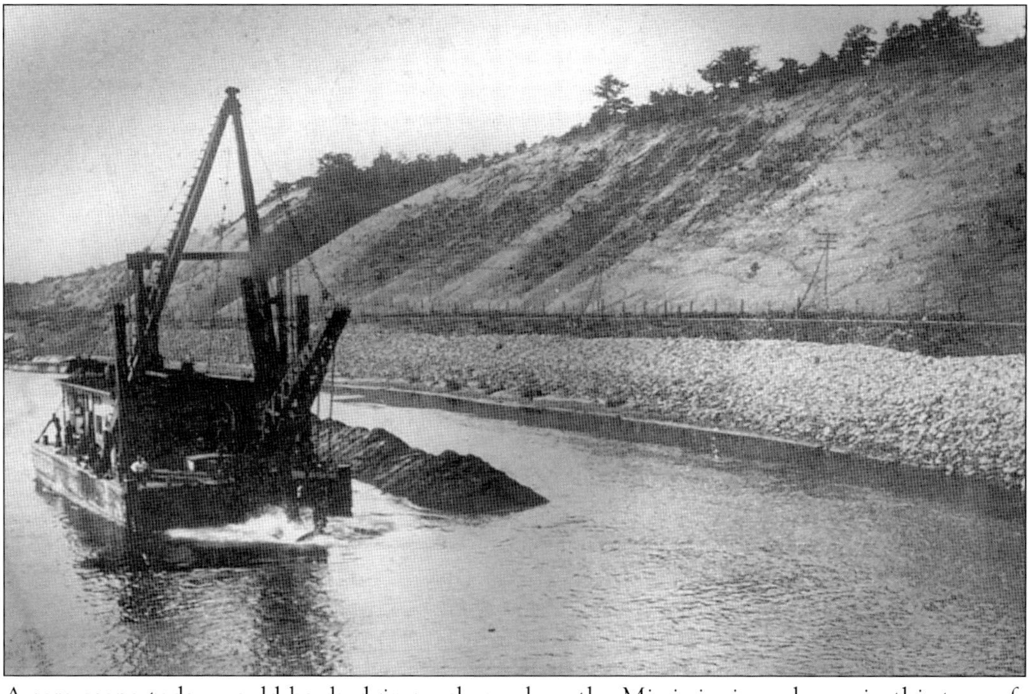

A rare scene today would be dredging a channel on the Mississippi, as shown in this turn-of-the-20th century photograph taken near Prescott, Wisconsin.

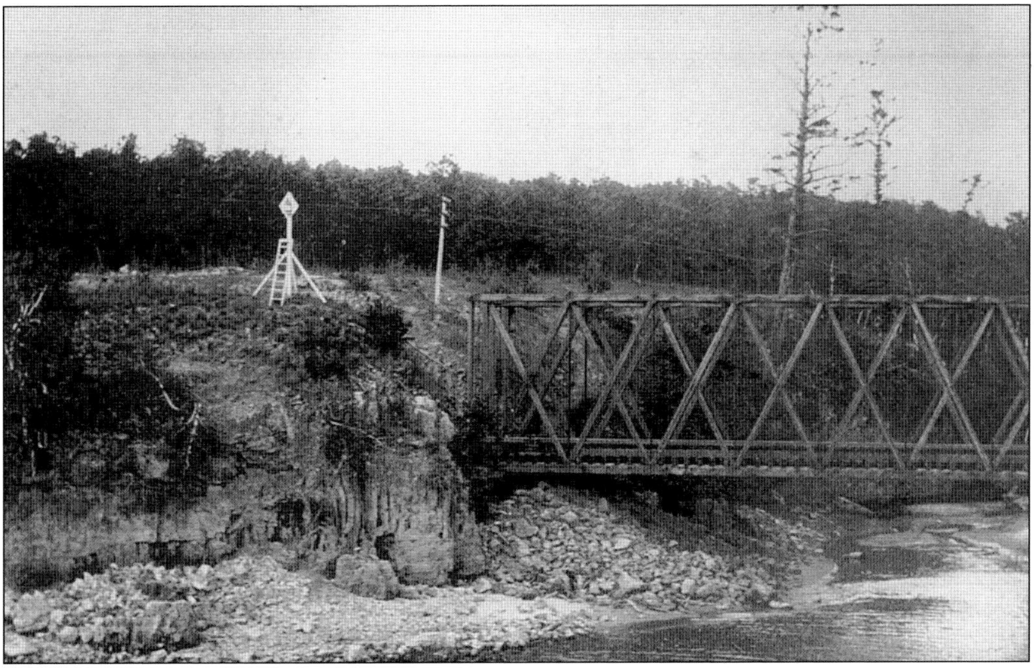

A wooden railroad truss bridge crosses a stream emptying into the Mississippi below Prescott, Wisconsin.

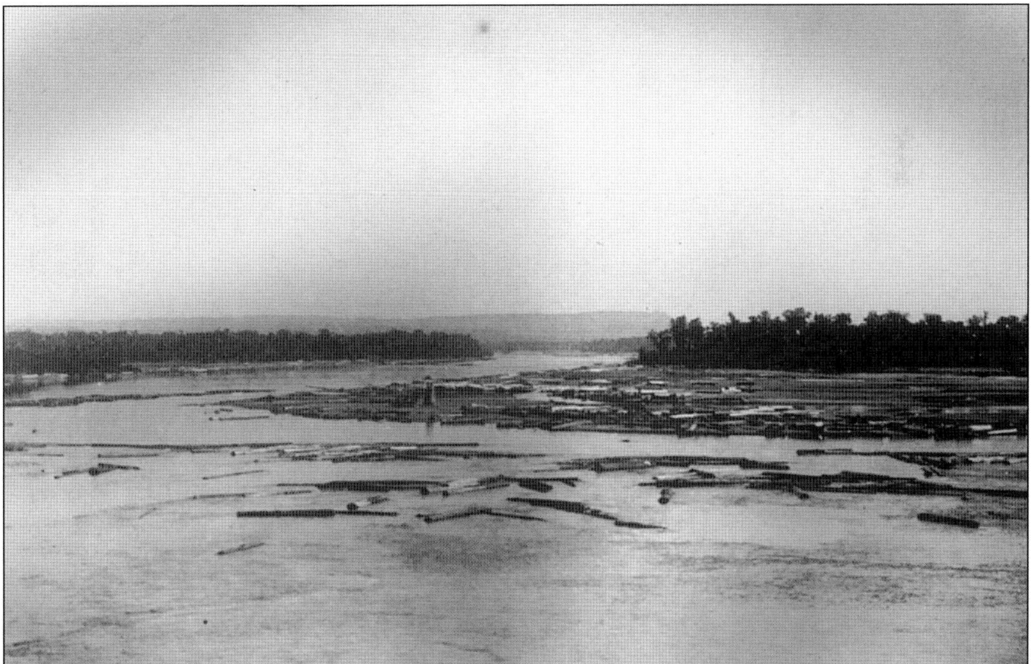

Logs float freely at the mouth of the Chippewa River. Millions of board feet were rafted down the Chippewa and into the Mississippi to be taken south to one of the lumber mills.

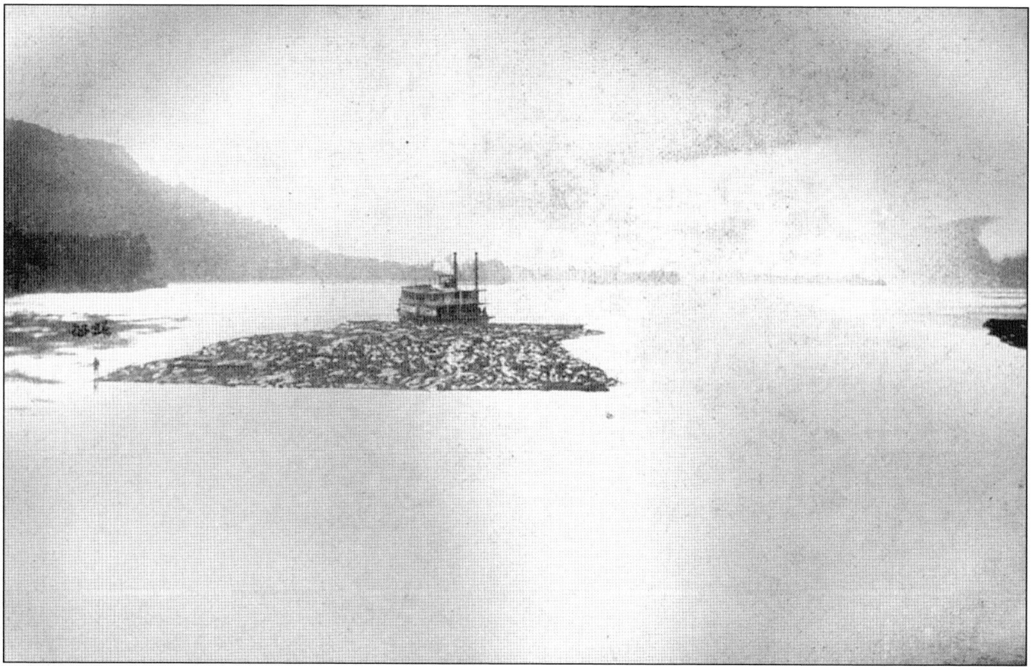

A rafter at the mouth of the Chippewa River is captured in this photograph. Notice the boat is at an angle to the raft to direct the logs to port, or left, enabling the boat and raft to turn into the Mississippi and head south. Three pike men ride the front of the raft, ready to push those logs out of the way, such as the man on the left is about to do.

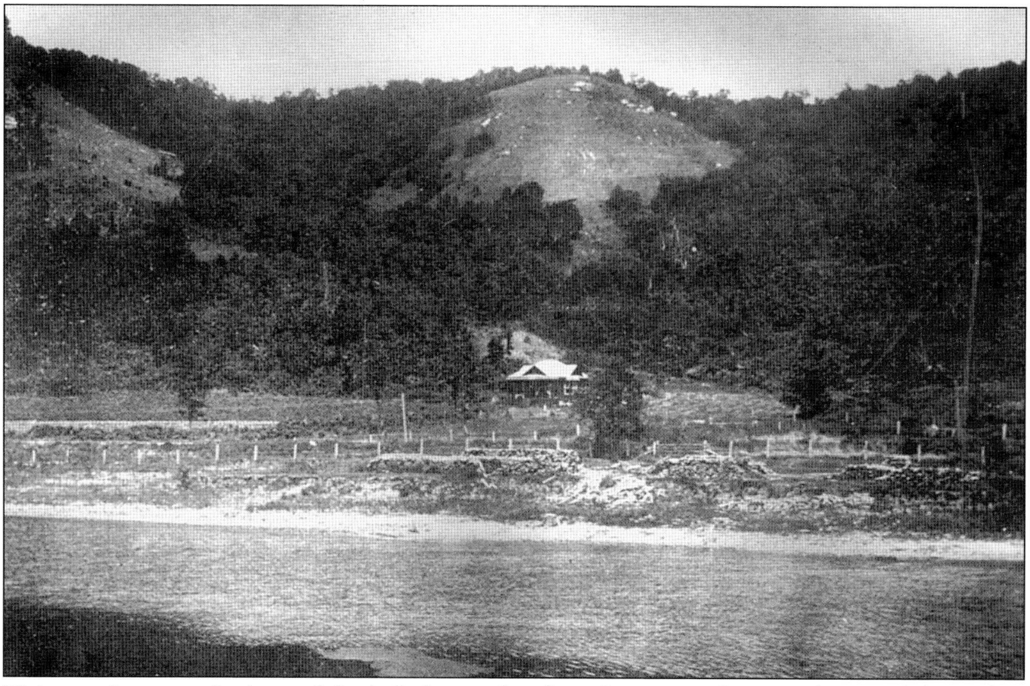

This cozy home at the base of the hills lining the shore has an unobstructed view of the Father of Waters.

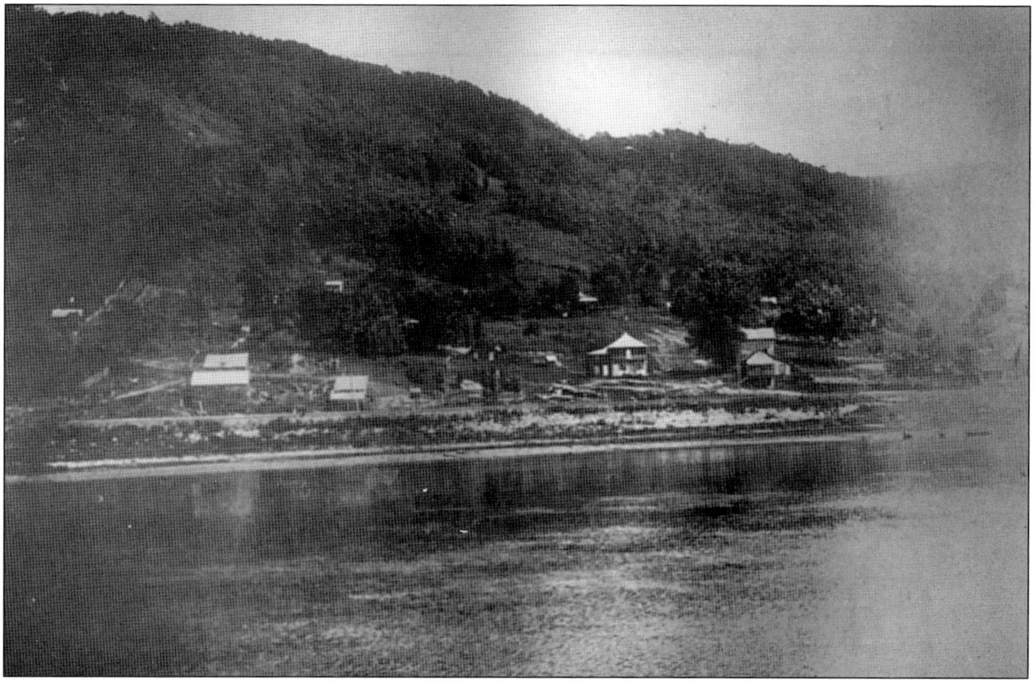

Victory, Wisconsin has expanded in the one hundred years since the above photograph was taken. Like many river towns, it extends along the shore, north and south, building inland only when necessary.

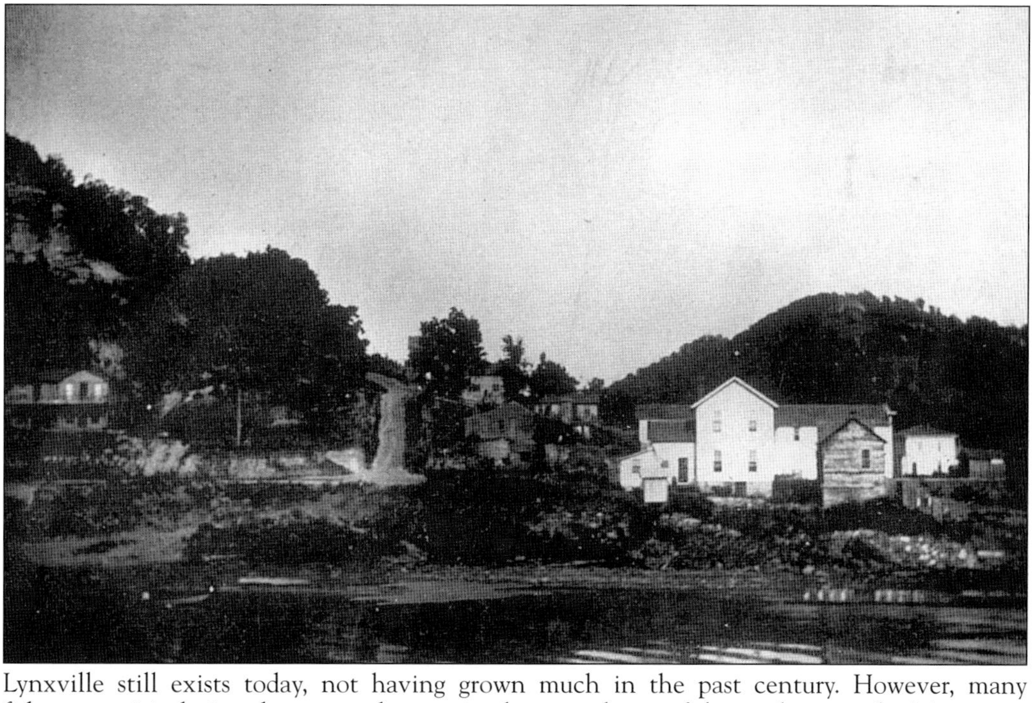

Lynxville still exists today, not having grown much in the past century. However, many fishermen visit during the year today, storing boats and sport fishing whatever the Mississippi is ready to offer.

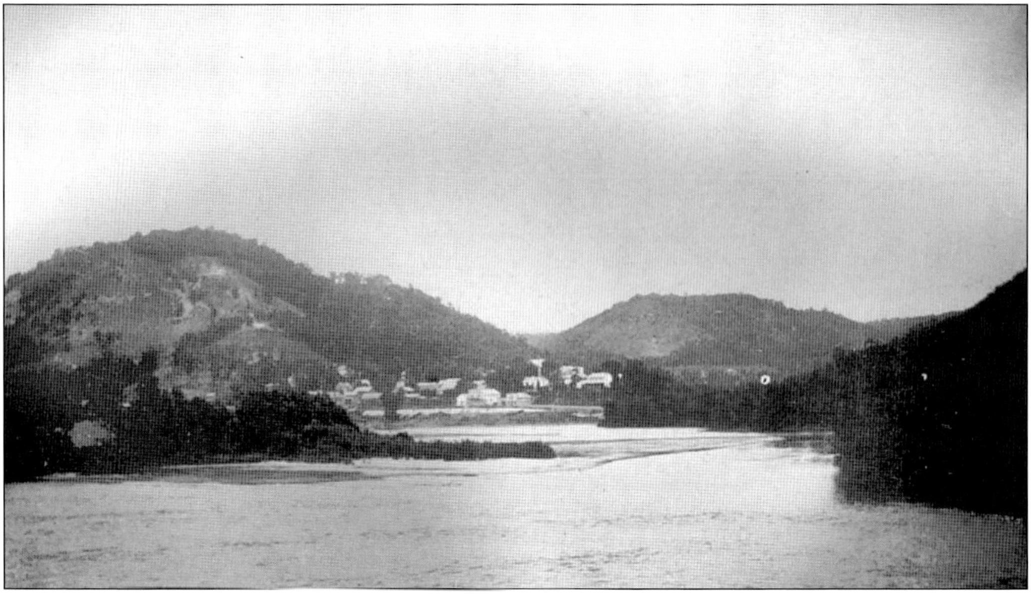

South of Lynxville, the community of DeSoto nestles among the hills and currently welcomes tourists and travelers who might stop for camping provisions and gasoline for their automobiles.

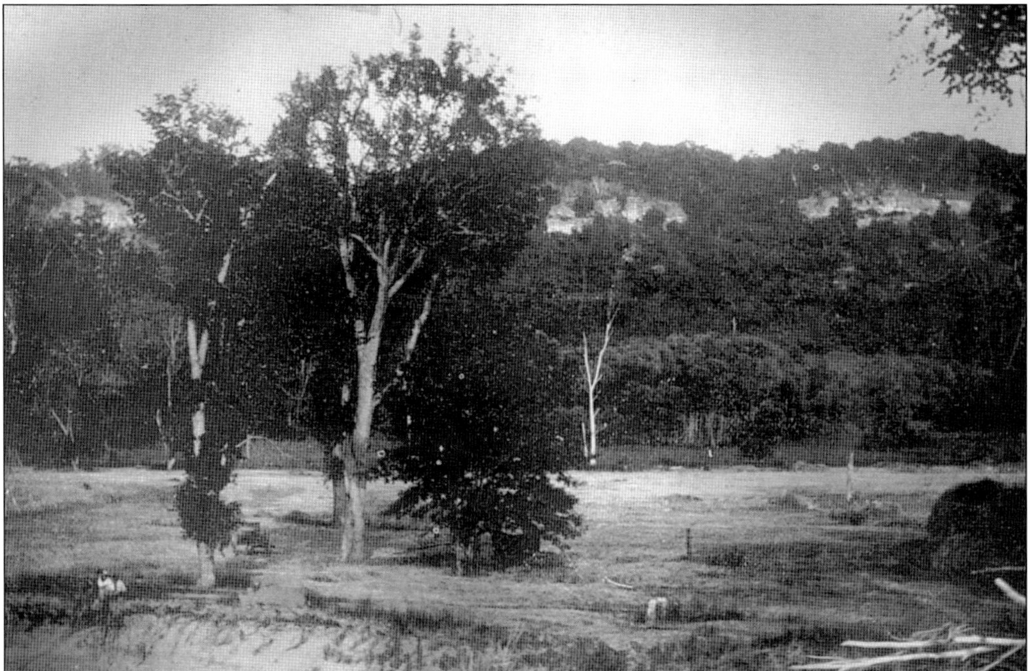

This scene is as peaceful as anyplace in the world, and two people are enjoying it, sitting on the bank to the left of the small strand of trees.

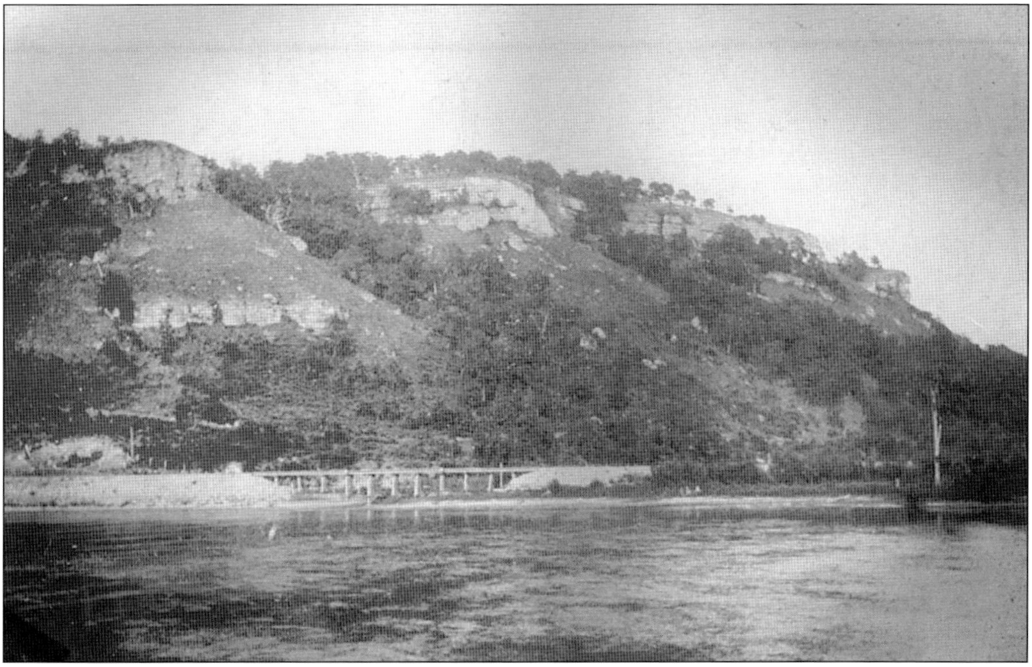

The Chicago, Burlington, and Quincy Railroad's wooden trestle bridge has long since been replaced with a steel one. Long freights of the Burlington Northern Santa Fe Railroad haul freight north and south many times daily.

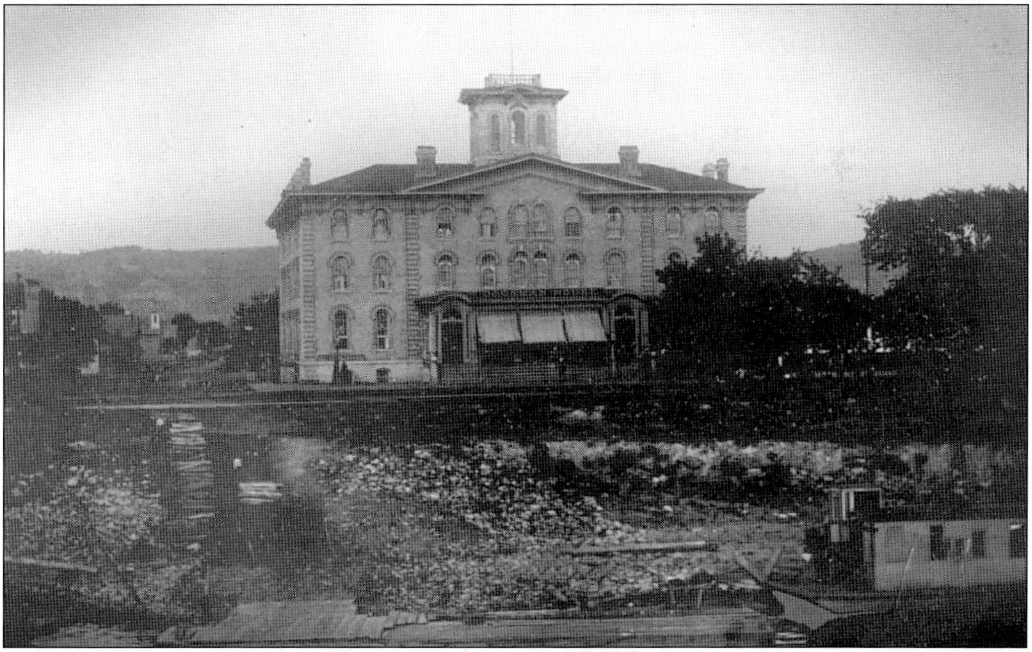

The boat landing at Prairie du Chien, Wisconsin, is shown here. Notice the wood neatly stacked to allow rivermen to load the fuel on board while freight and passenger business is conducted. The three-storied building is the largest in town, with the exception of the Dousman Mansion, which rivals it in size.

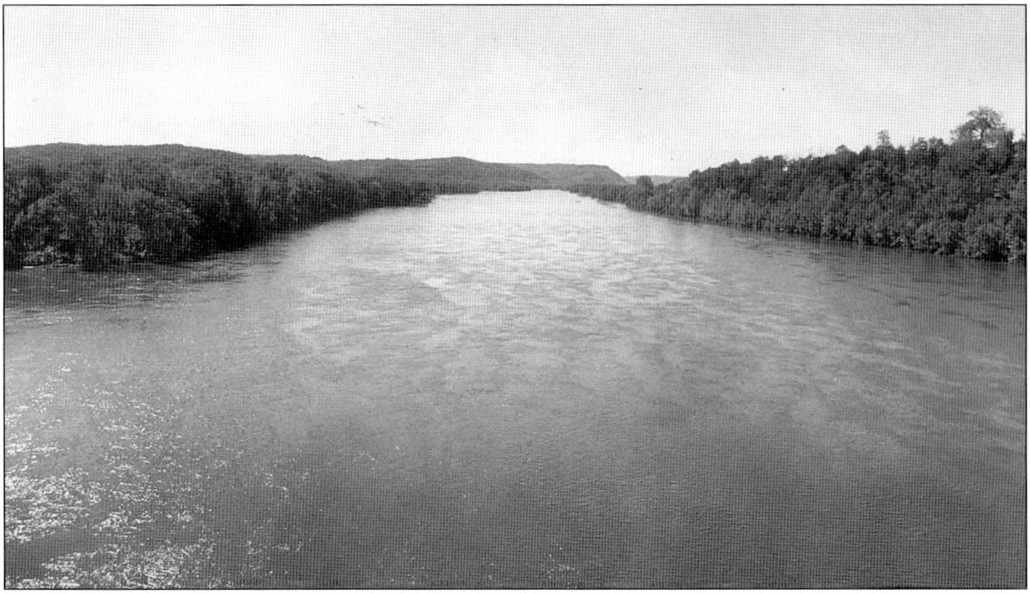

The Wisconsin River empties into the Mississippi a mile or so south of Prairie du Chien, which is opposite McGregor and Marquette, Iowa.

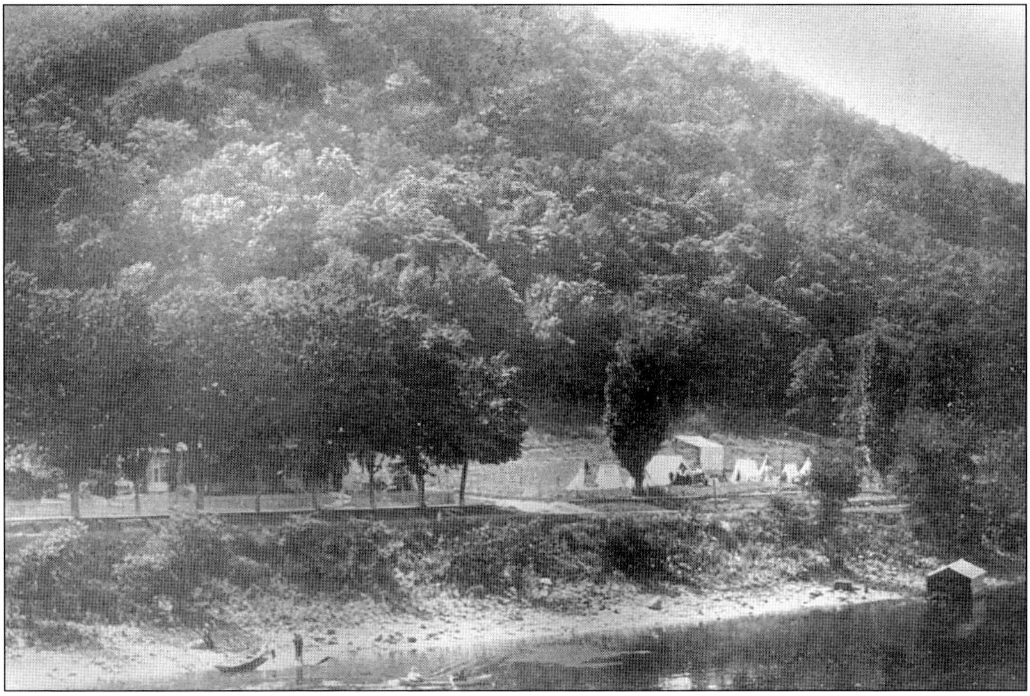

A Kickapoo camp near Lansing, Iowa, is pictured here. Originally part of a tribe of Algonquin Indians, the Kickapoo broke into two separate tribes. One went west and the other remained in the Midwest. Some of the eastern tribe followed B lack Hawk in 1832.

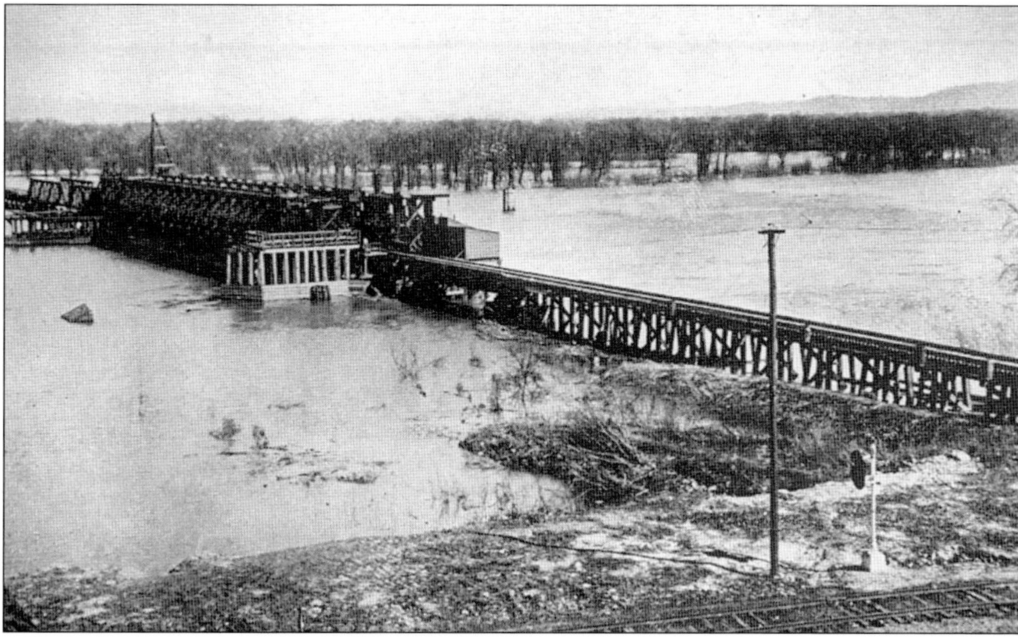

The Chicago, Milwaukee, St. Paul, and Pacific pontoon bridge is located at Marquette, Iowa. The bridge is in a closed position.

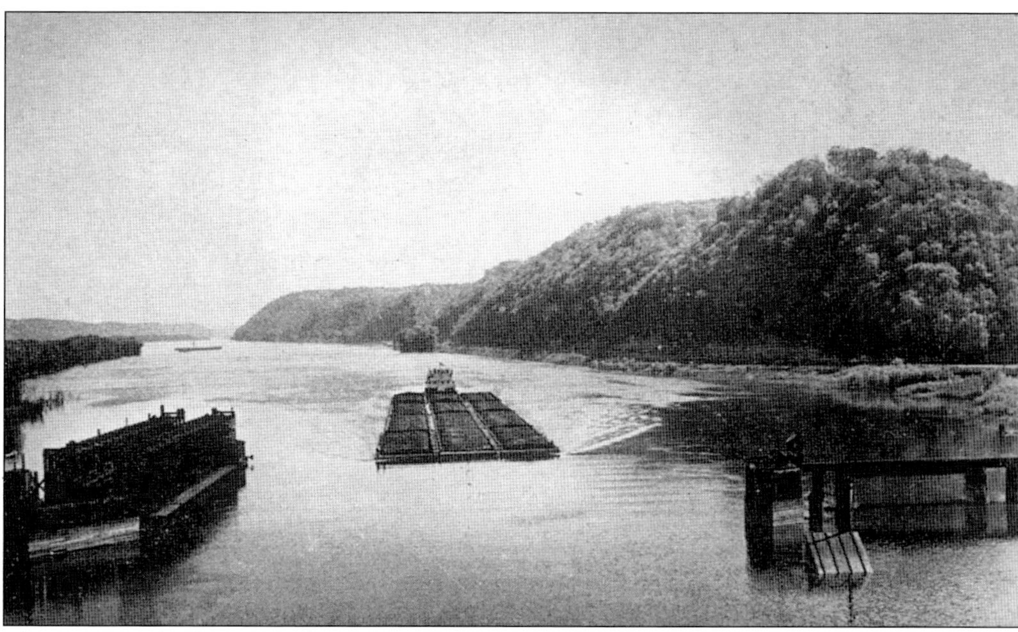

The pontoon bridge's swing portion opened by the current and closed by mechanical means. The bridge spanned the Iowa, or west, channel of the Mississippi at Marquette.

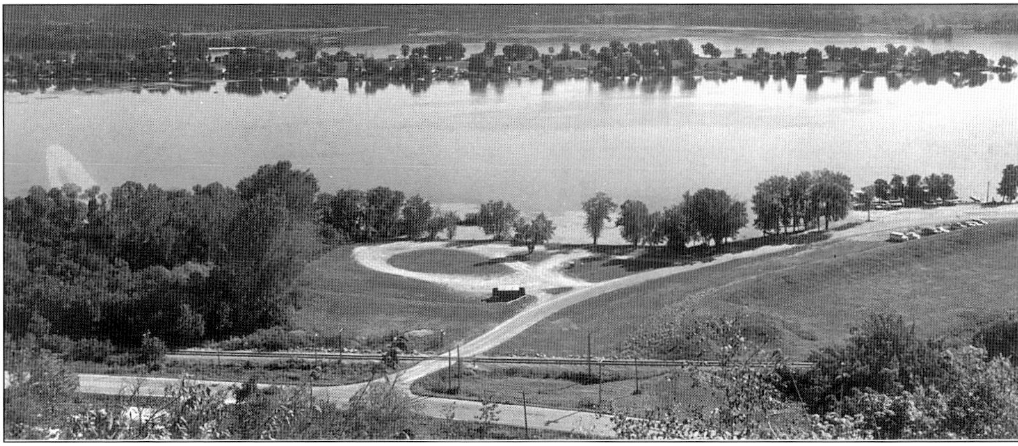

This park on the north edge of Guttenberg, Iowa, is opposite an island that is home to many summer visitors as well as year-round residents. Wisconsin lies on the distant shore.

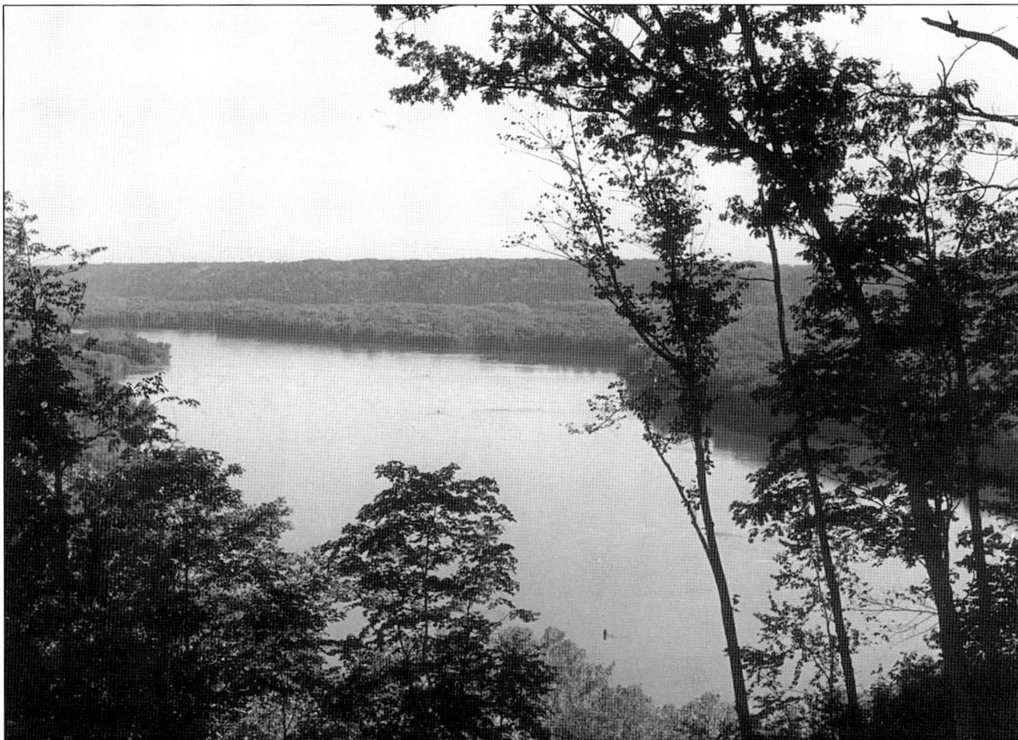

This vantage point south of Guttenberg, looking north, upriver, offers a beautiful view.

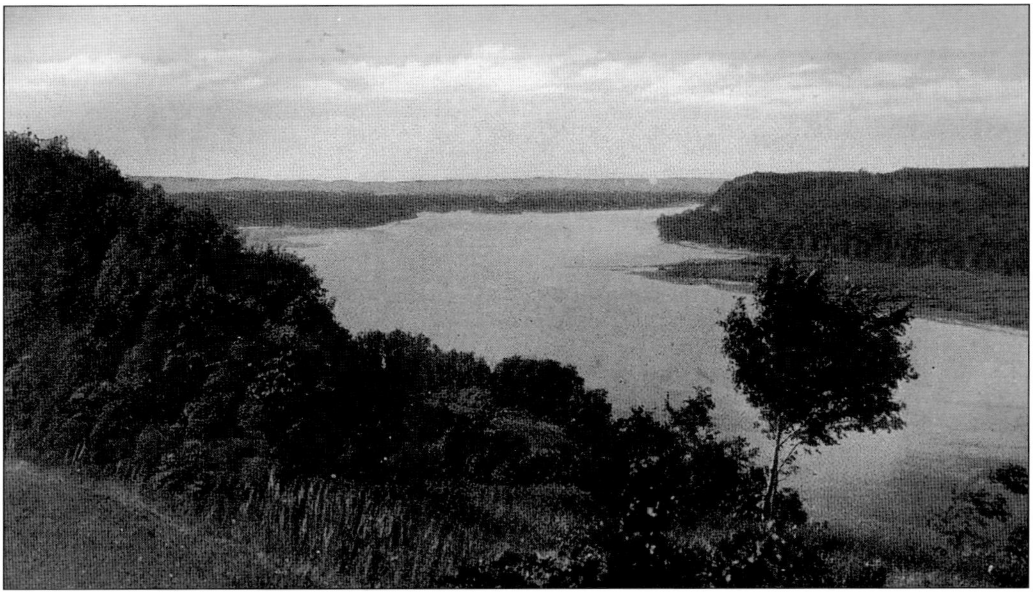

This view looks north up the Mississippi from Eagle Point Park in Dubuque, Iowa.

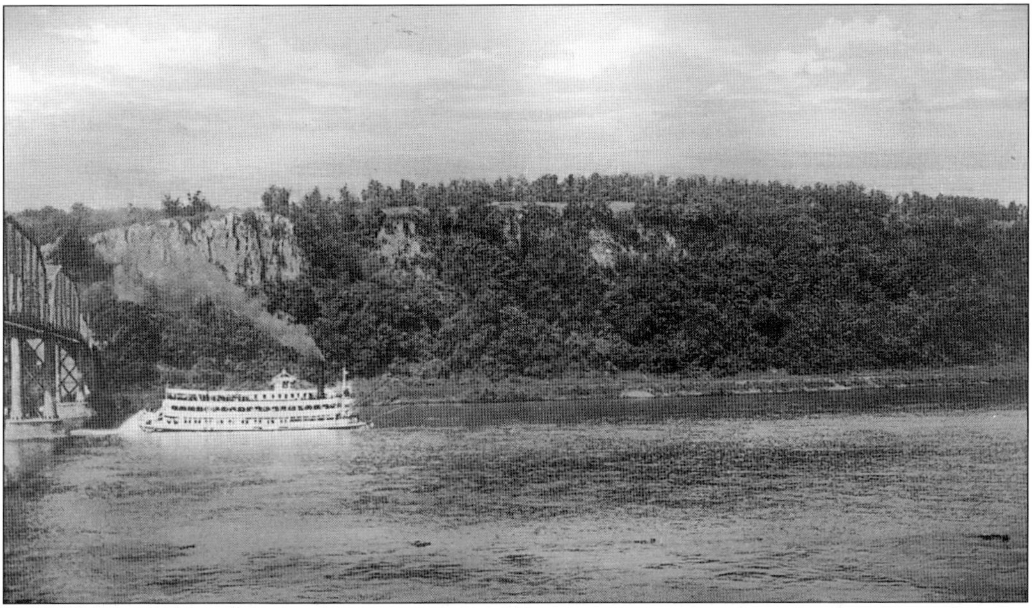

From the shore of Wisconsin, a camera catches not only the middle section of Eagle Point Park, but three modes of transportation in the 1920s as well—an automobile bridge, a river excursion boat, and the Milwaukee Railroad tracks on the shore opposite.

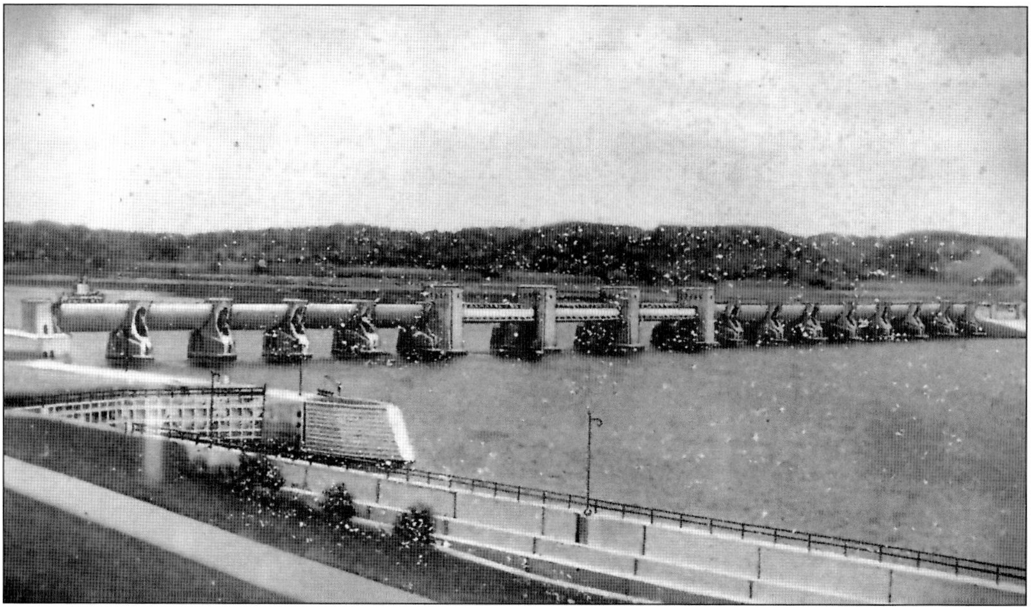

Numbered from upriver, the Zebulon Pike Lock and Dam is number 11, and number 12 is at Bellevue, Iowa, approximately 20 miles south. The dams were built in the 1930s.

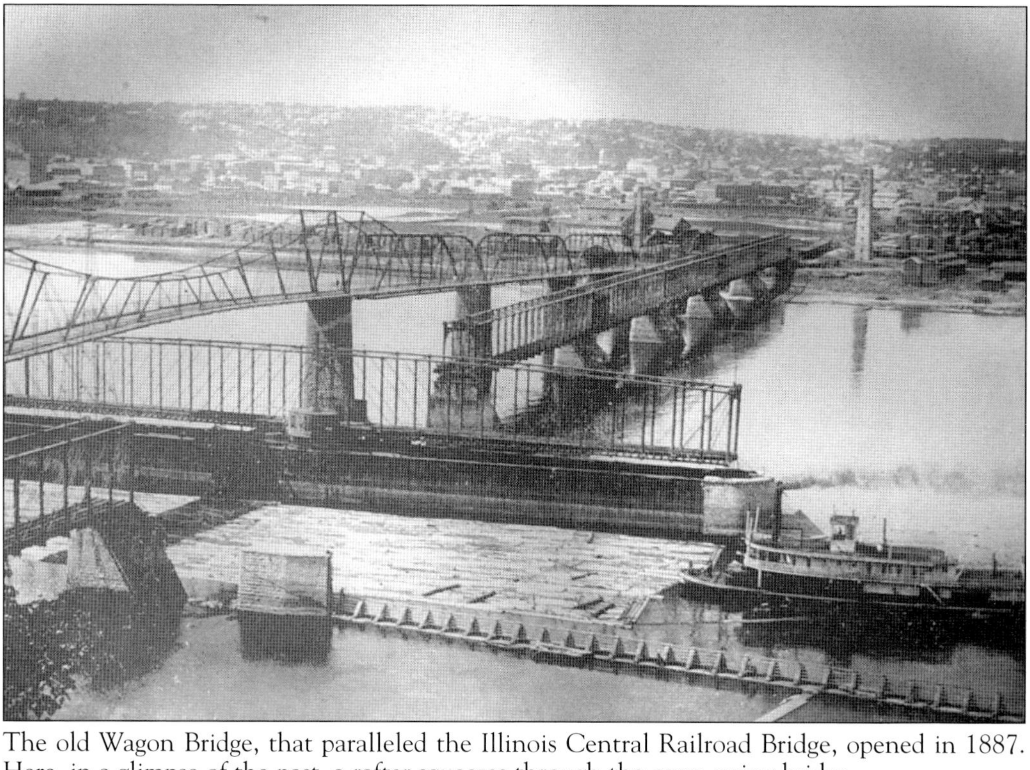

The old Wagon Bridge, that paralleled the Illinois Central Railroad Bridge, opened in 1887. Here, in a glimpse of the past, a rafter squeezes through the open swing bridge.

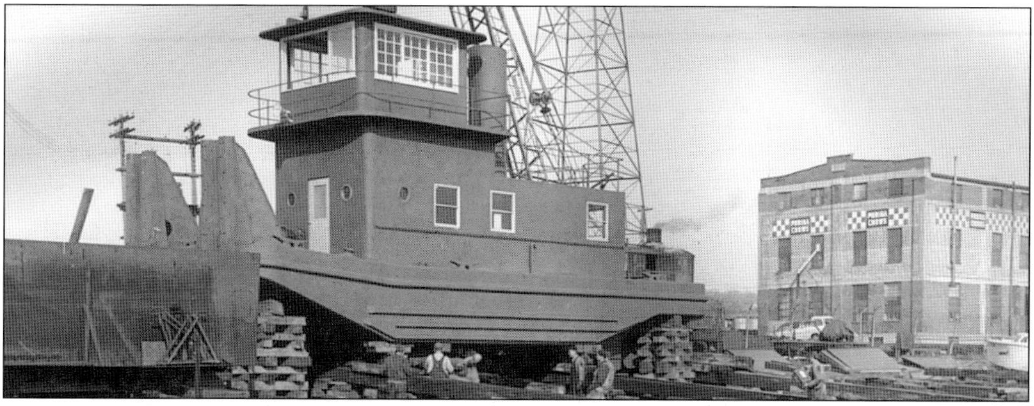

A tow switcher that will handle one or two barges at a time sits on shore, waiting to be launched.

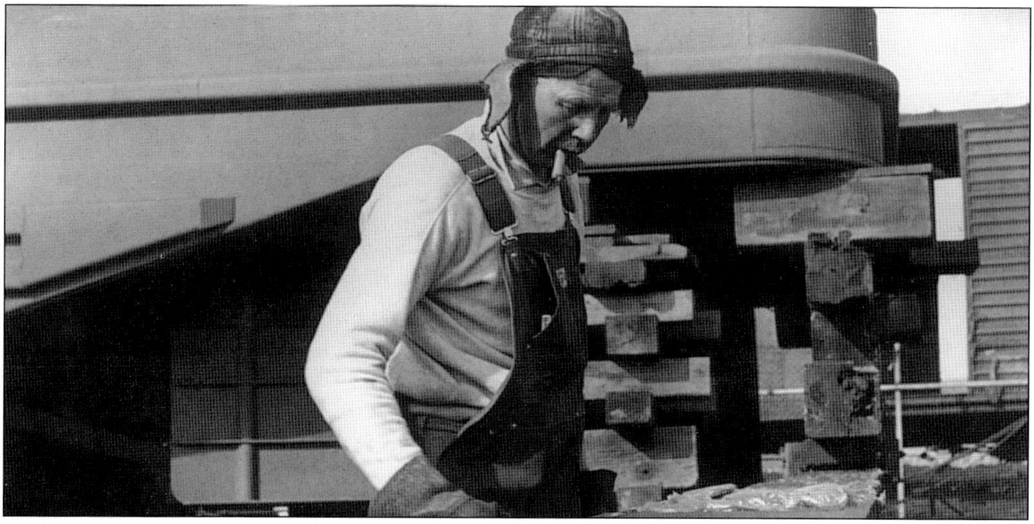

A Dubuque Boat and Boiler Works employee greases the runway, or skid rails.

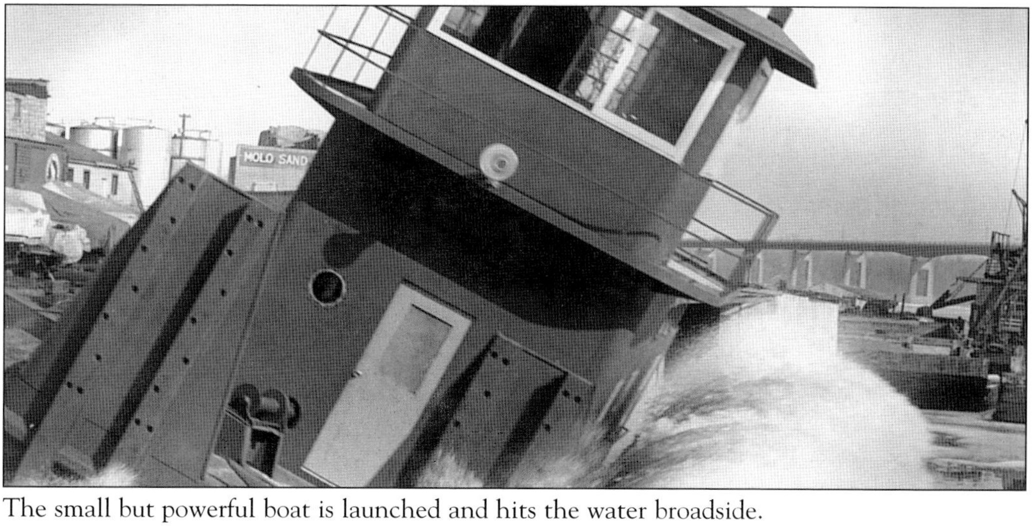

The small but powerful boat is launched and hits the water broadside.

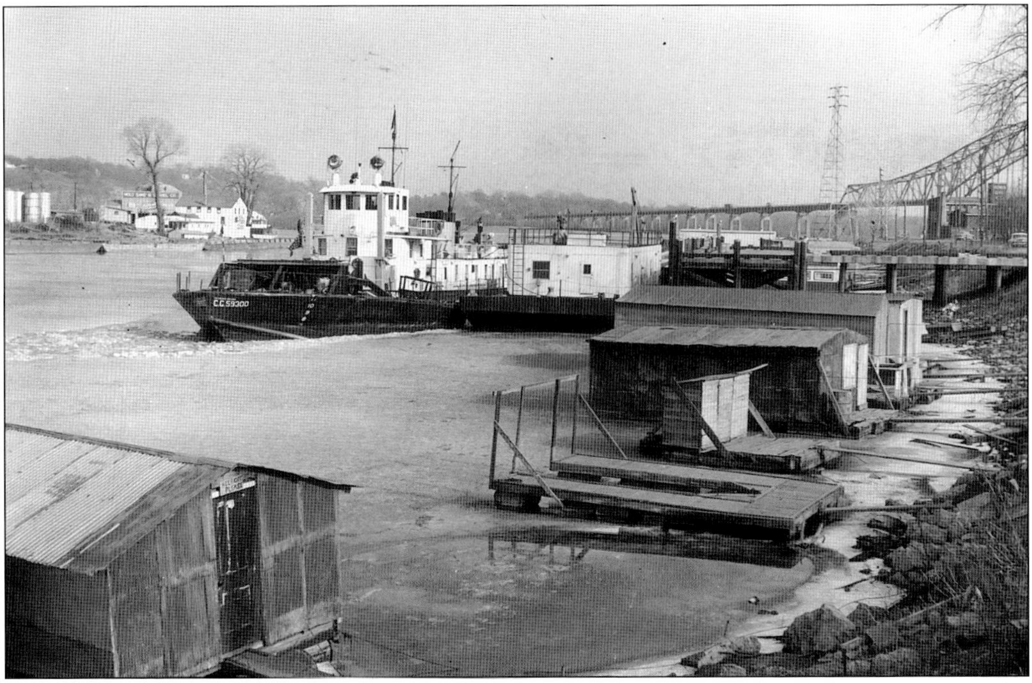

The Dubuque Ice Harbor, in winter, holds coast guard cutter #59300 in place with ice. The small buildings hold private boats. The flood wall had not yet been built, and the river might rise again, causing millions of dollars worth of damage.

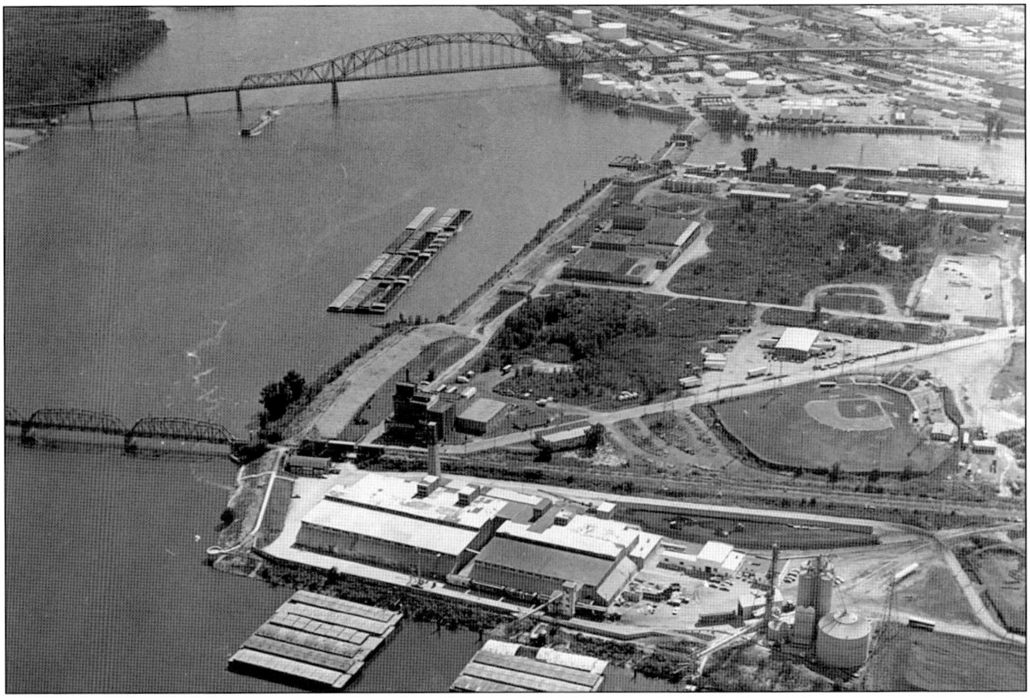

An air view of Dubuque shows the city's flood wall in place. It isn't that obvious, except across the mouth of the Ice Harbor, at top right.

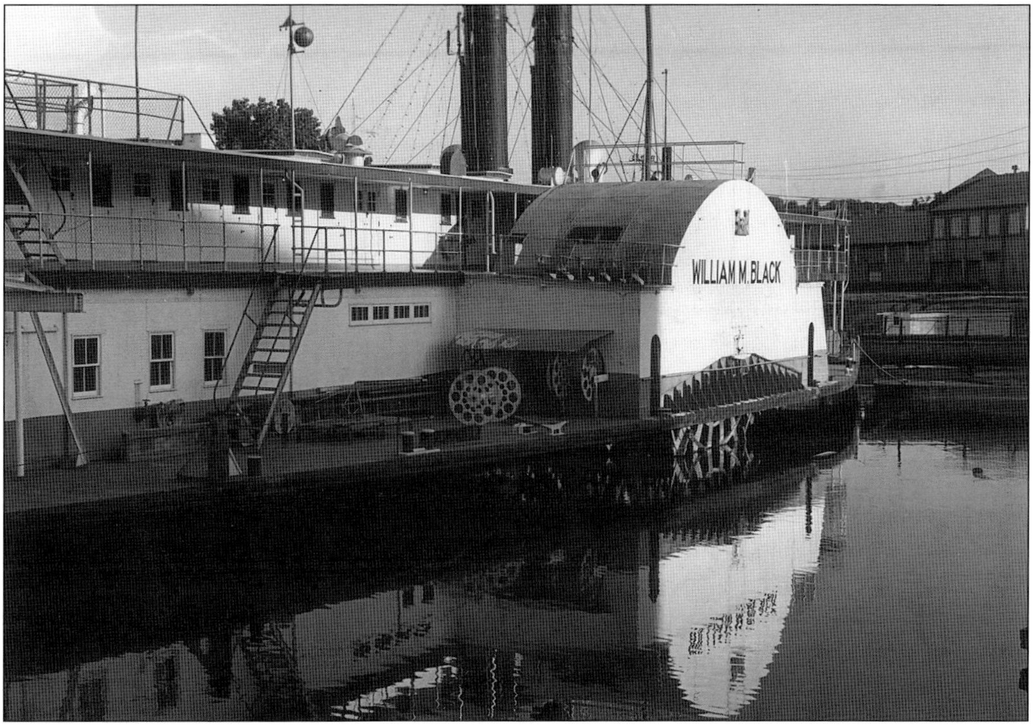

The *William M. Black* was obtained through the efforts of Jerry Enzler, curator/director of the Dubuque County Historical Society and Riverboat Museum.

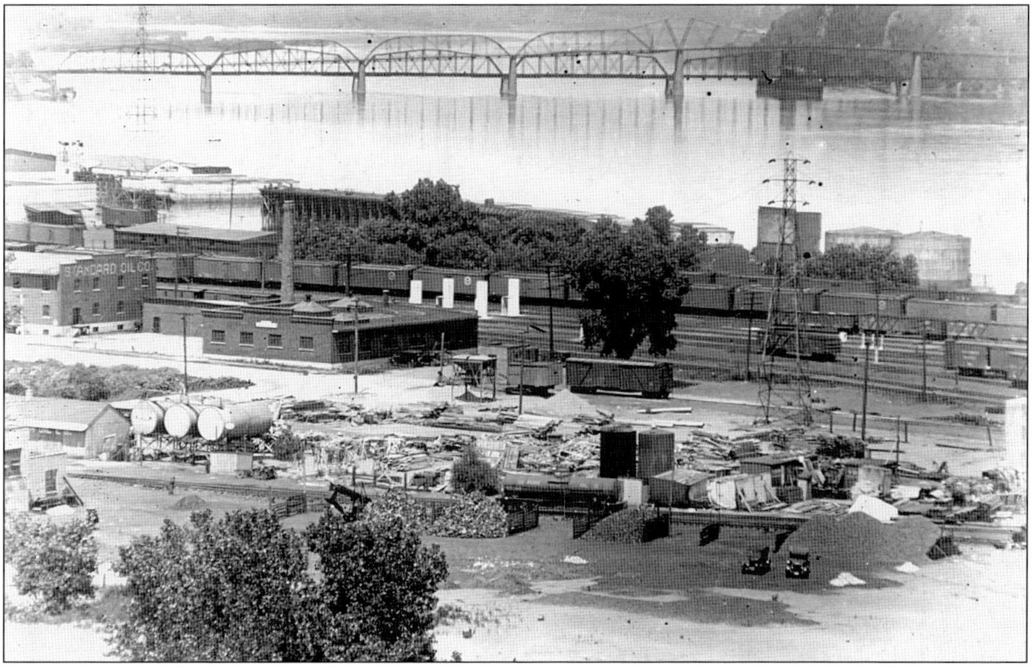

Here is a final, 1920s–1930s look upriver before leaving Dubuque. The river and railroad bridge remain the same. Most everything else has changed.

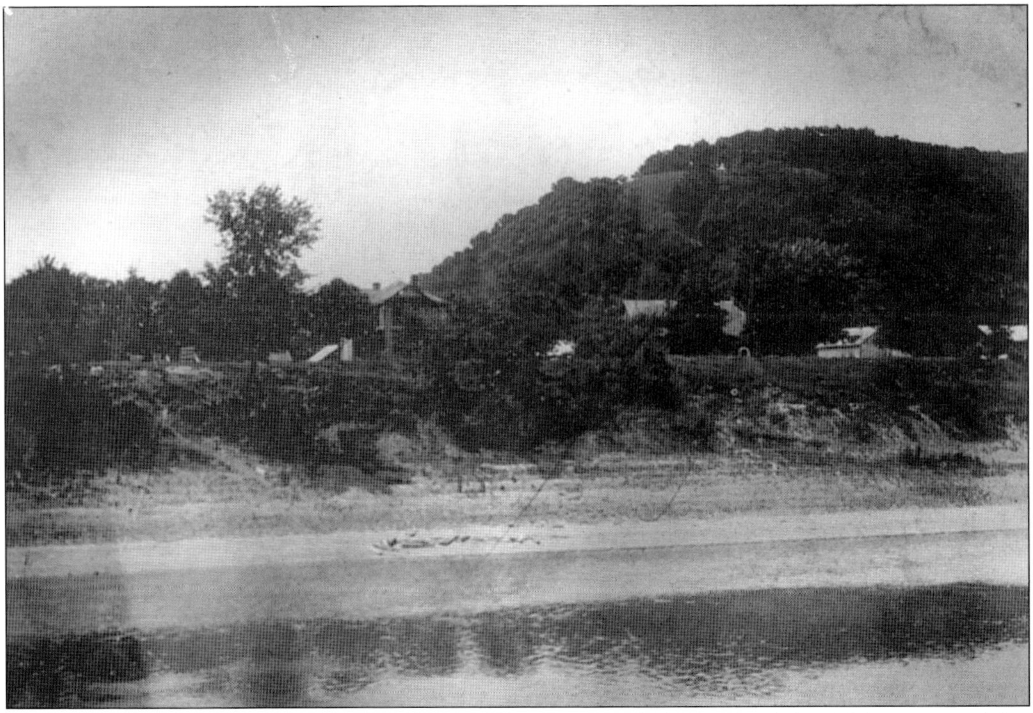

This photograph shows the area north of Bellevue around the turn of the 20th century. The water is low, because the dams have not yet been built.

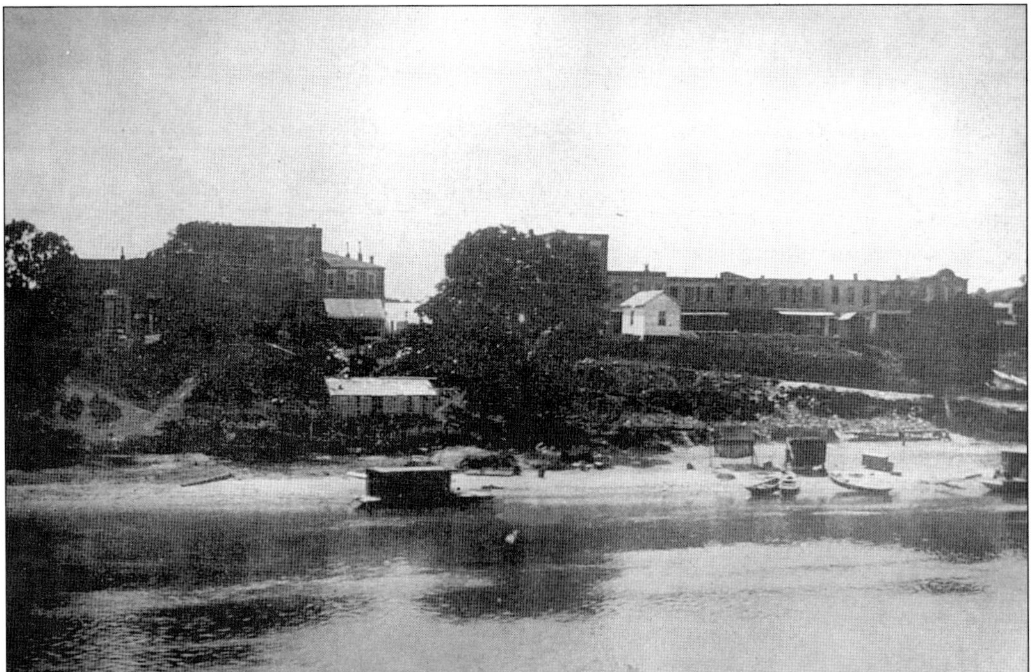

This is the town of Bellevue before 1909. While it resembled many such river towns of the time, today Bellevue is a beautiful community, and Lock and Dam number 12 is located there.

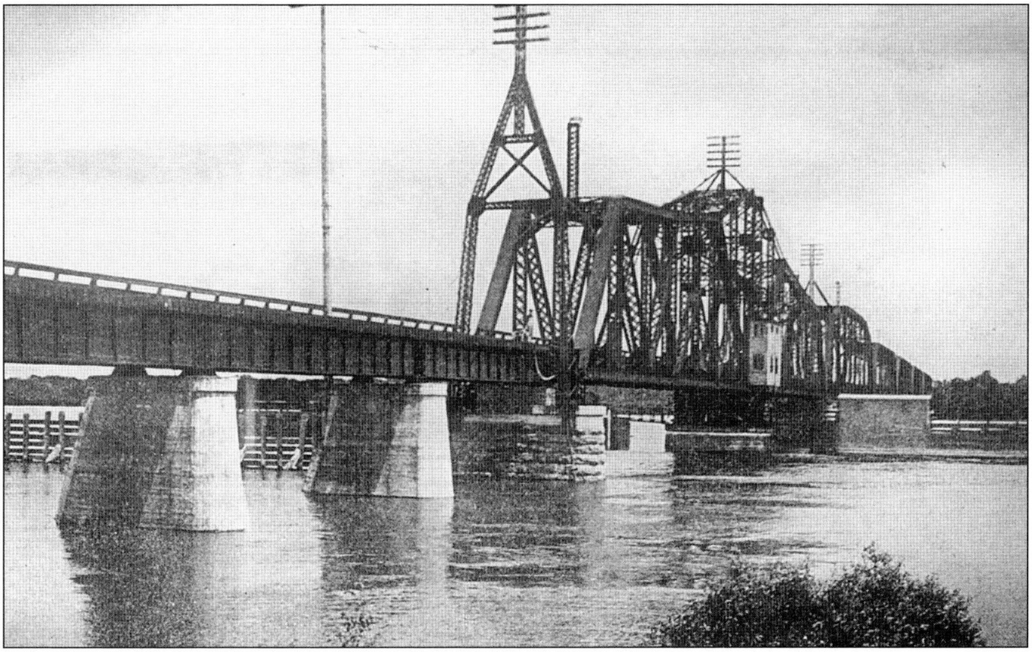

The Milwaukee Road Bridge that spans the Mississippi River was built before 1930 and is still in use today. The first span, with the five-barred electric line pole on top, is the swing span that opens for river traffic. It passes Sabula, Iowa on its way north.

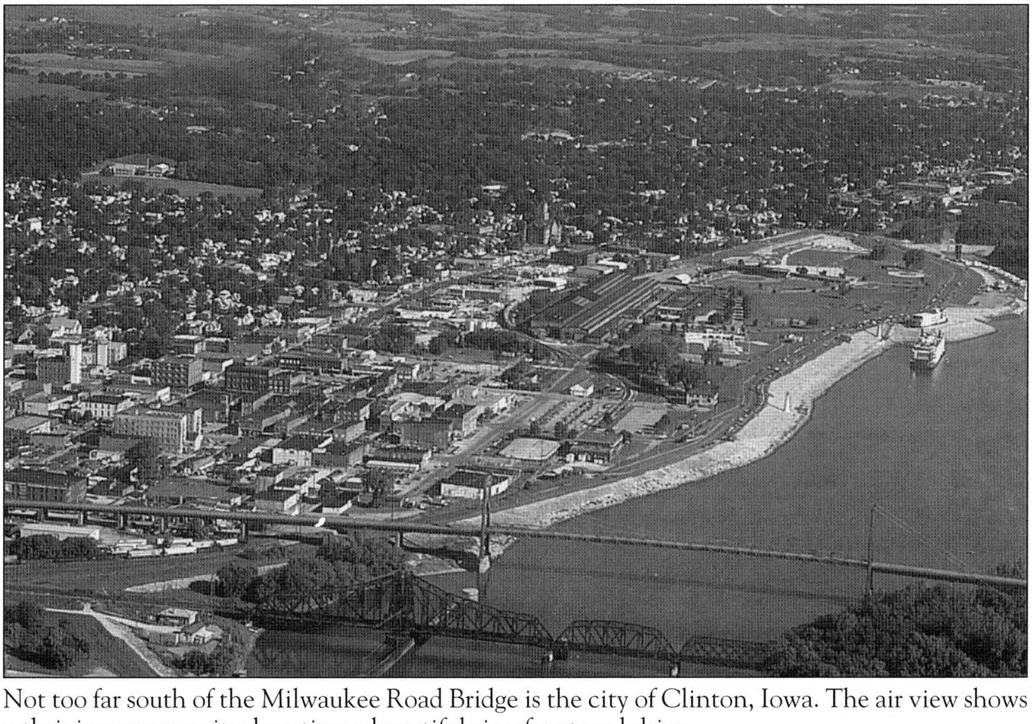

Not too far south of the Milwaukee Road Bridge is the city of Clinton, Iowa. The air view shows a thriving community, boasting a beautiful riverfront and drive.

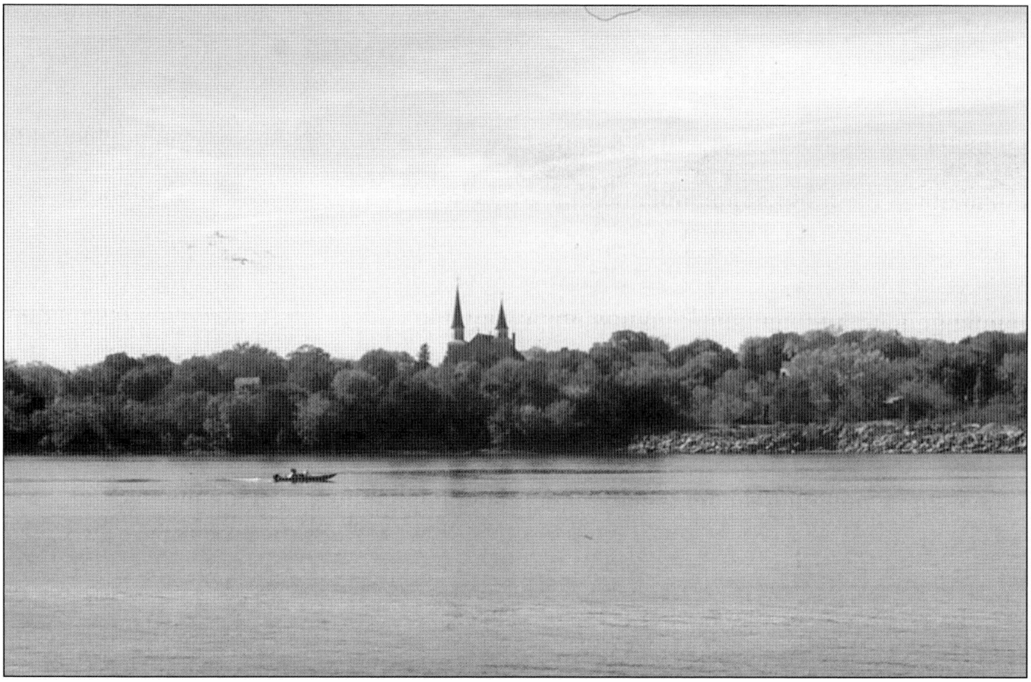

The steeples of St. Irenaeus Roman Catholic Church rise out of the trees, while two fishermen head upriver to find a better fishing hole.

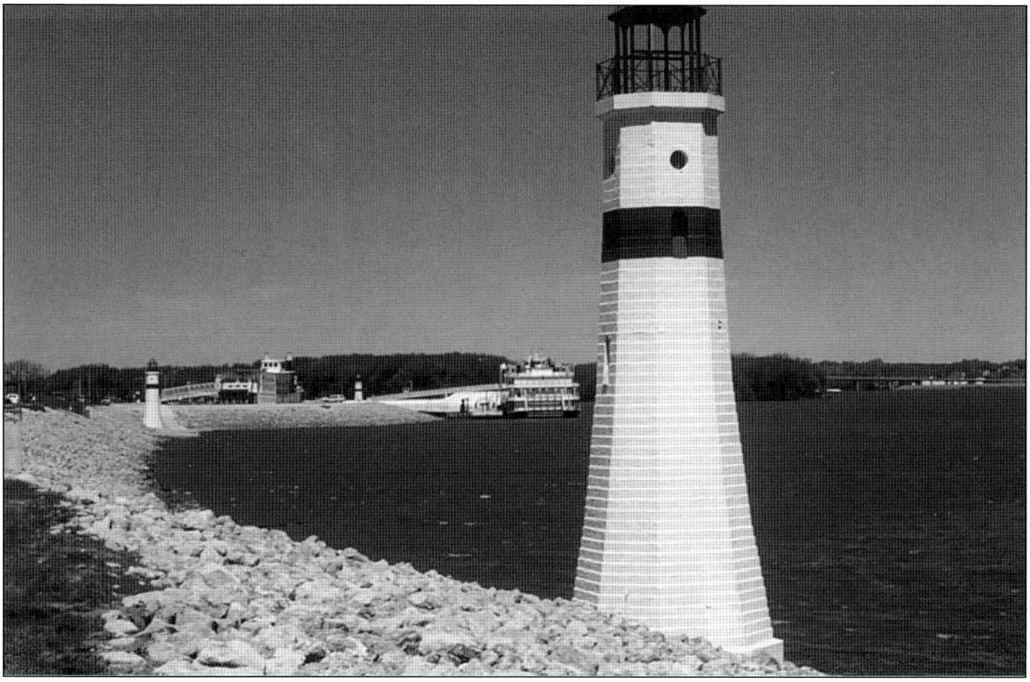

One of two small, non-functional lighthouses at Clinton's River Front Park is pictured here. The beautiful park was part of the W.P.A project under President Roosevelt in the 1930s.

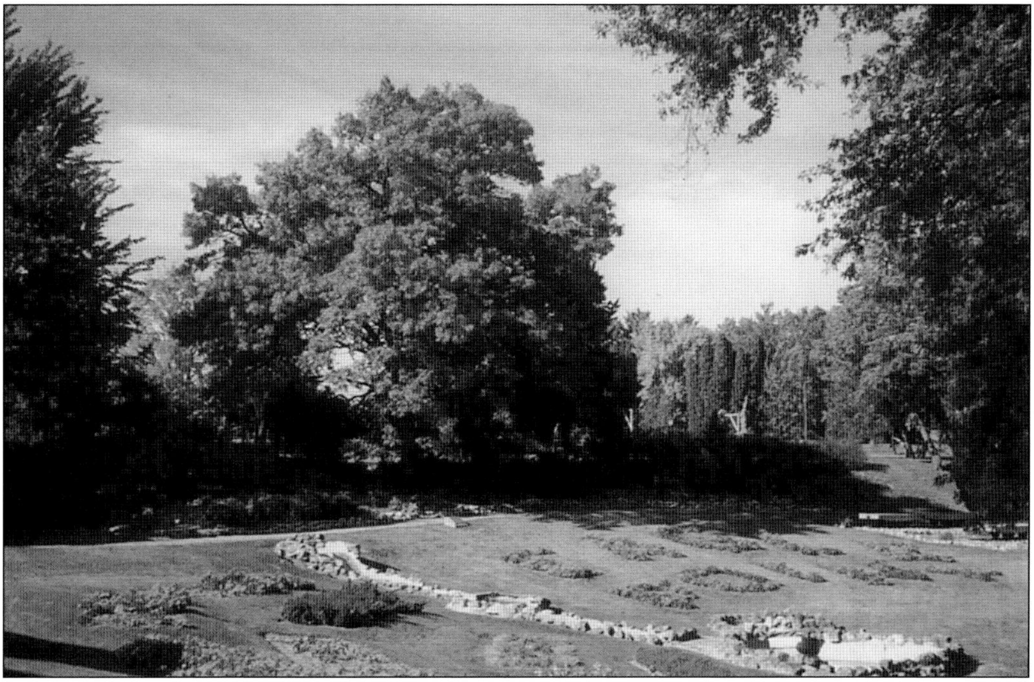

This is one of two Eagle Point Parks that line the Mississippi. One is in Dubuque, and the other in Clinton, Iowa. Both are beautiful, especially in autumn as shown in Clinton's park above.

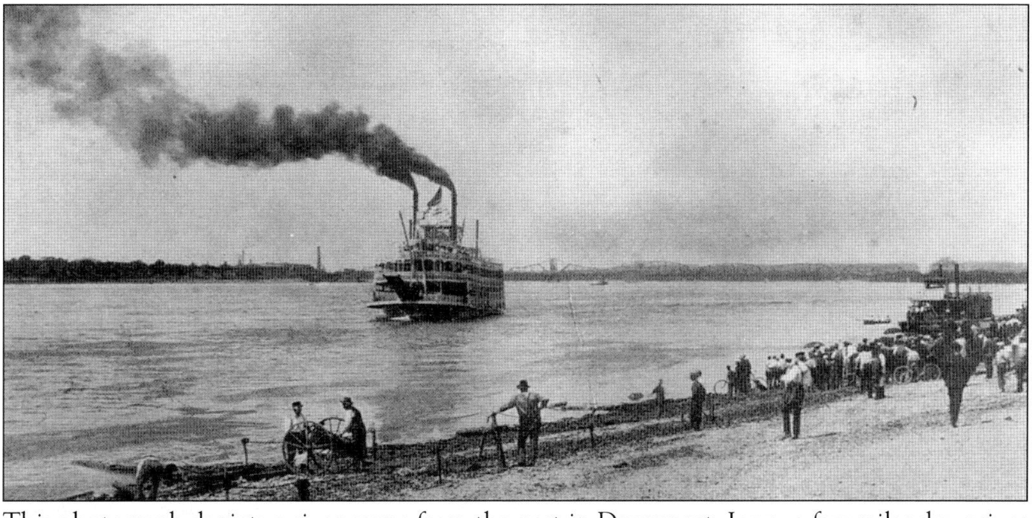

This photograph depicts a river scene from the past in Davenport, Iowa, a few miles downriver from Clinton. Cries of "River boat comin'!" always brought curious people along with those who had business with the boat's captain.

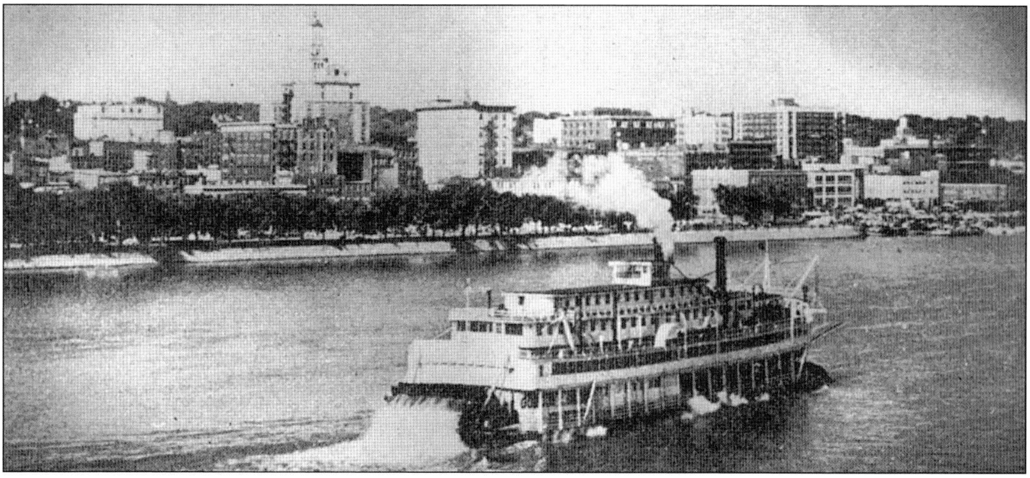

Here is a more modern shot of a stern-wheeler passing Davenport, which, as indicated by its buildings, is a thriving city.

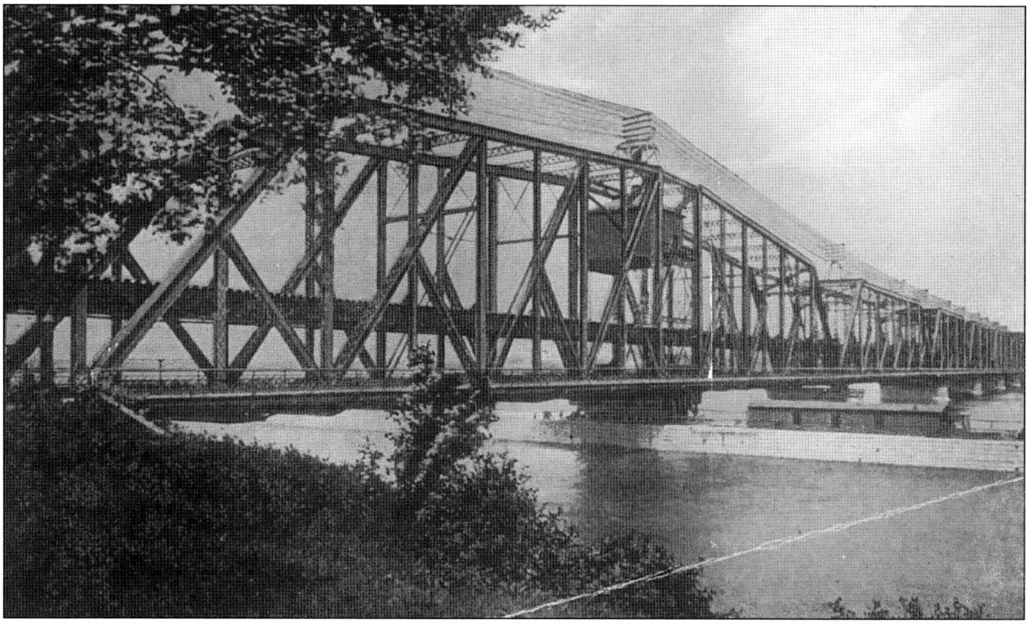

The Government Bridge connects Davenport, Iowa, and Rock Island, Illinois. The latter was famous for its arsenal and was well-known because of the Chicago, Rock Island, and Pacific Railroad. The bridge carries both auto and train traffic.

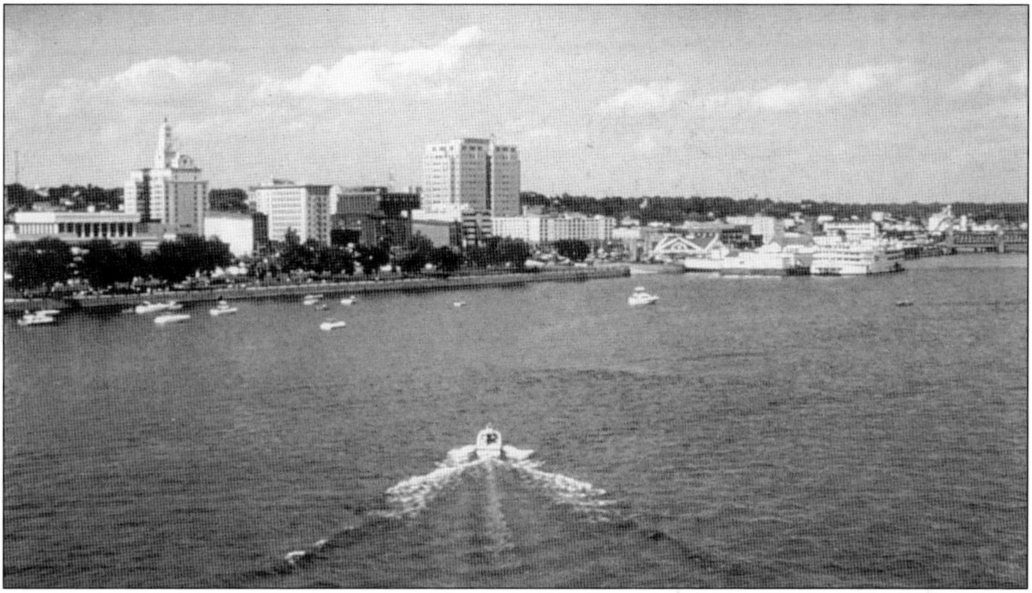

A modern look at Davenport shows many changes including a gambling boat(right, center), a pleasure craft (left, center), and new buildings.

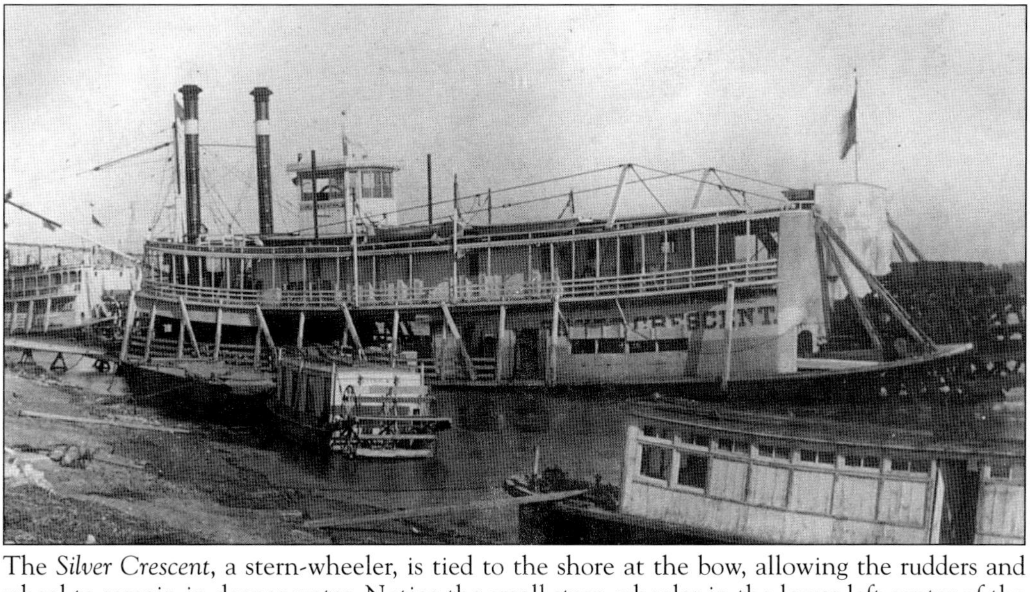

The *Silver Crescent*, a stern-wheeler, is tied to the shore at the bow, allowing the rudders and wheel to remain in deeper water. Notice the small stern-wheeler in the lower left center of the photograph. The location is Burlington, Iowa.

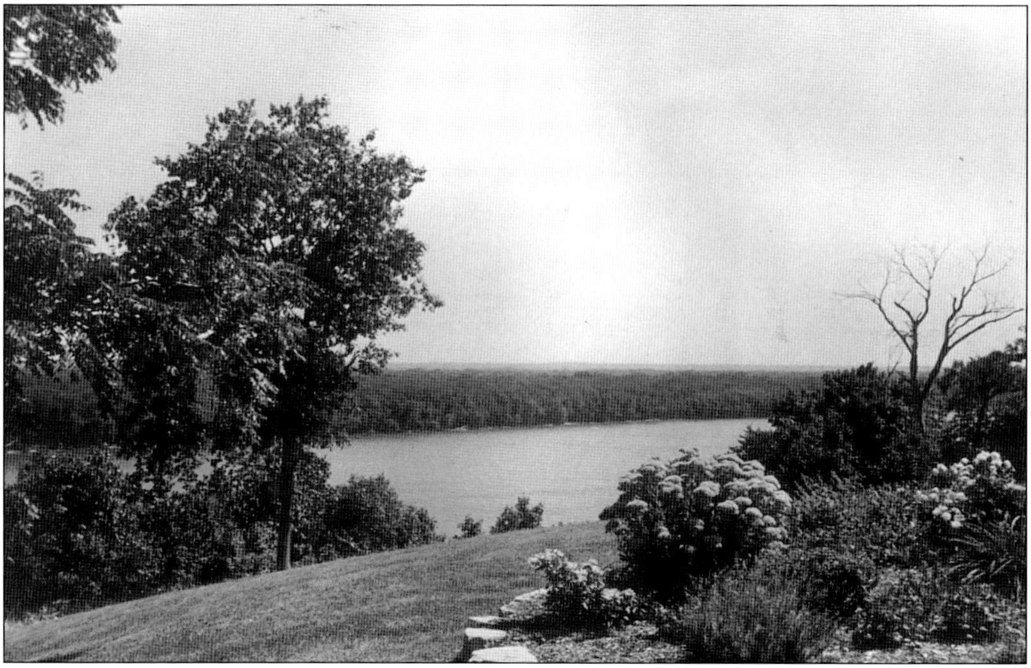

This park overlooks the Mississippi at Burlington, Iowa. Burlington became renowned when the Chicago, Burlington, and Quincy seemed to go "Everywhere West," which was the railroad's motto. Most referred to it as the Burlington; railroaders called it the "Q."

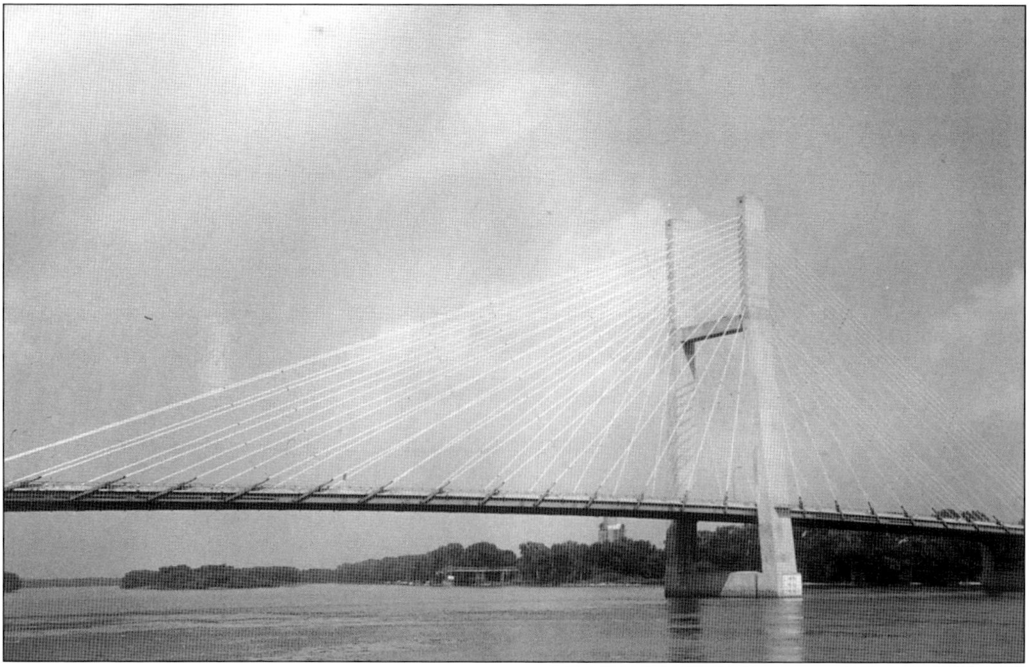

The Great River Bridge is probably one of the more uniquely designed bridges to span the Mississippi River at Burlington, Iowa.

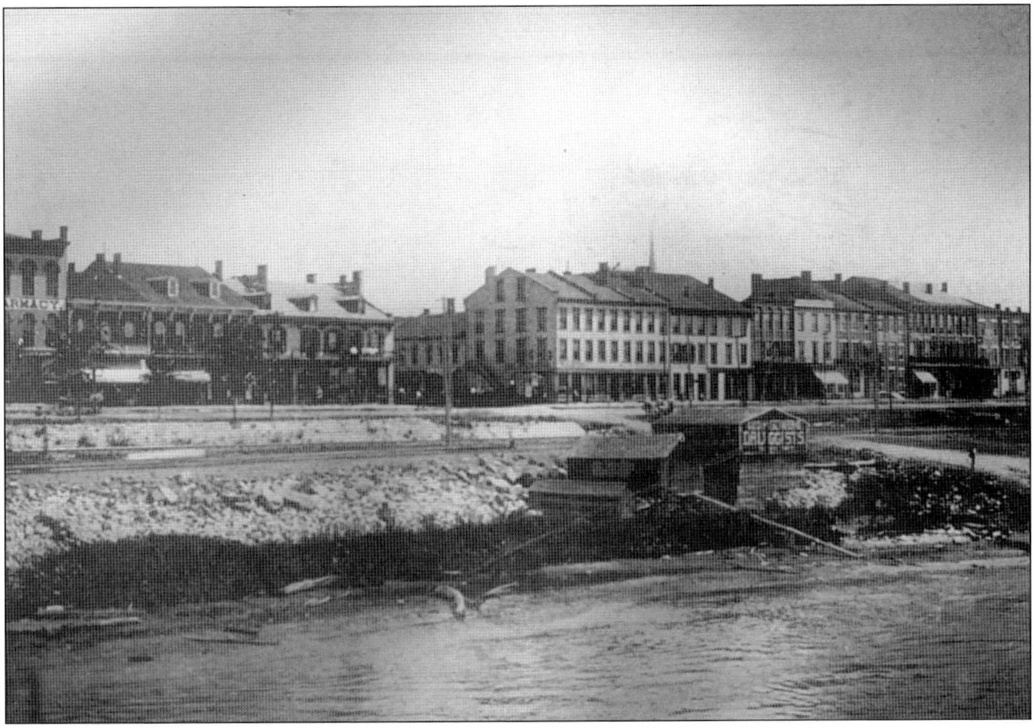

This is a view from the river of a turn-of-the-century Fort Madison, Iowa. Notice the sign advertising a druggist. The extreme left shows a pharmacy. Even then, Fort Madison was an attractive town.

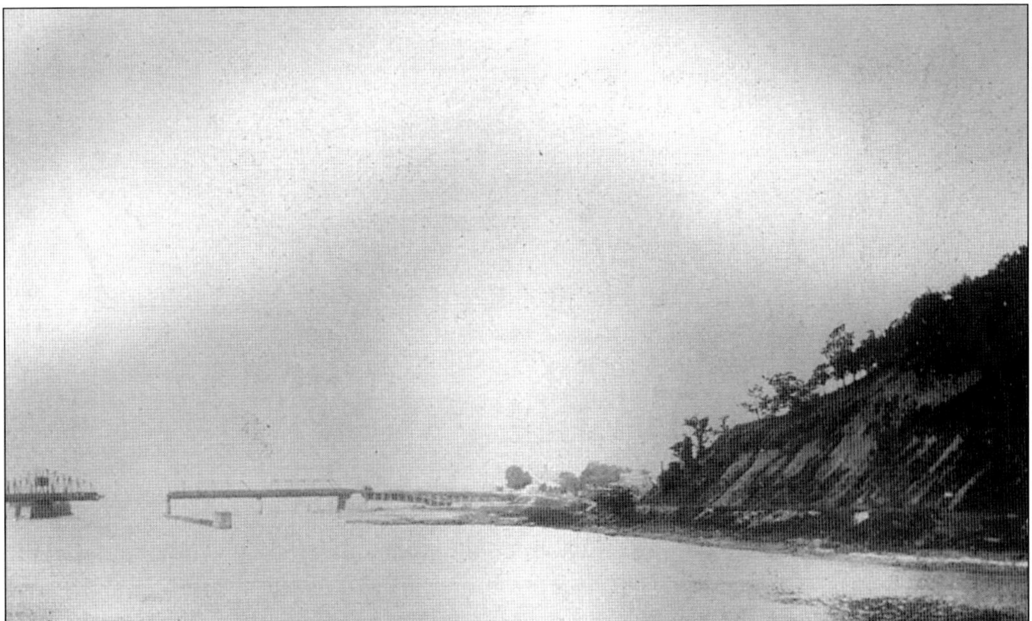

The swing bridge at Fort Madison is either opening or closing for a riverboat that is not yet in view.

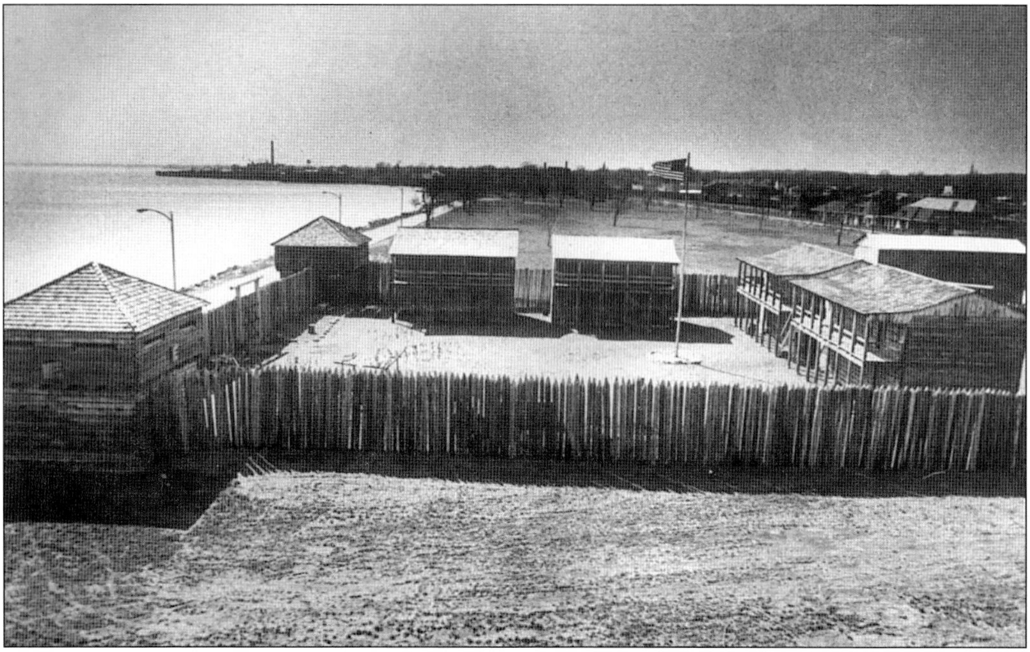

This is a replica of the original Fort Madison, built near the Mississippi. The block houses at each corner afforded protection, even from attack by boat.

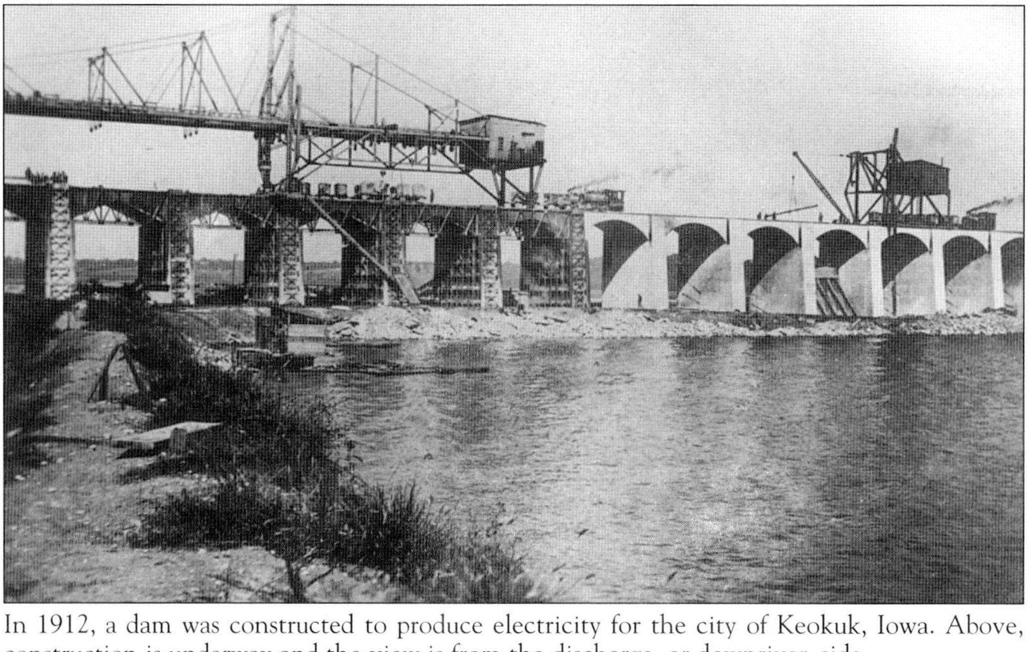

In 1912, a dam was constructed to produce electricity for the city of Keokuk, Iowa. Above, construction is underway and the view is from the discharge, or downriver, side.

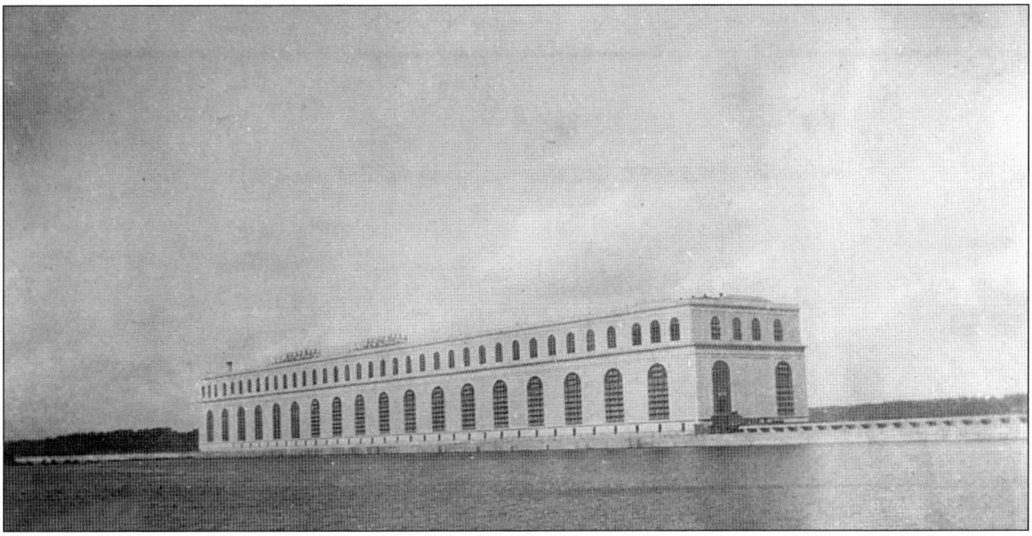

The completed Keokuk powerhouse is shown here from the upriver side where the water is 40 feet deep, the deepest on the upper Mississippi.

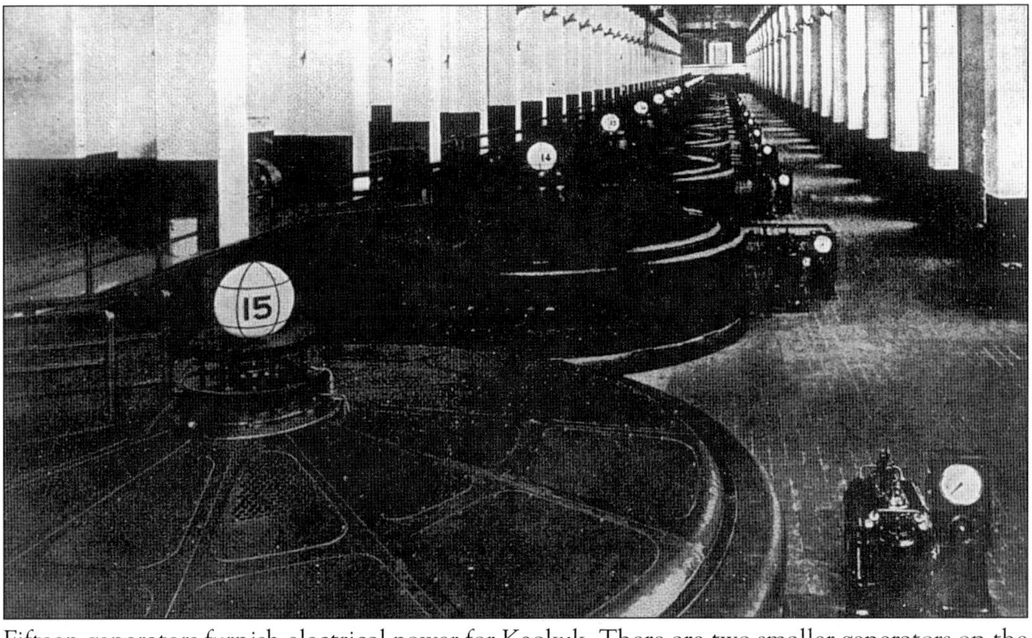

Fifteen generators furnish electrical power for Keokuk. There are two smaller generators on the left side of the larger ones that were used by the powerhouse while it was completed. Today, they contribute to the overall output of electricity. Boats bypass the dam through locks on the Iowa side.

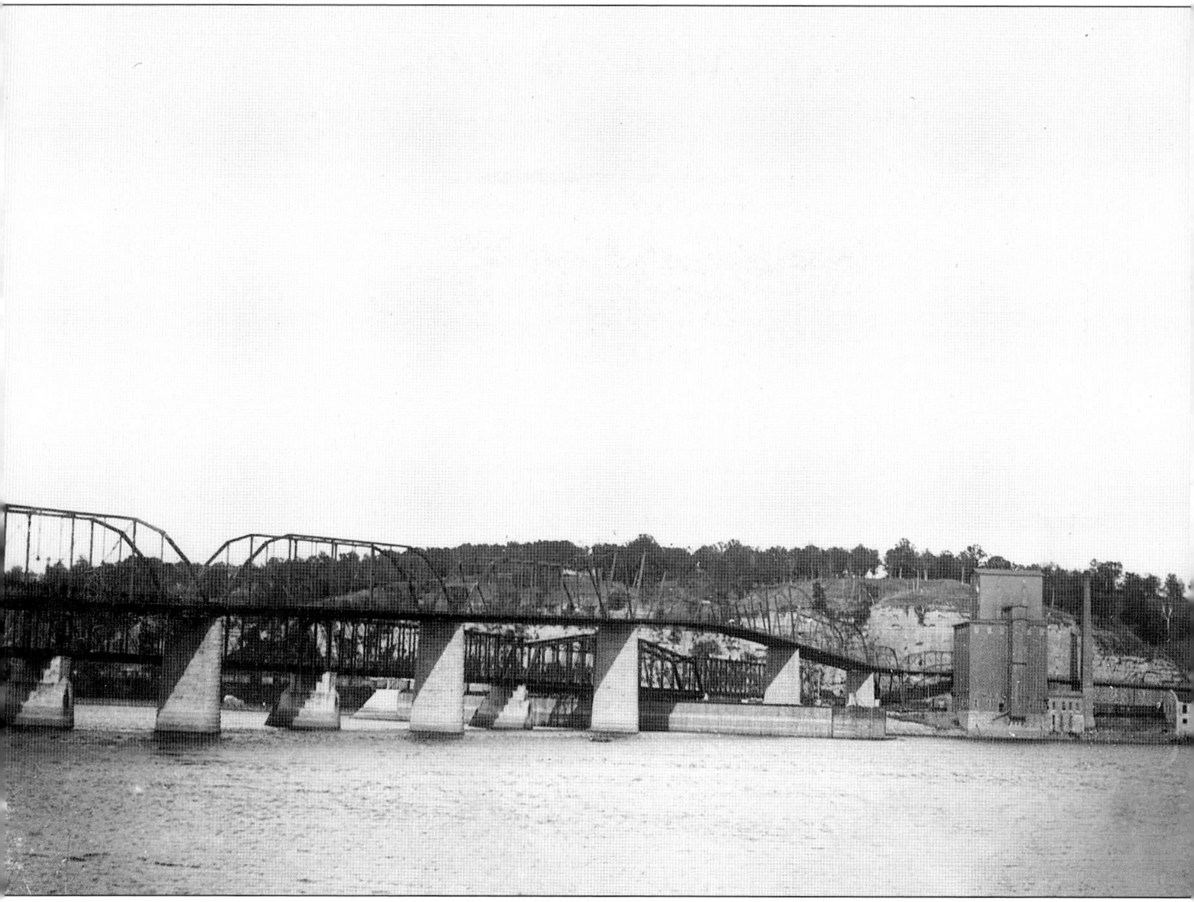

The huge grain elevator on the Illinois side of the Mississippi is in East Dubuque, formerly called Dunleith. The elevator, owned by the Diamond Jo Lines, received grain from Illinois farmers to ship out on barges. The elevator was higher than the top of the High Bridge or the Wagon Bridge.

STEAMBOAT PILOT'S CERTIFICATE.

6th RENEWAL.

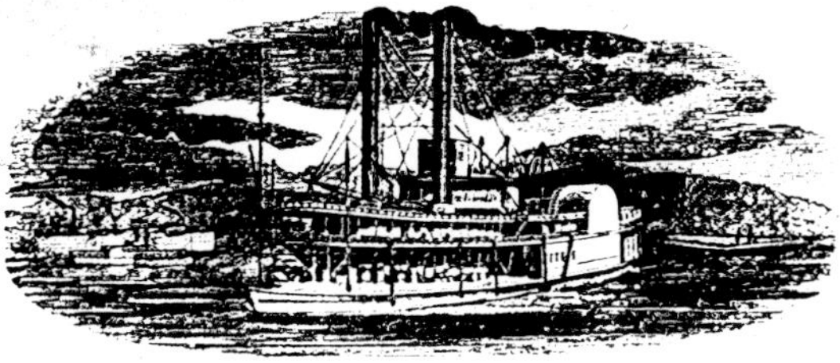

No.

In Accordance with the Act of Congress, approved August 30th, 1852.

The Undersigned, Supervising Inspector for the District of Galena certify that William J Dolson having been by me this day duly examined, touching his qualifications as a Pilot of a Steamer on Mississippi River,
To and from Le Claire, to Galena, Dubuque Stillwater and Saint Paul
I am satisfied he possesses the requisite skill as a Pilot, and is trustworthy and faithful, and do license him to act as such, within the said bounds, for one year from this date.

Given under my hand this 12th day of June 1864

Chas L Stephenson

I, Chas L Stephenson Supervising Inspector for the District of Galena certify that the above named William J Dolsen this day, before me, solemnly swore that he would faithfully and honestly, according to his best skill and judgment, without concealment or reservation, perform all the duties required of him as Pilot, by the Act of Congress, approved Aug. 30th, 1852, entitled "An act to amend an act entitled An act to provide for the better security of the lives of passengers on board of vessels propelled in whole or in part by steam, and for other purposes."

Here is a Steamboat Pilot's Certificate as issued in 1864 for William J. Dolson. He was qualified to pilot steamers on the Mississippi River to and from LeClaire, to Galena, Dubuque, Stillwater, and St. Paul. The certificate was good for one year.

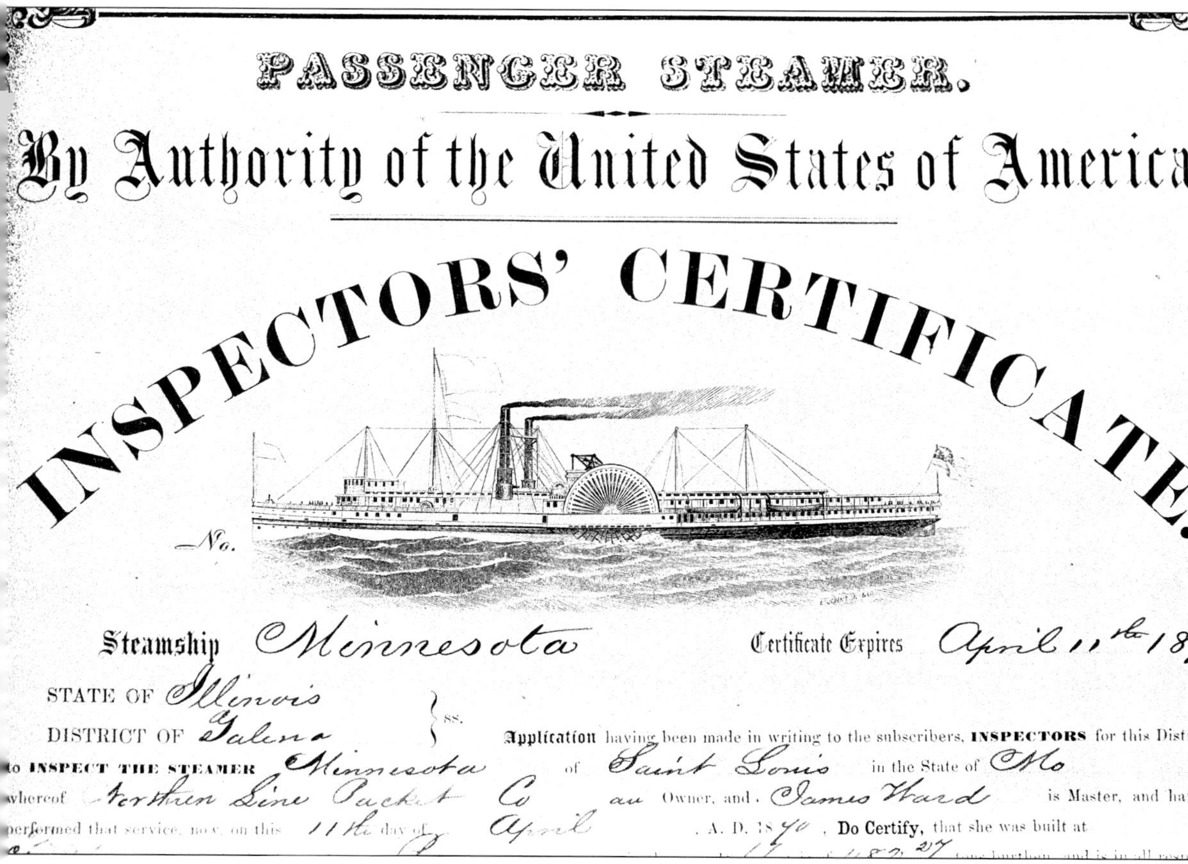

PASSENGER STEAMER.

By Authority of the United States of America

INSPECTORS' CERTIFICATE.

No.

Steamship Minnesota Certificate Expires April 11th 187

STATE OF Illinois }
DISTRICT OF Galena } ss. Application having been made in writing to the subscribers, INSPECTORS for this Distri

to INSPECT THE STEAMER Minnesota of Saint Louis in the State of Mo

whereof Northern Line Packet Co as Owner, and James Ward is Master, and hav

performed that service, now, on this 11th day of April, A. D. 1870, Do Certify, that she was built at

This is an Inspector's Certificate of the steamboat *Minnesota*, which expired April 11, 1871, one year from date of issue.

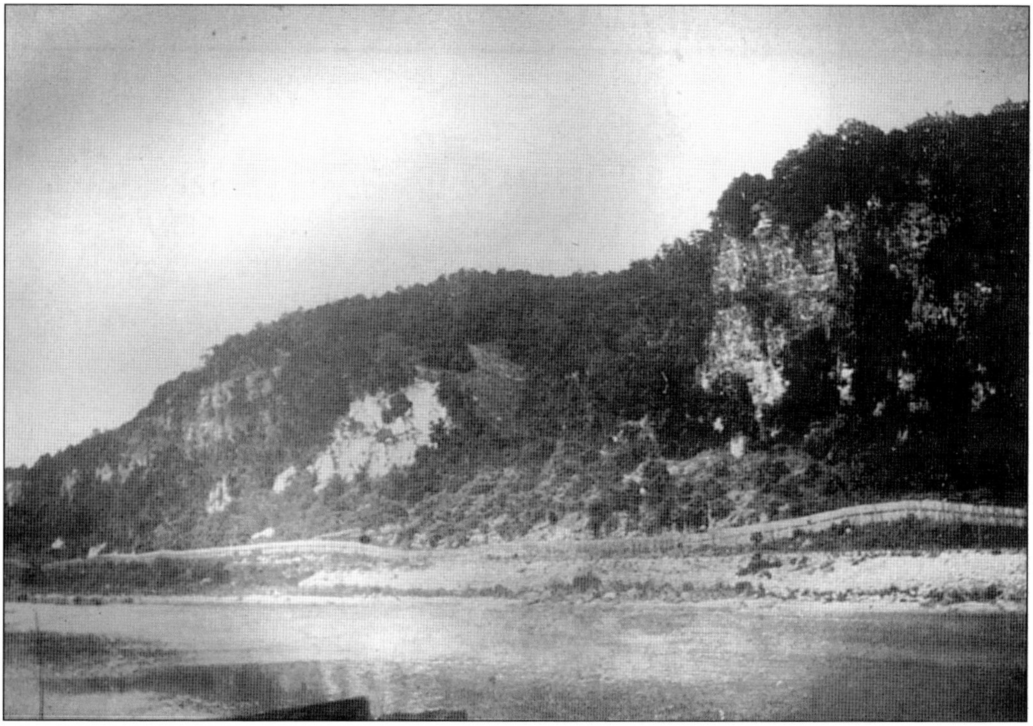

The bluffs north of Savanna, Illinois were palisade-like in formation, and a park, built on top, was named Palisades Park.

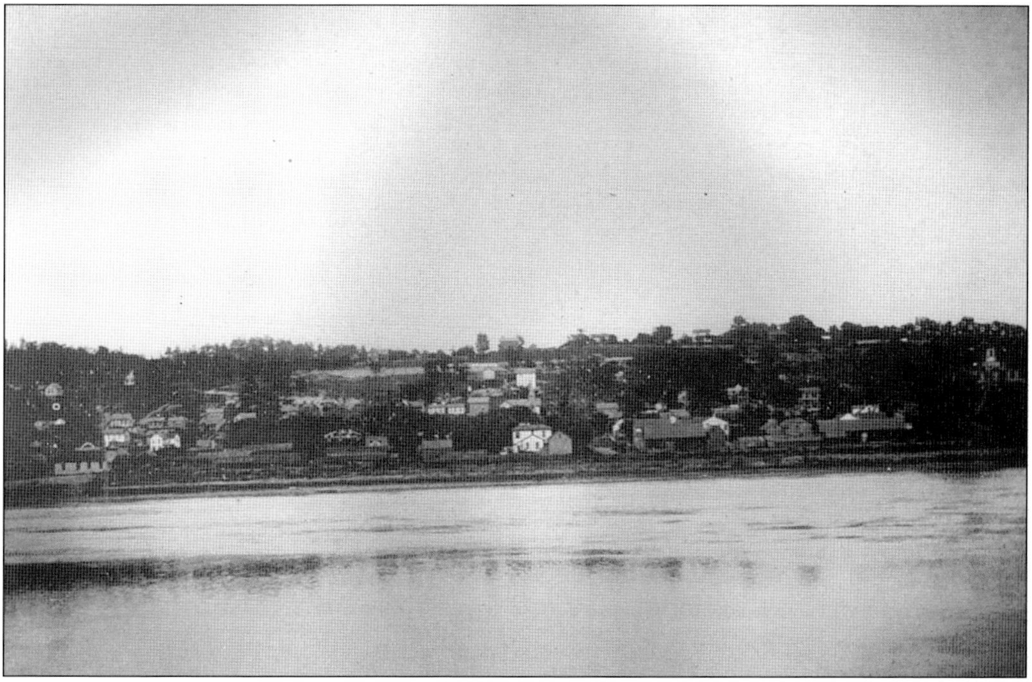

Here we see the town of Savanna, Illinois, prior to 1909. Savanna became a large rail center for the Milwaukee Road and the Burlington Route.

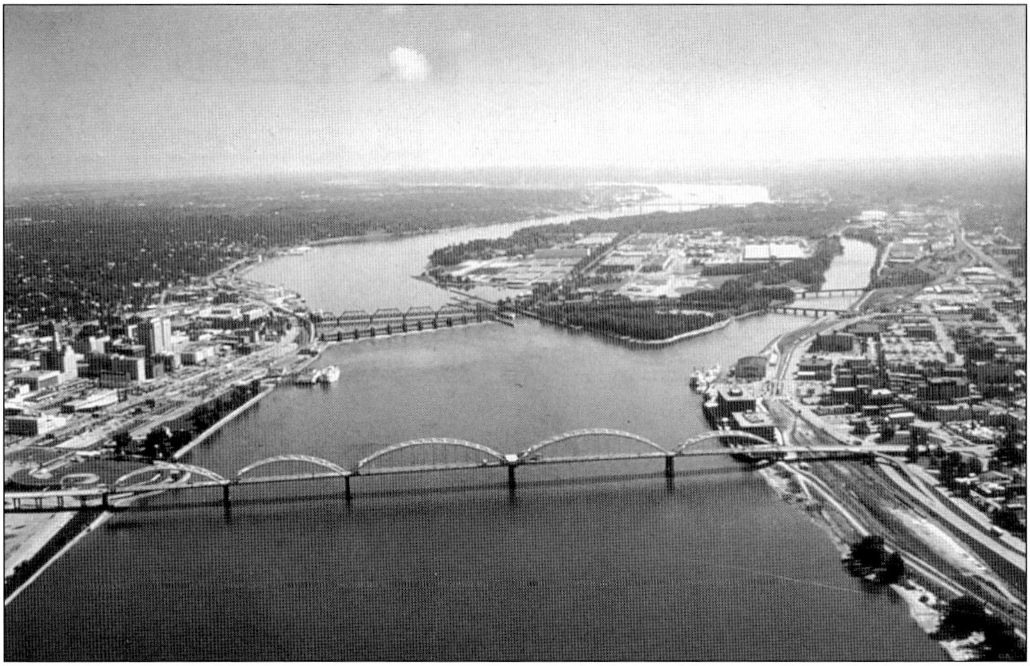

This view shows the Quad Cities: Davenport and Bettendorf, Iowa, are on the left, and Moline and Rock Island, Illinois, are on the right. A United States arsenal and fort have been part of Rock Island's history, and are quite noticeable in the photograph above.

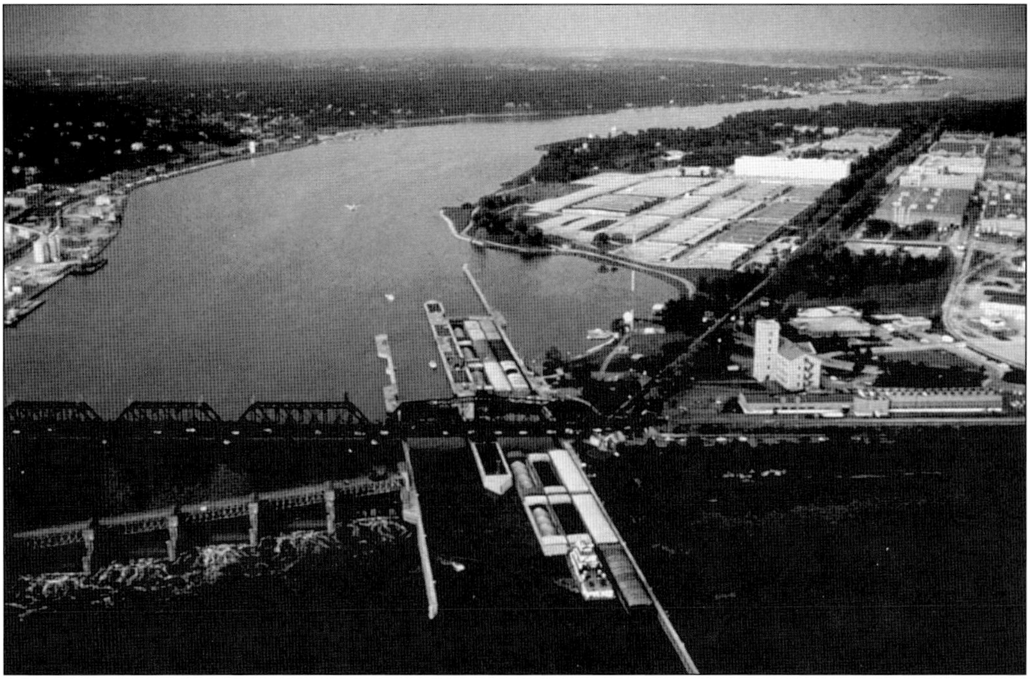

Here is a closer view of not only Rock Island, Illinois, but the angled Dam and Lock number 15. The dam is the largest roller dam in the world. At the Quad Cities, the Mississippi flows westerly before turning and heading south.

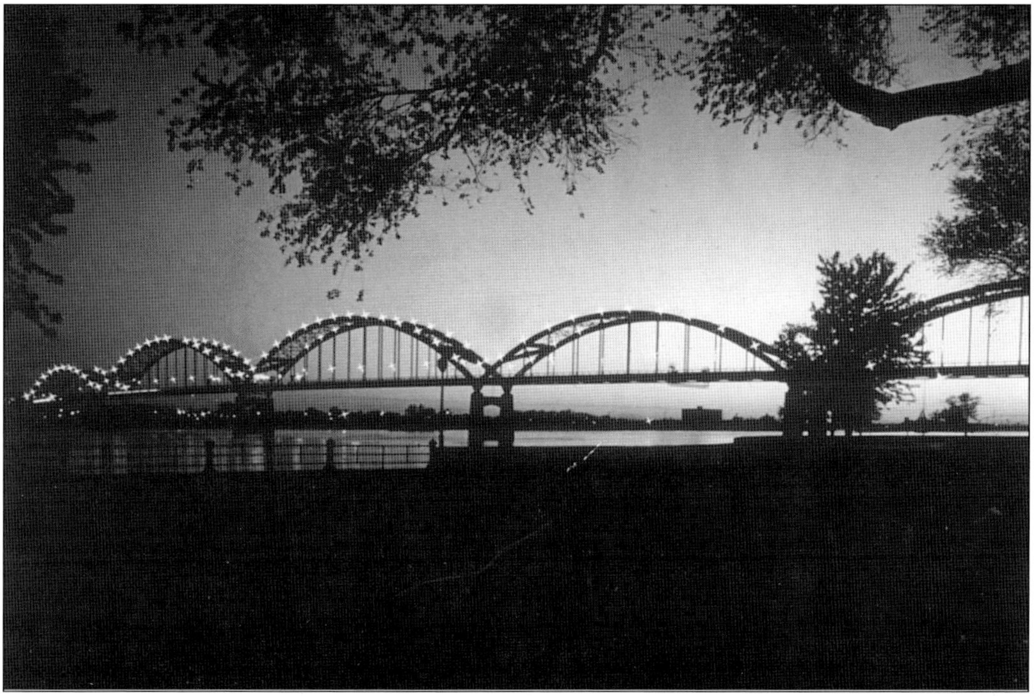

The Davenport–Moline Bridge displays lights, outlining each arched span.

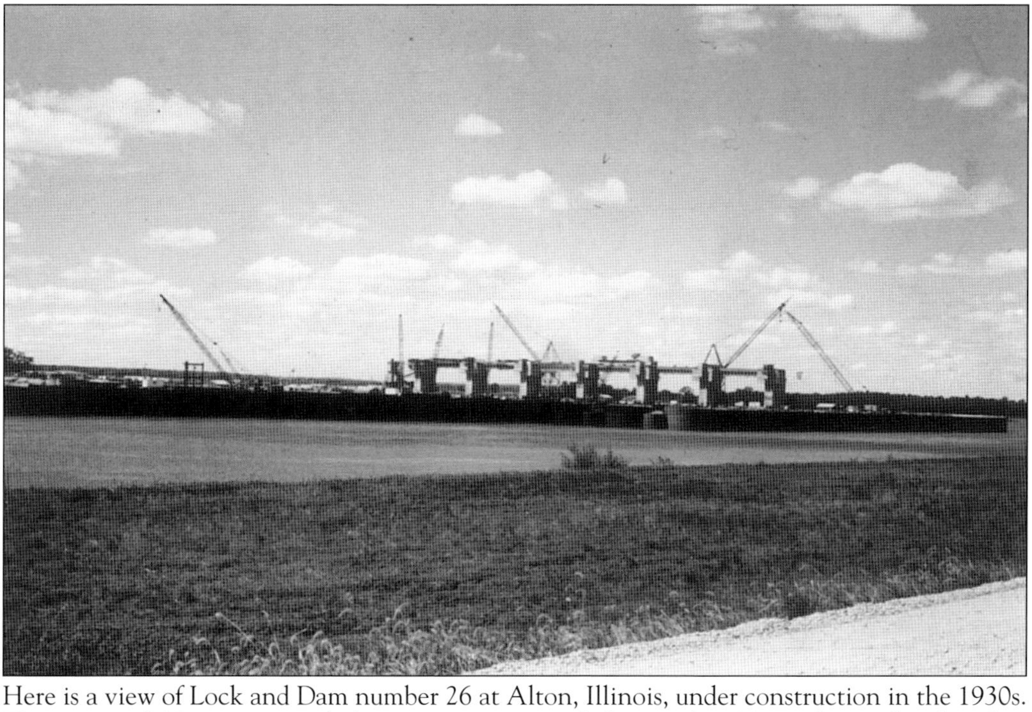

Here is a view of Lock and Dam number 26 at Alton, Illinois, under construction in the 1930s. The series of 29 navigational dams was constructed during the '30s and completed within ten years.

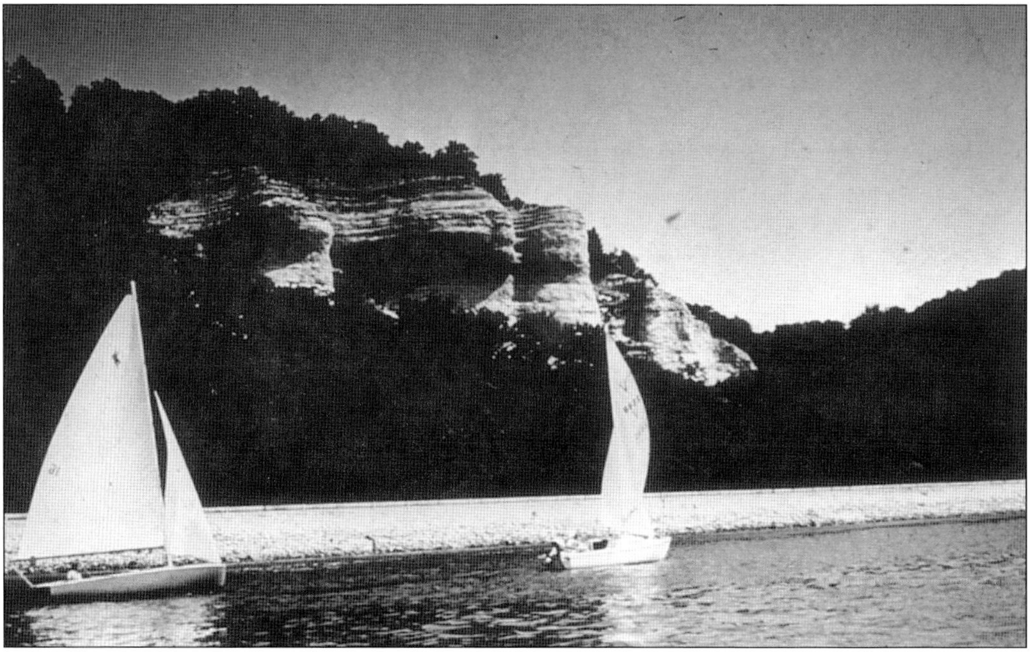

Because the 29 navigational dams held back water, the upper Mississippi became, in reality, a series of lakes, some as wide as a mile. Sailboating has become popular in the last 30 or 40 years of the 20th century.

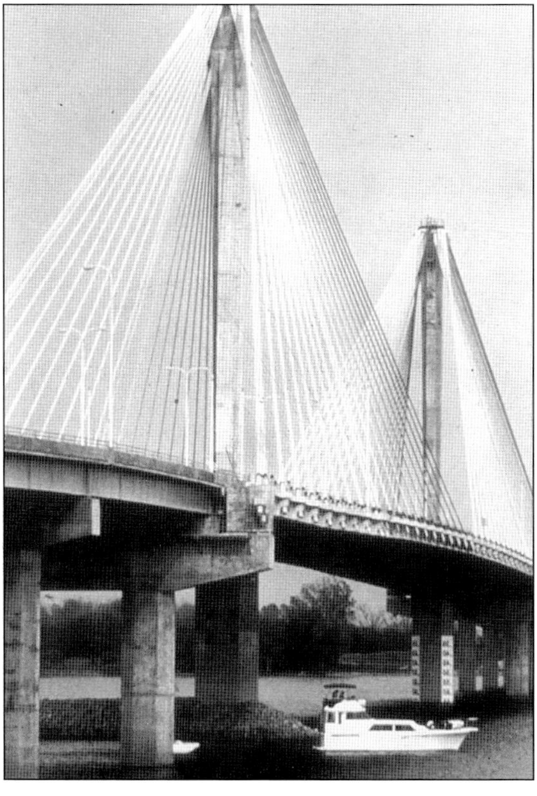

Here is a view of the Clark Bridge that crosses the Mississippi from Alton, Illinois, to Missouri. It almost appears like a two-masted sailing ship and most definitely resembles the Great River Bridge in Burlington, Iowa.

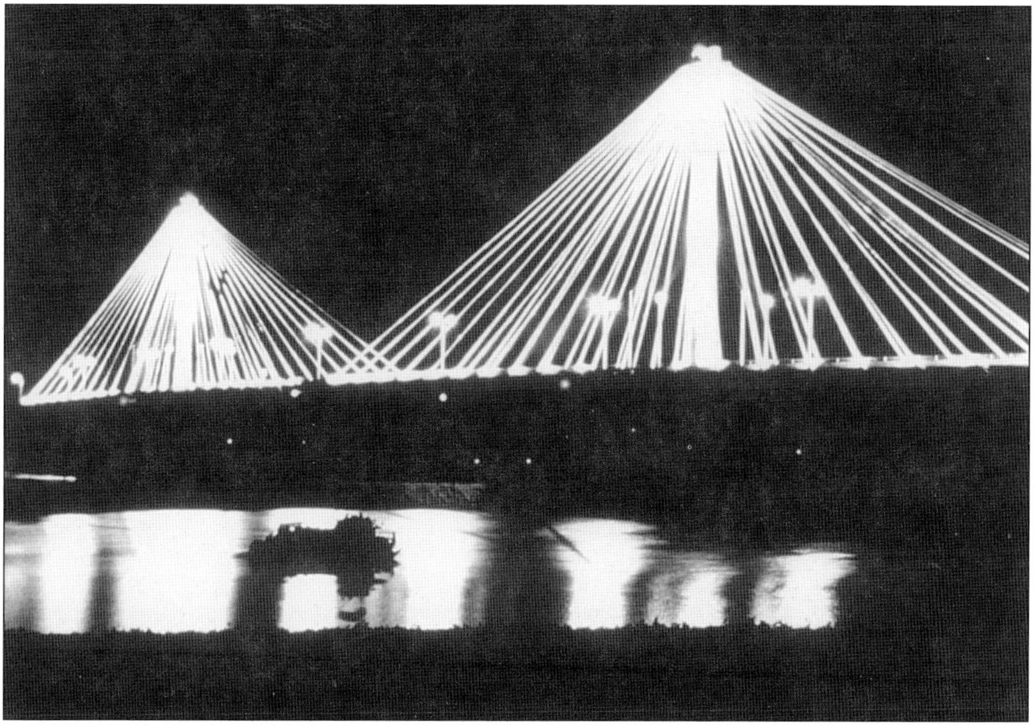

A night view of the Clark Bridge is a breathtaking sight when the lighted cables and bridge lights reflect off the Mississippi River. The bridge was named for William Clark of the Lewis and Clark Expedition.

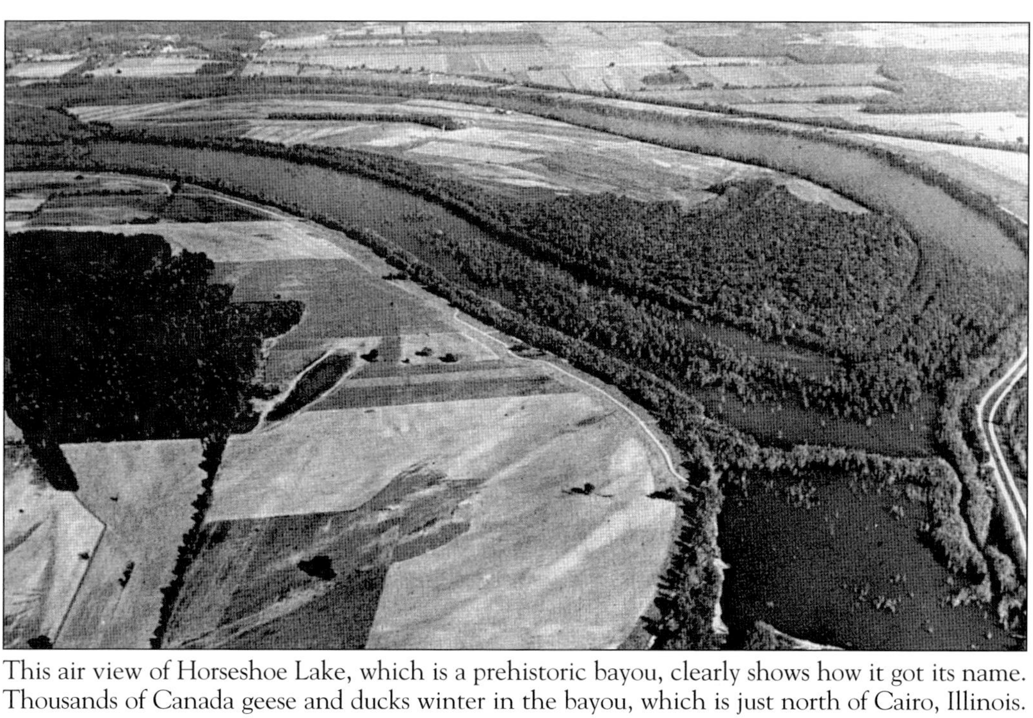

This air view of Horseshoe Lake, which is a prehistoric bayou, clearly shows how it got its name. Thousands of Canada geese and ducks winter in the bayou, which is just north of Cairo, Illinois.

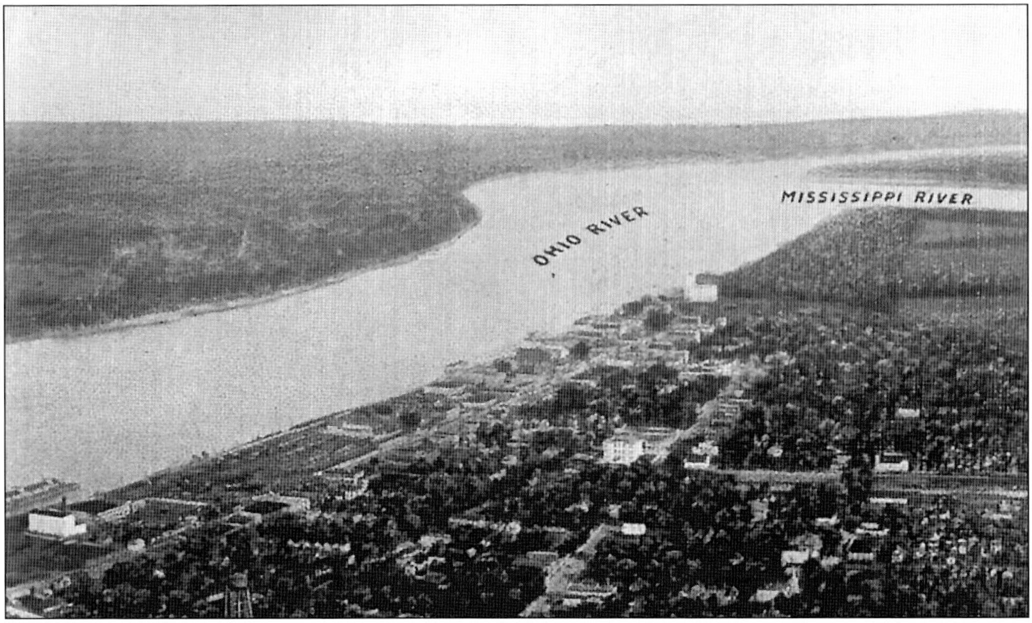

Here is a view looking south over the city of Cairo, Illinois, where the confluence of the Ohio and Mississippi Rivers is located.

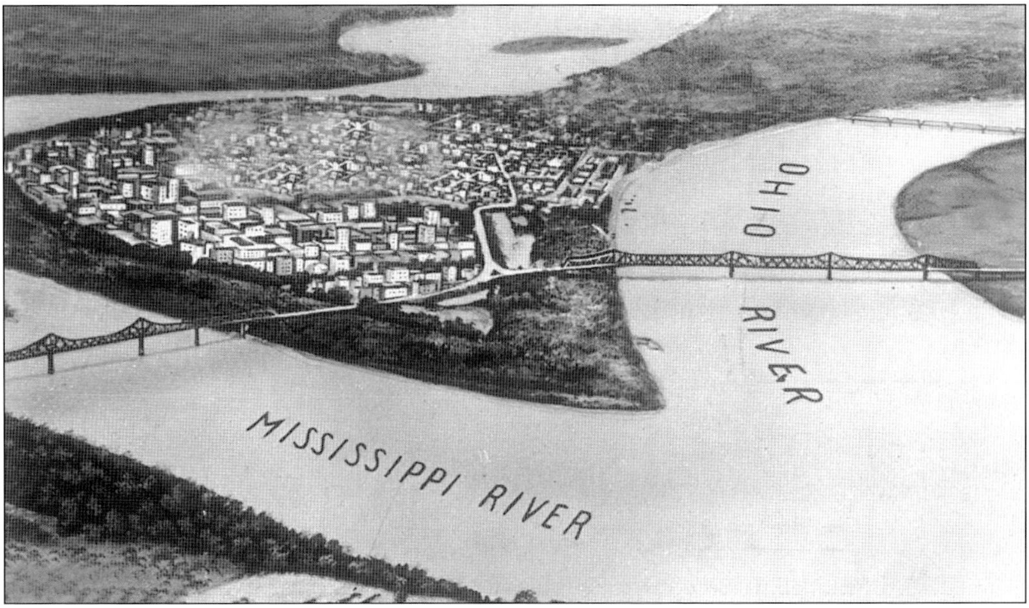

Another view of the Ohio–Mississippi confluence shows three states: Illinois, Missouri, and Kentucky. This location is one of the narrower widths of the Mississippi.

Four

The Lower Mississippi

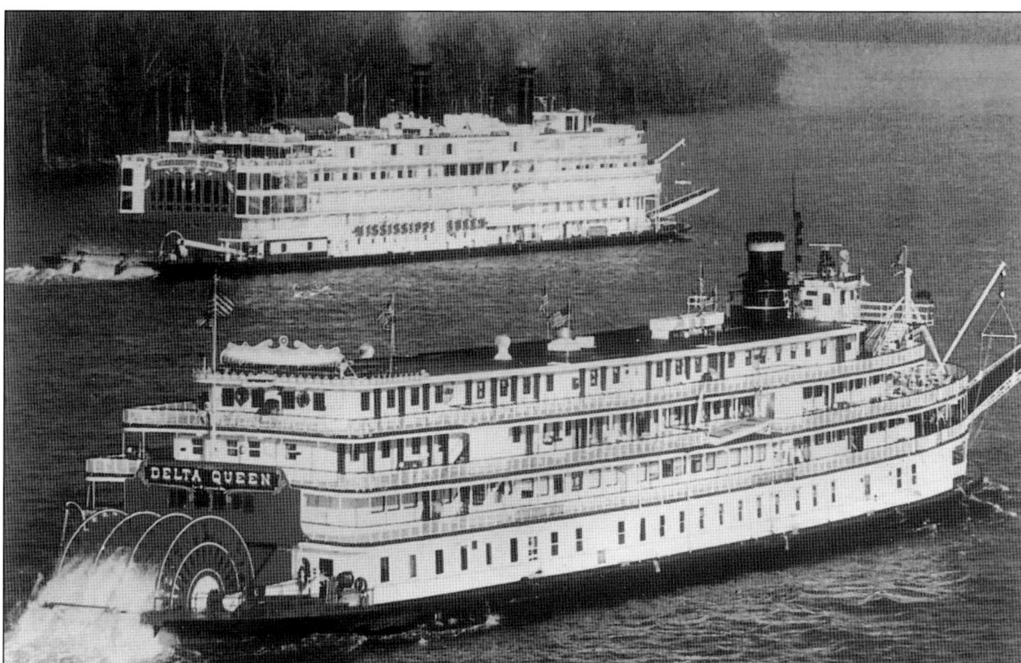

Captains of Mississippi riverboats were a proud lot, and if challenged to a race by another captain, the gauntlet was picked up and the race set. Above, the *Delta Queen* and the *Mississippi Queen* have at it in the annual race of the *Queens*.

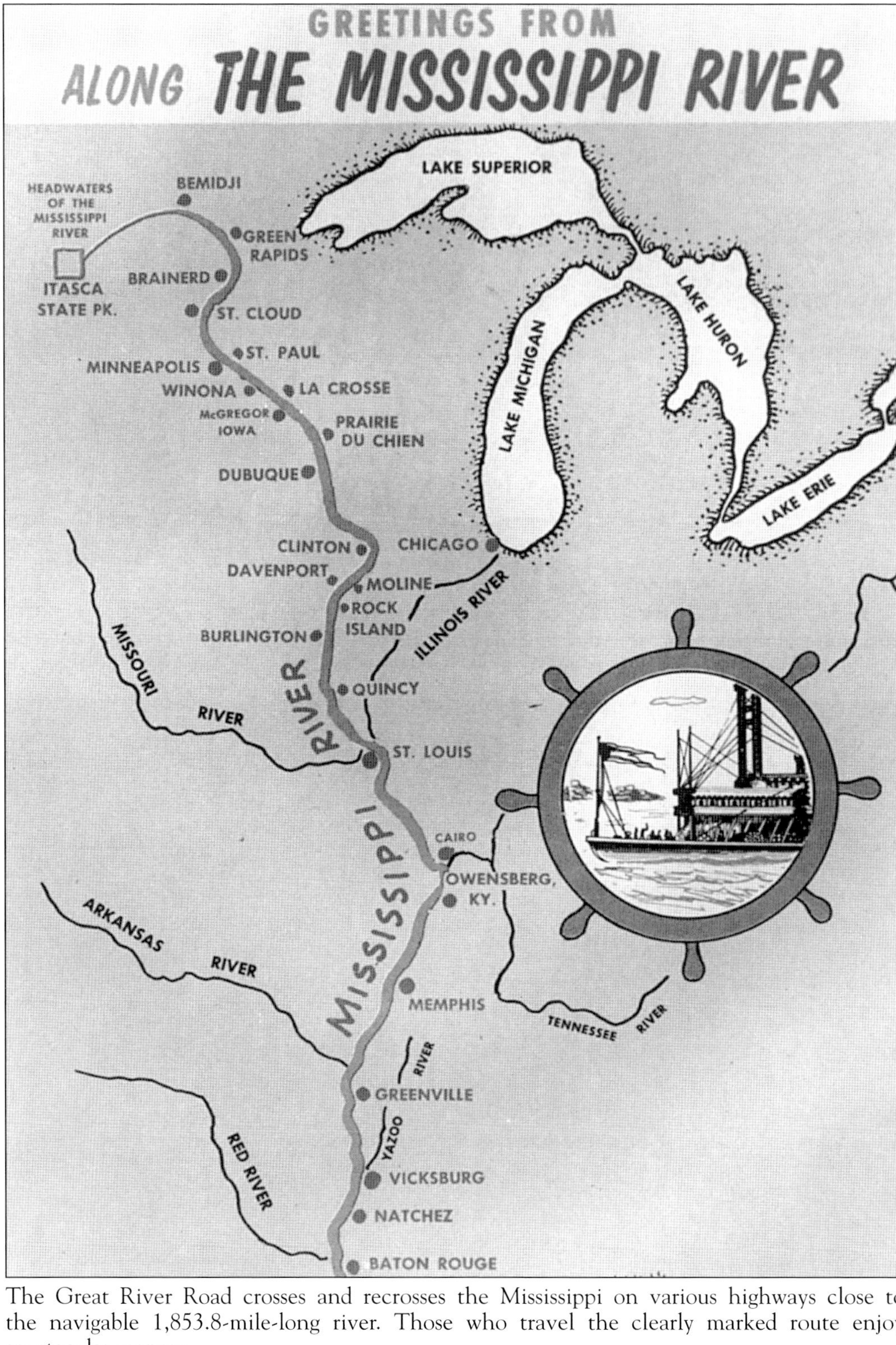

The Great River Road crosses and recrosses the Mississippi on various highways close to the navigable 1,853.8-mile-long river. Those who travel the clearly marked route enjoy spectacular scenery.

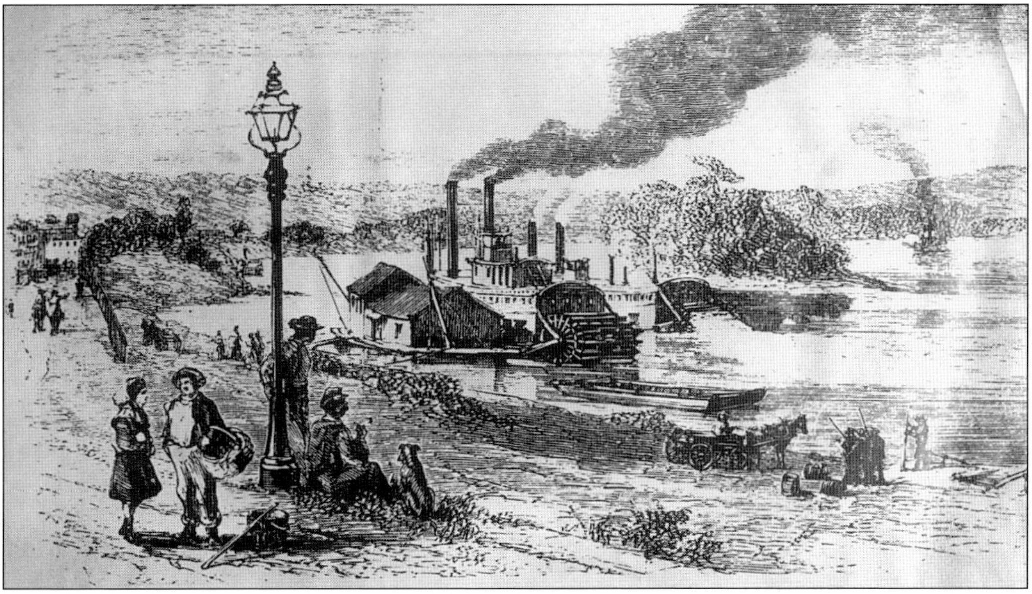

This is a lithograph of life on the lower river in the 19th century. Riverboats coming to town always produced excitement.

Readers of all river town newspapers kept track of arrivals and departures of boats to and from their town, as seen in this example here, which is dated 1843.

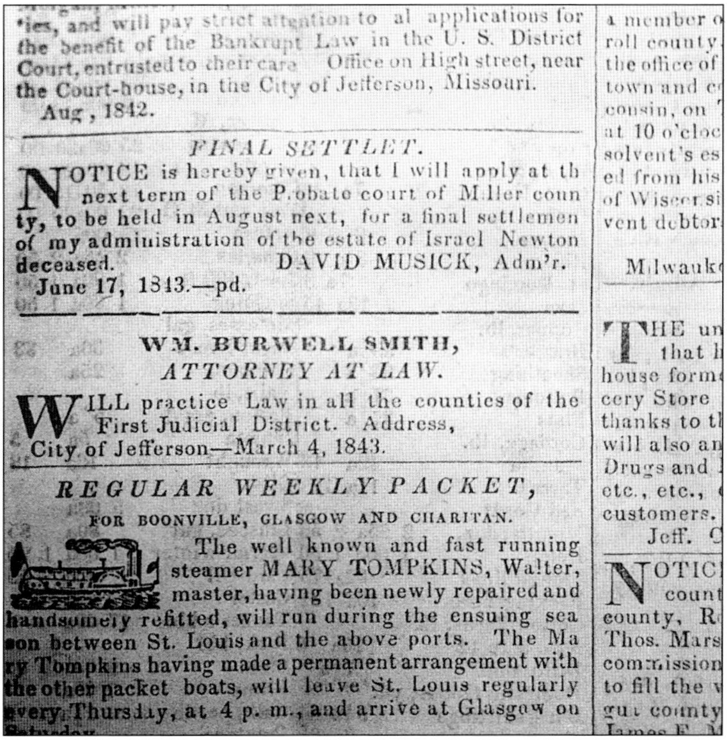

ies, and will pay strict attention to al applications for the benefit of the Bankrupt Law in the U. S. District Court, entrusted to their care Office on High street, near the Court-house, in the City of Jefferson, Missouri.

Aug , 1842.

FINAL SETTLET.

NOTICE is hereby given, that I will apply at th next term of the Probate court of Miller county, to be held in August next, for a final settlemen of my administration of the estate of Israel Newton deceased. DAVID MUSICK, Adm'r.

June 17, 1843.—pd.

WM. BURWELL SMITH,

ATTORNEY AT LAW.

WILL practice Law in all the counties of the First Judicial District. Address, City of Jefferson—March 4, 1843.

REGULAR WEEKLY PACKET,

FOR BOONVILLE, GLASGOW AND CHARITAN.

The well known and fast running steamer MARY TOMPKINS, Walter, master, having been newly repaired and handsomely refitted, will run during the ensuing season between St. Louis and the above ports. The Mary Tompkins having made a permanent arrangement with the other packet boats, will leave St. Louis regularly every Thursday, at 4 p. m., and arrive at Glasgow on

a member o
roll county
the office of
town and c
consin, on
at 10 o'cloc
solvent's es
ed from his
of Wisconsi
vent debtor

Milwauk

THE un
that h
house form
cery Store
thanks to th
will also an
Drugs and
etc., etc.,
customers.
Jeff.

NOTIC
count
county, R
Thos. Mars
commission
to fill the
gu county

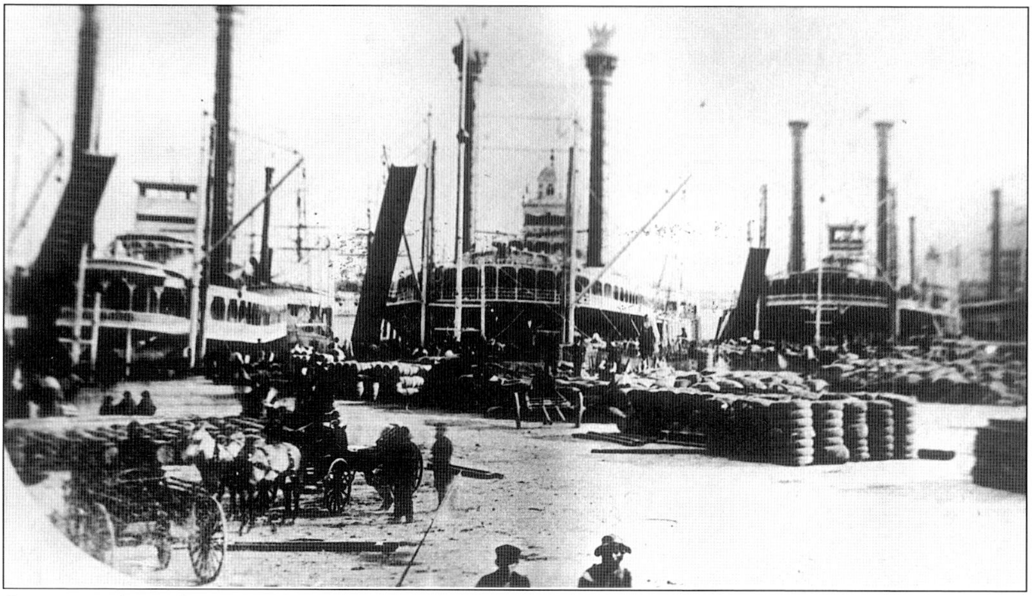

Scenes such as this one were common along the lower Mississippi. Notice the bales of cotton filling the dock. The beautiful, tall stacks would give way to shorter, hinged ones, when the railroads spanned the river with their bridges.

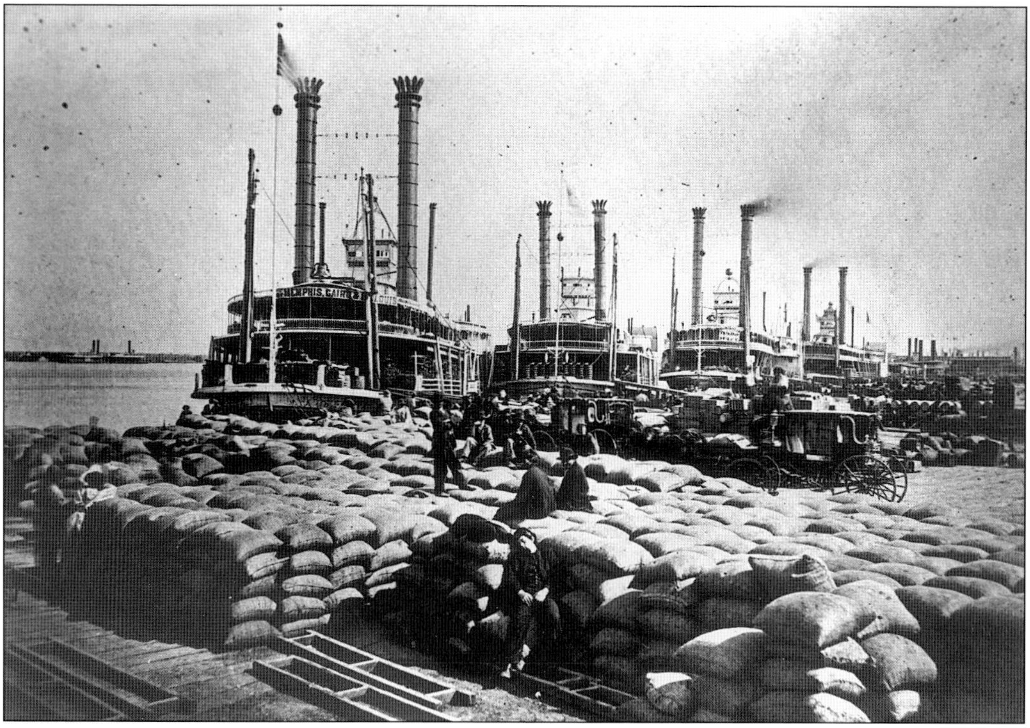

Here, a half-dozen boats have tied up to find cargo. The boat nearest the camera, although unidentified, has strung a banner across the top deck showing her destinations: Memphis, Cairo, and St. Louis.

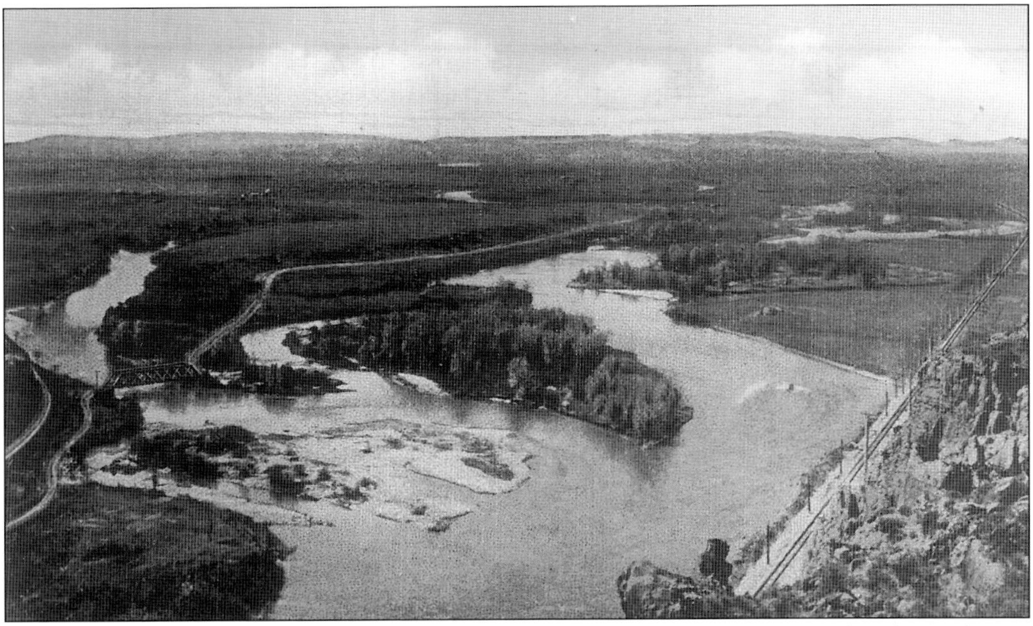

These are the head waters of the Missouri River near Three Forks, Montana. The chief tributary of the Mississippi forms where the Gallatin, Madison, and Red Rock-Jefferson (the main headstream of the Missouri) Rivers join.

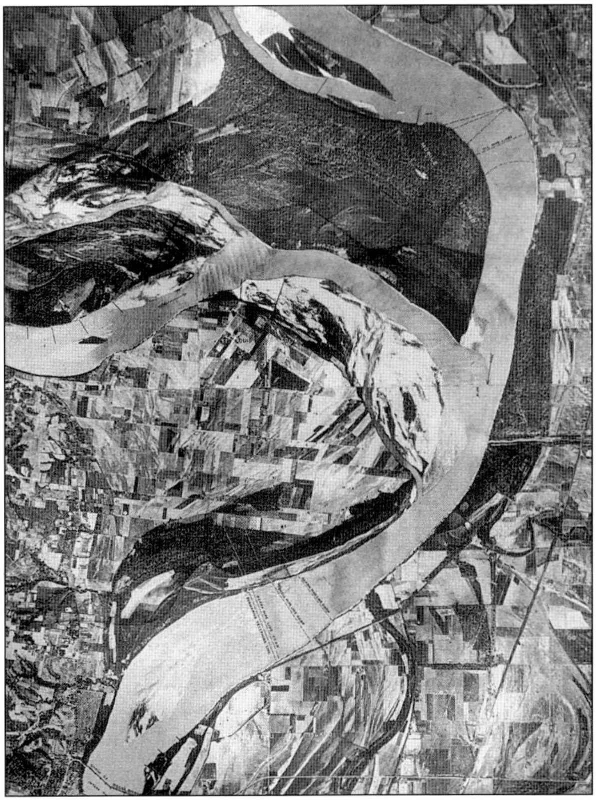

This high-altitude photograph of the Missouri/Mississippi confluence will give the reader a small degree of understanding of the mighty Mississippi River.

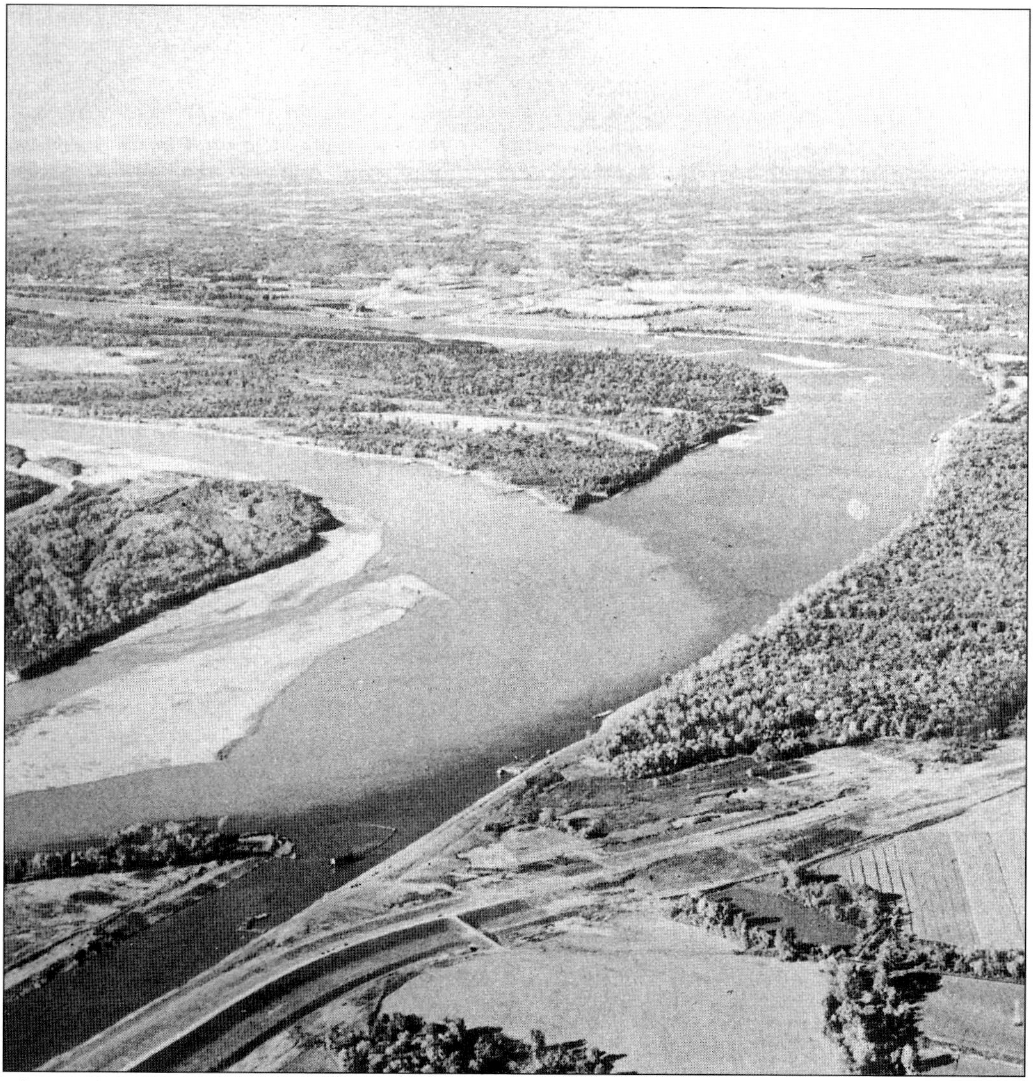

The reader can clearly see why the lower river is of a muddier color than the upper. While the Mississippi flows southward from Minnesota, it picks up rich, dark soil that gives the water a deep gray color. When the two meet, the lighter-colored Missouri is more dense than the upper Mississippi water, and the two don't combine until the Ohio enters the river.

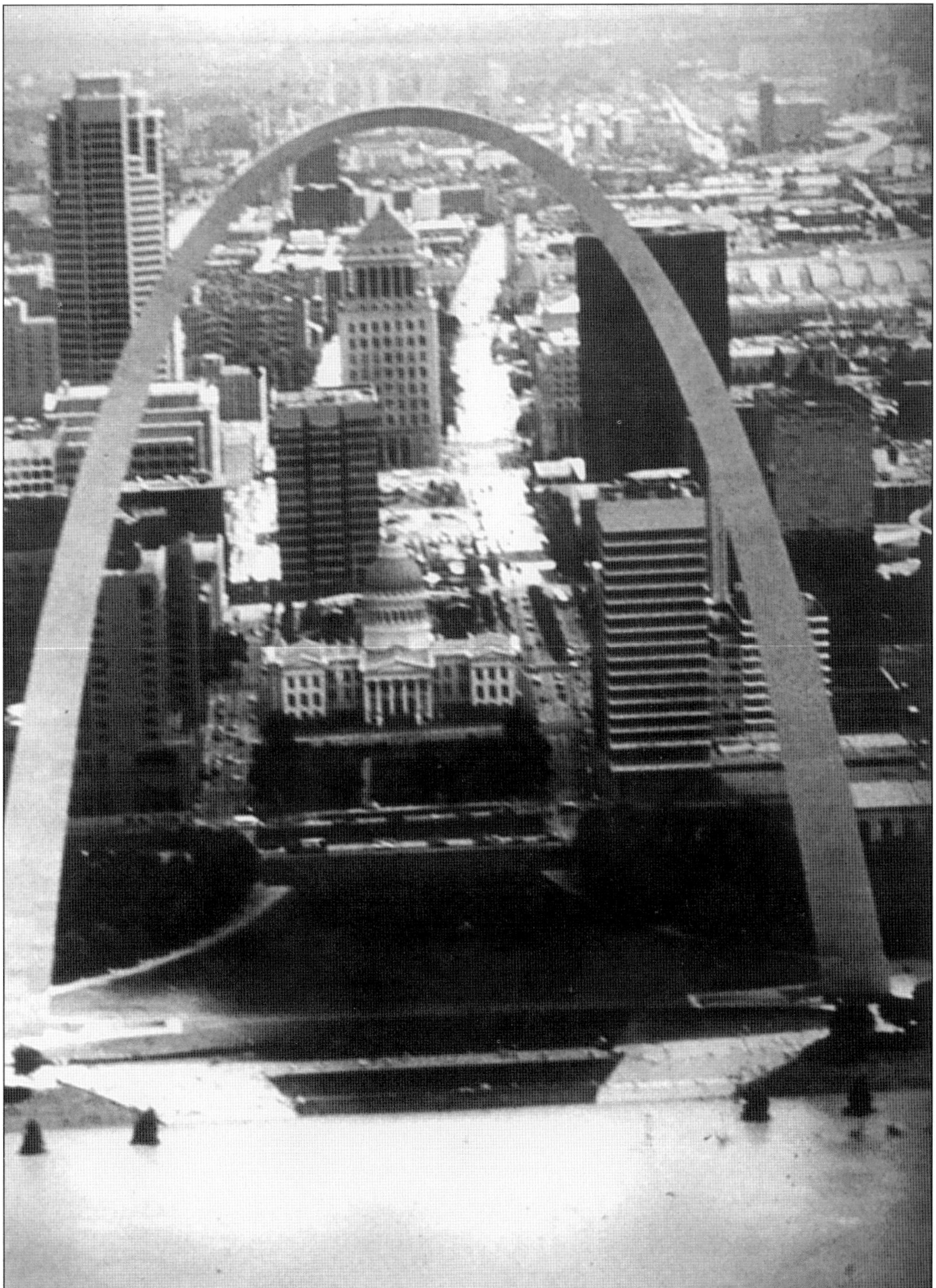

In this photograph, the Gateway Arch frames the buildings behind it, towering over most of them. The arch is 630 feet high and is visible from 30 to 40 miles away.

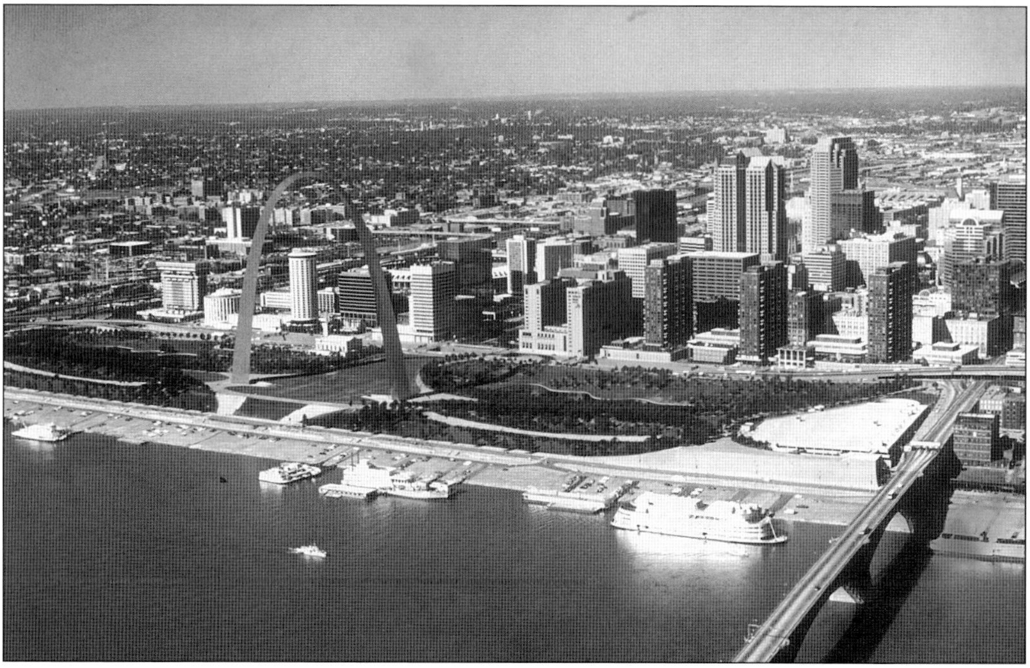

Here the reader can see the city of St. Louis spreading out behind the Gateway Arch.

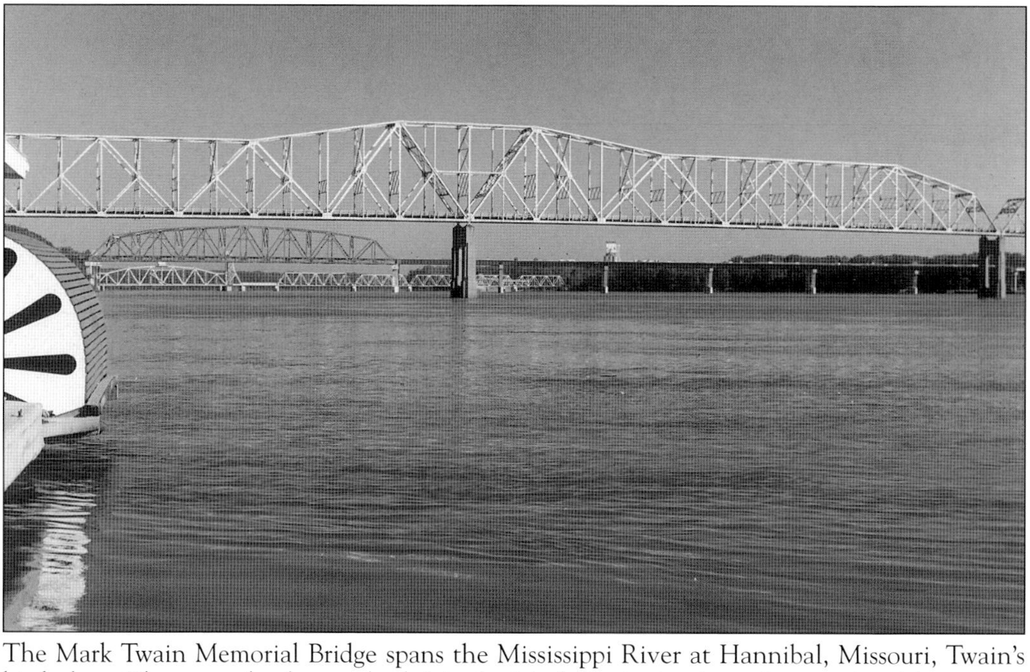

The Mark Twain Memorial Bridge spans the Mississippi River at Hannibal, Missouri, Twain's birthplace. The sternwheeler on the left is the *Mark Twain* riverboat that carries sightseers on the Father of Waters.

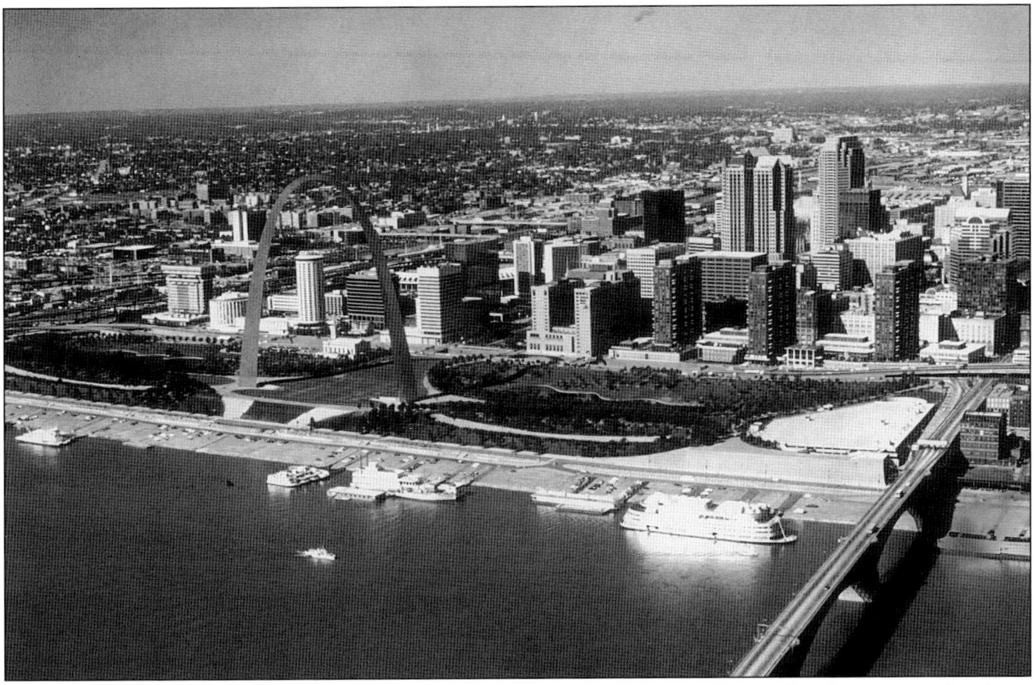

This is a view the reader could see of the Mississippi River from the Riverview Park in Hannibal, Missouri.

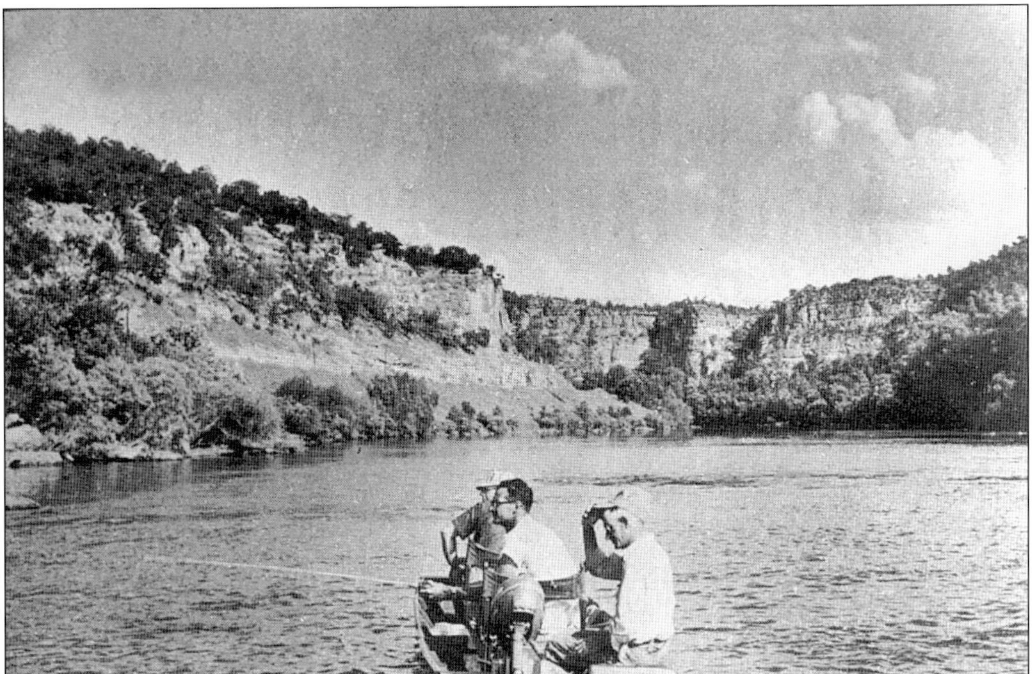

The Mississippi drains every waterway and river in Arkansas, including the White River pictured above. I wonder how the fish are biting.

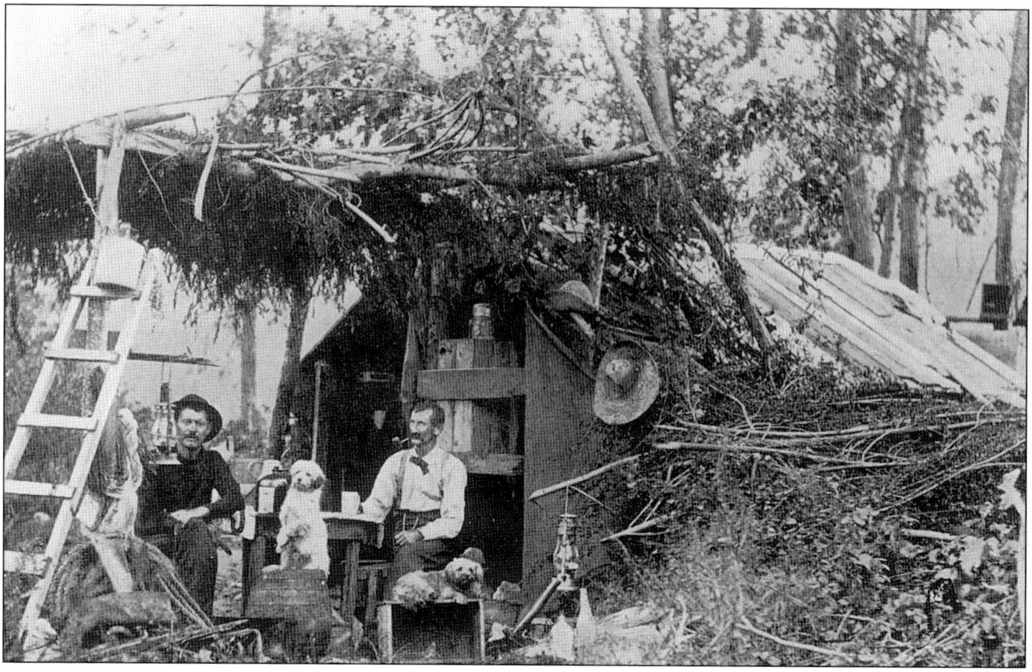

Here is a fisherman's cabin along the Mississippi River shortly after the turn of the 20th century. As primitive as it appears, it seems cozy.

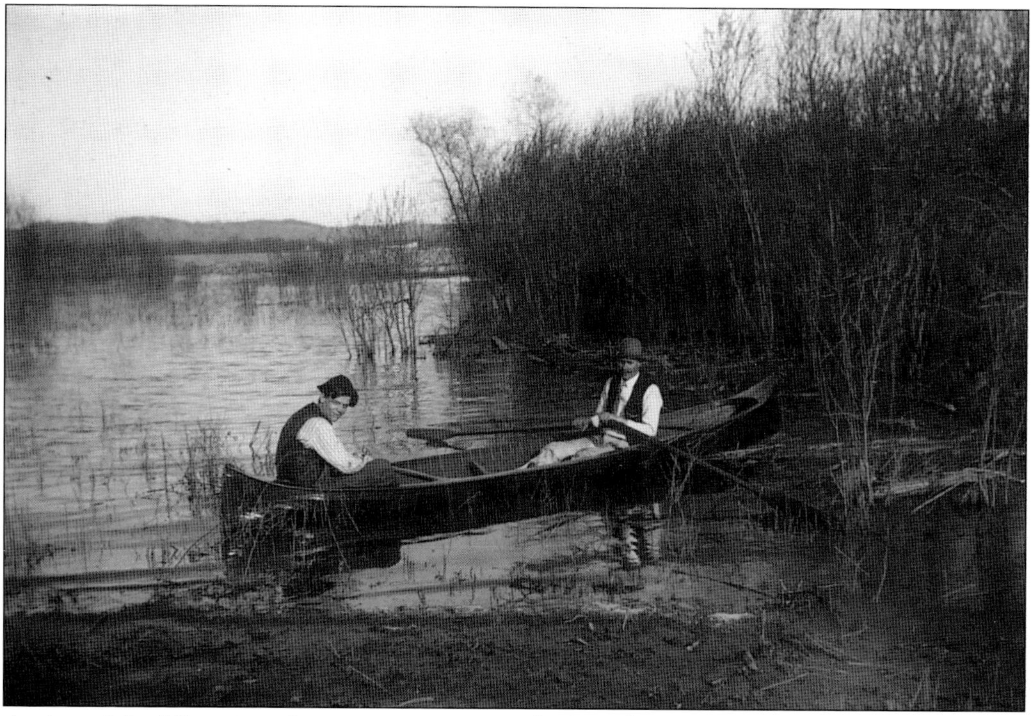

A view of the Mississippi shore, sometime around 1909, shows two men about to set out for a boat ride. They have no fishing gear with them, and the canoe-like, double-bowed boat should move right along.

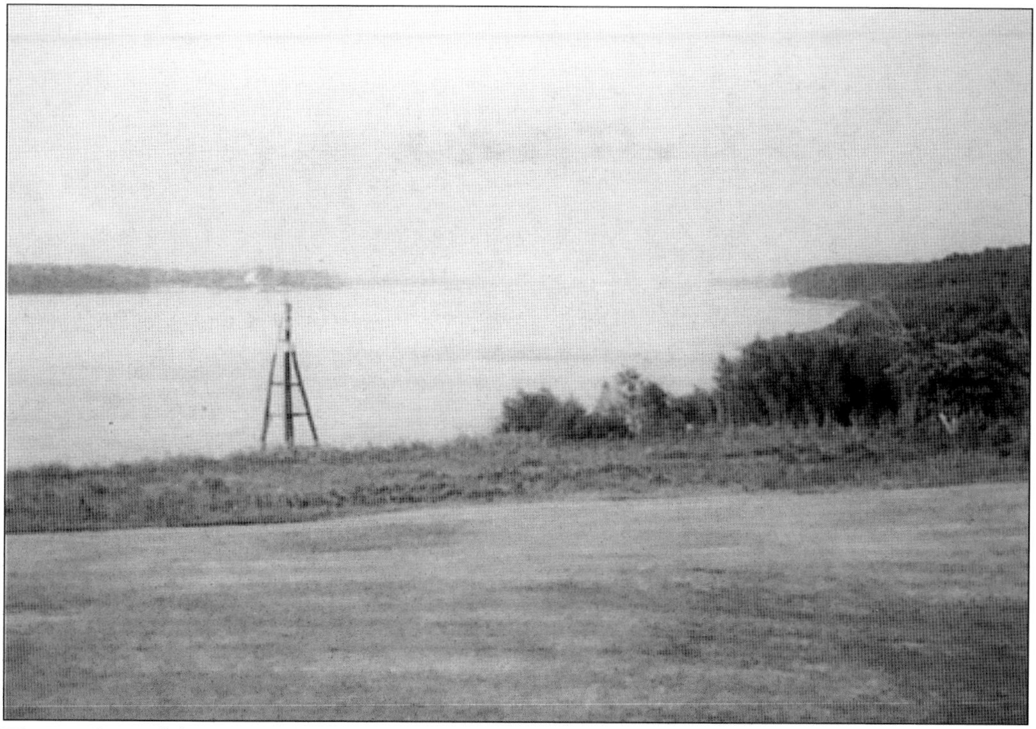

The reader will have to take the word of photographer Velva Yarbro, of Hickman, Kentucky, that a towboat with barges is in the picture. The fog bank that stretched from shore to shore engulfed it just when she took the picture. The small structure is milepost 921.

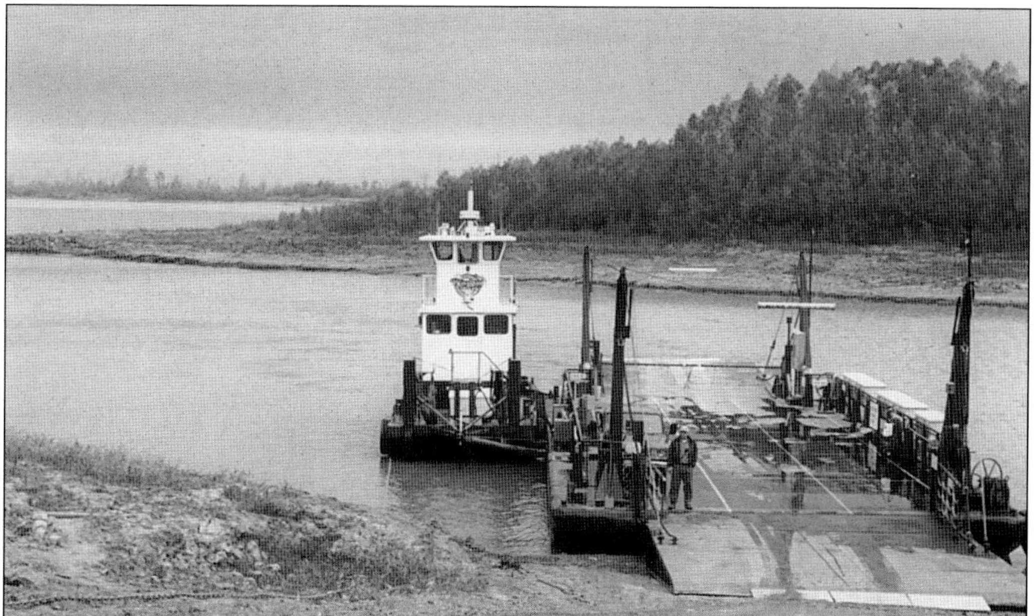

The Dorena, Missouri/Hickman, Kentucky ferry is shown here at the ferry landing, waiting for passengers and an auto or two. There are quite a few ferry boats still operating on both the upper and lower Mississippi.

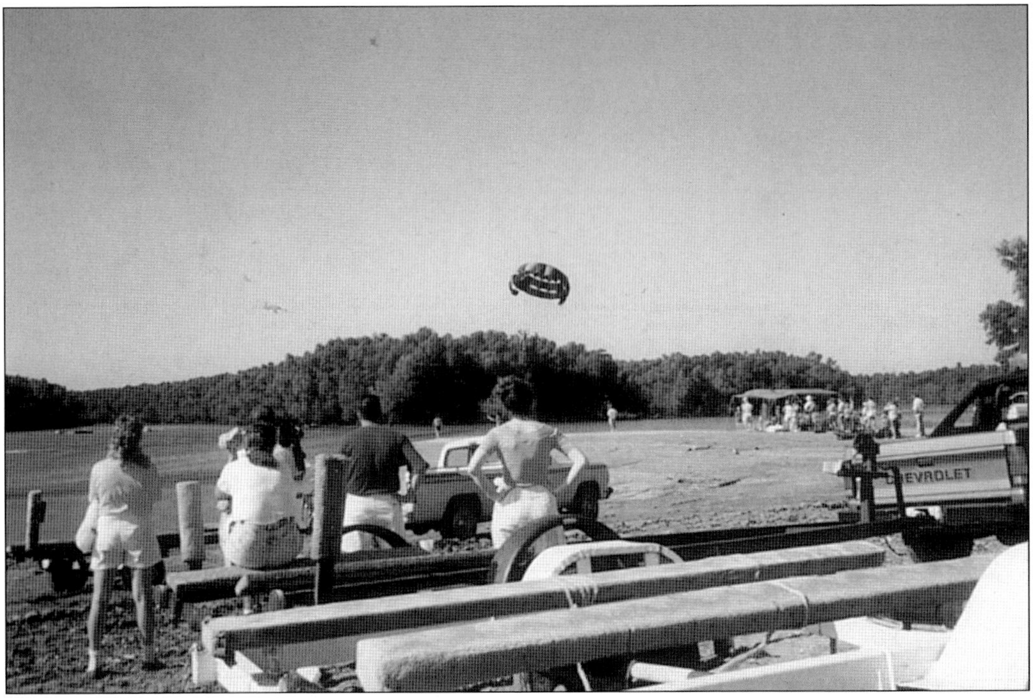

Water shows always attract people. Here, someone is taking off, harnessed to a parachute, while being towed by a motorboat.

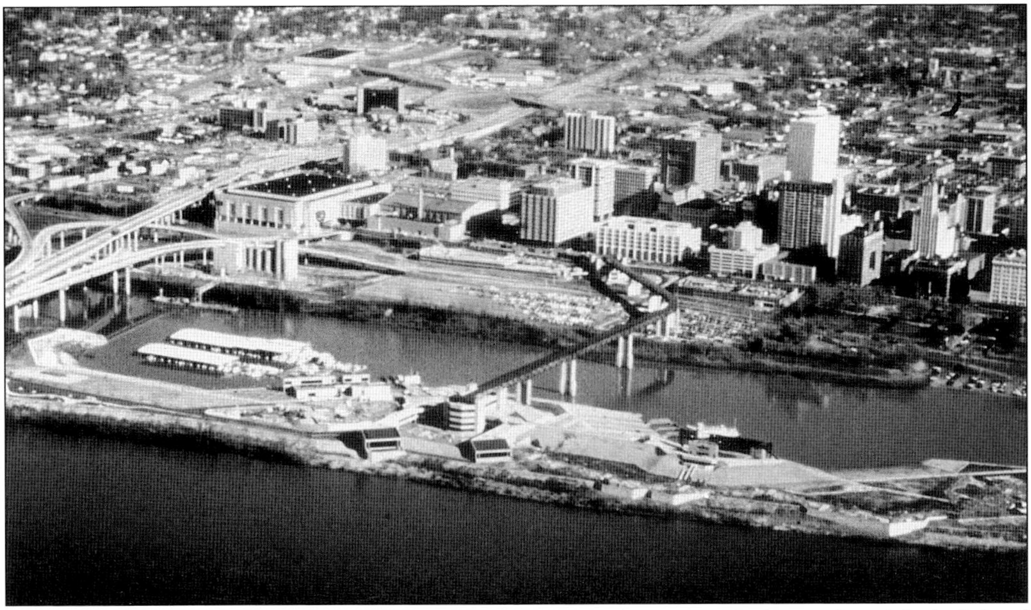

Here is a view of Memphis, Tennessee's waterfront, including the Mud Island Amusement Park.

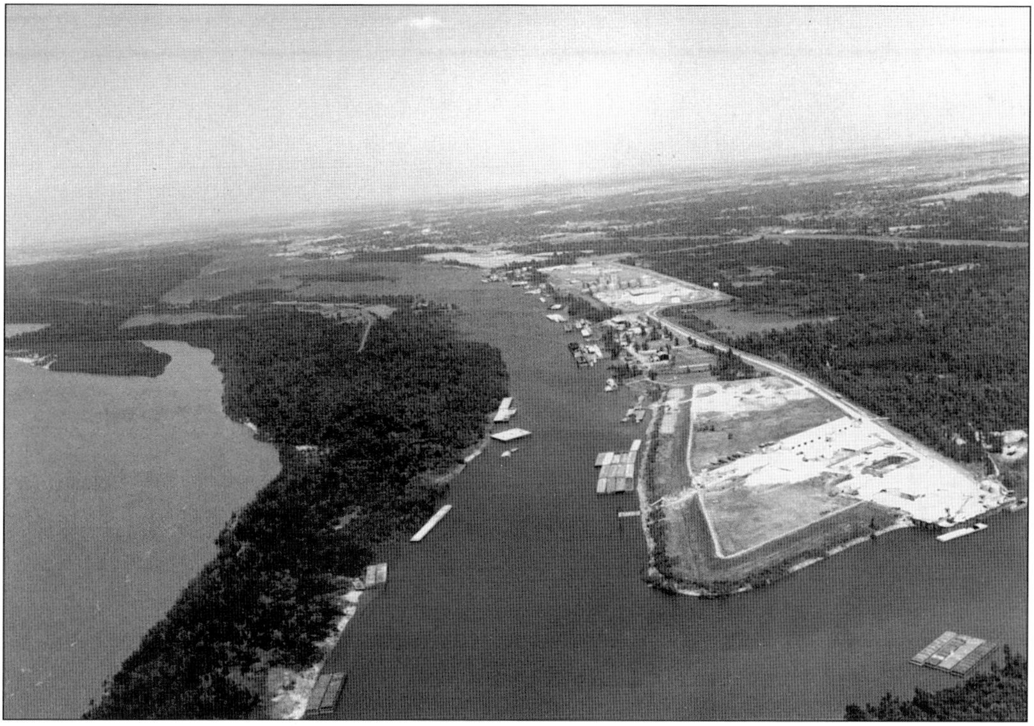

This view shows the port at Greenville, Mississippi, where barges are loaded, unloaded, and made into tows.

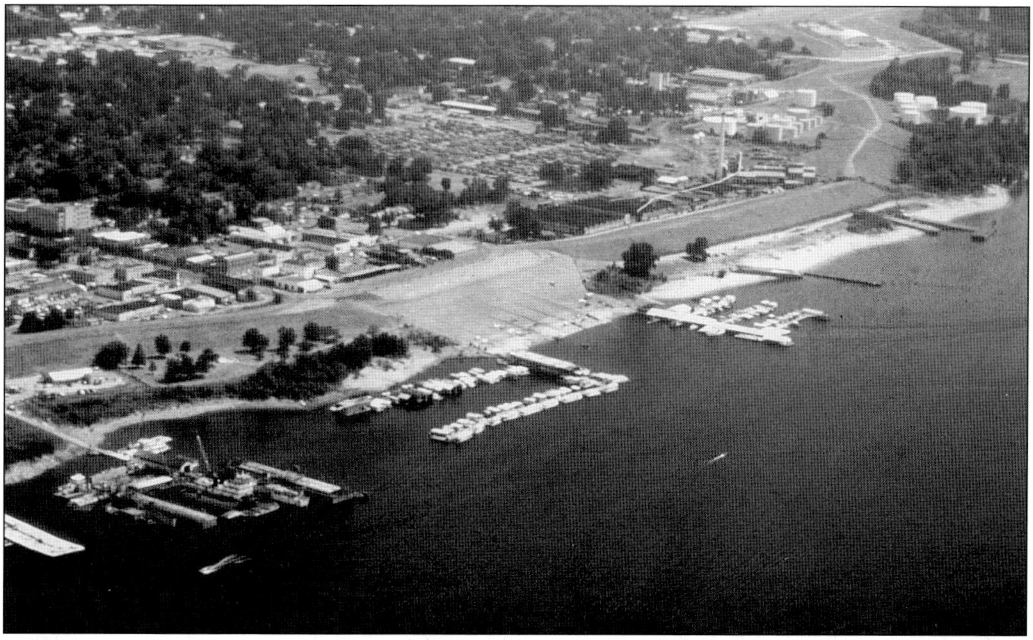

The city of Greenville lies beyond the port where tows arrive and depart. The town, which shows a tidy waterfront and several marinas, can be seen at left and right in the upper center of the photograph.

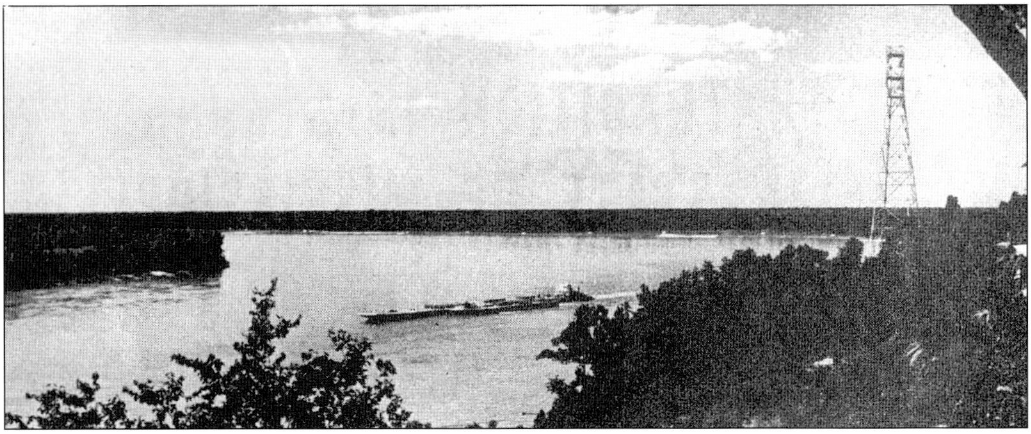

This view shows a towboat leaving the Yazoo River and entering the Mississippi. The boat has just left Vicksburg, Mississippi.

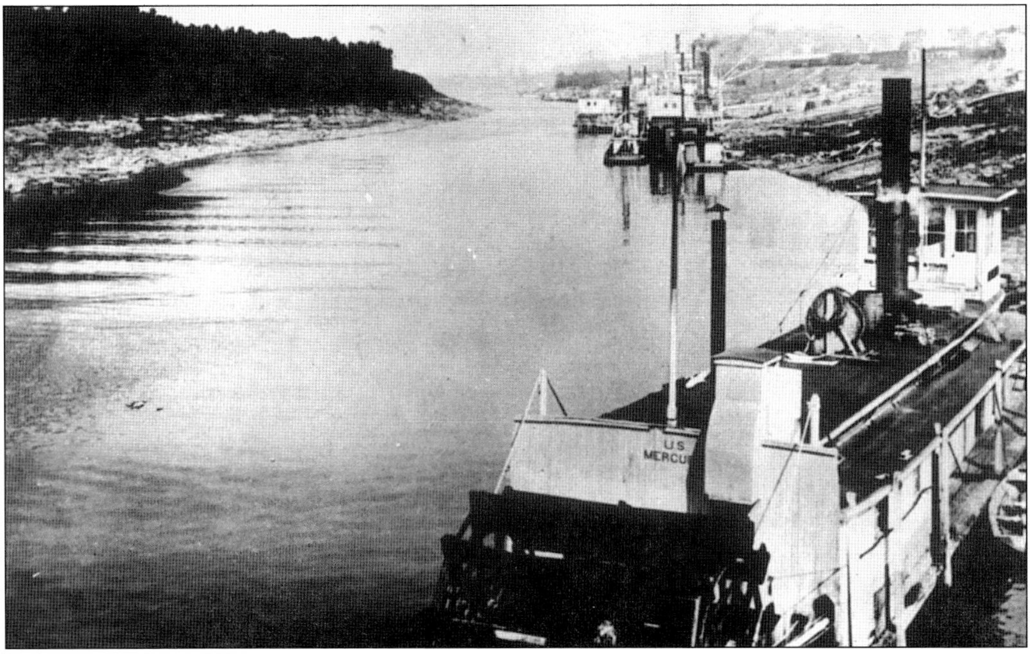

This 1908 photograph pictures steamboats tied up at Vicksburg's canal.

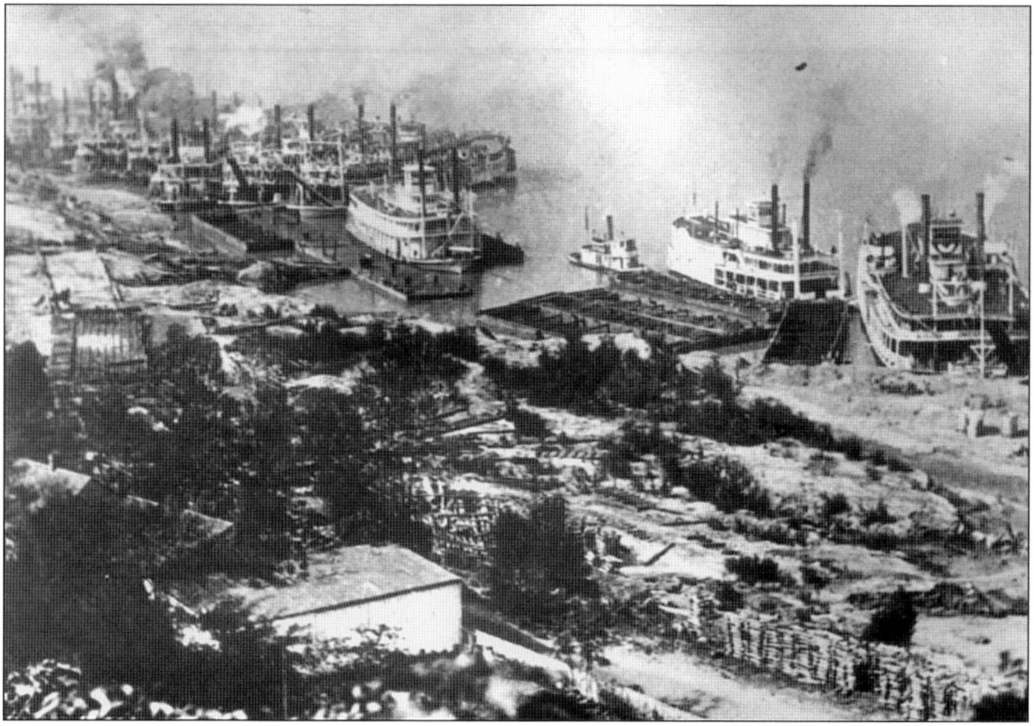

This busy scene is a 19th century river port, possibly Vicksburg. There are at least 12, if not more, steamboats in port.

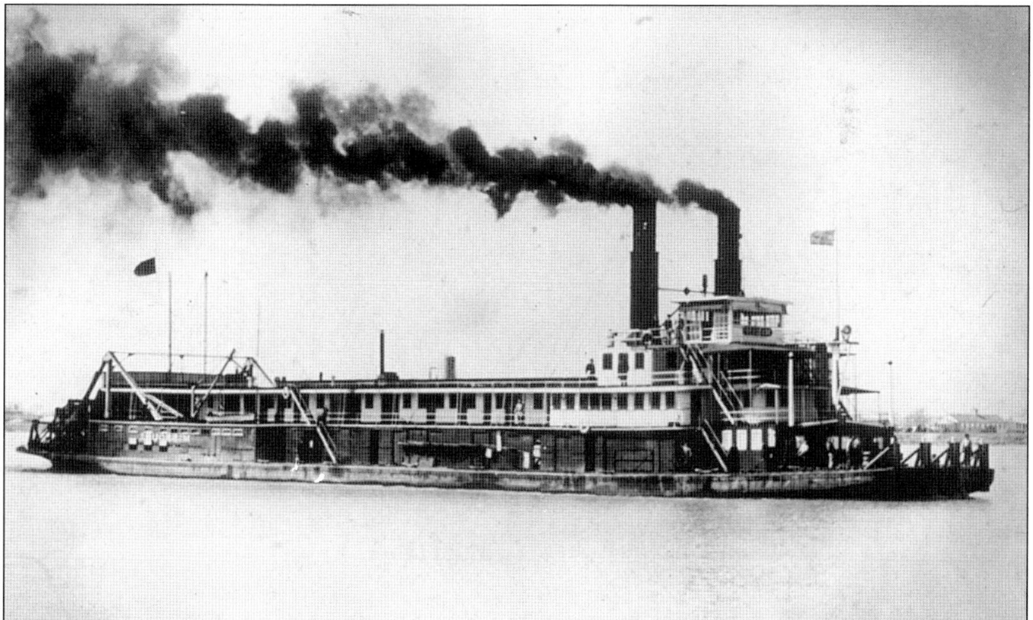

Here we see a steamboat of yesteryear, proudly plying the waters of the Mississippi, with black smoke plumes trailing behind.

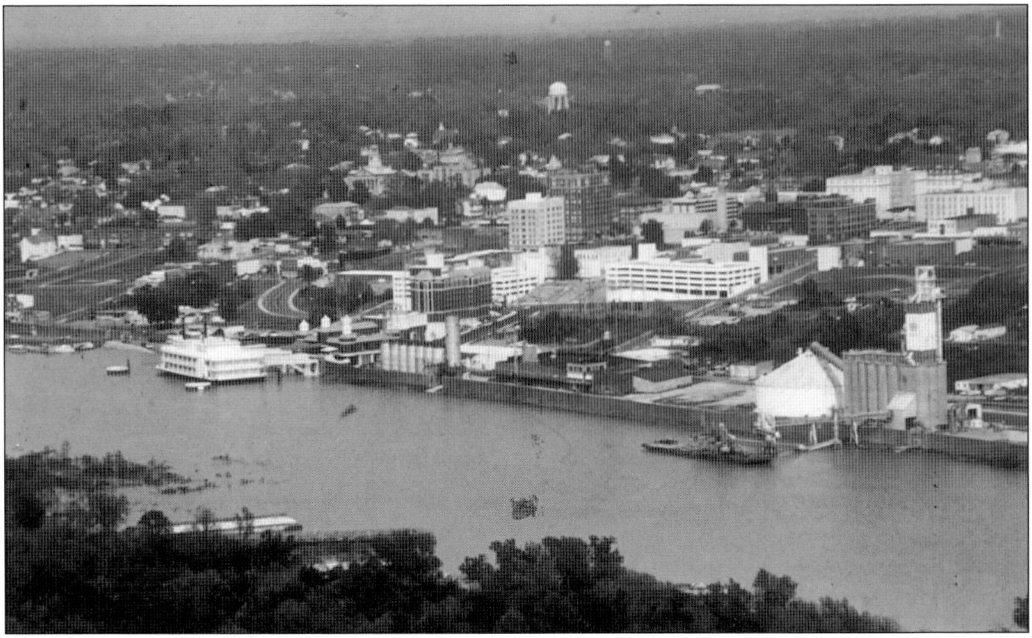

Vicksburg, which suffered an unbelievable siege during the Civil War, is shown here as it appeared in April, 1994. A beautiful city, its citizens keep alive the memory of that siege by maintaining the battleground.

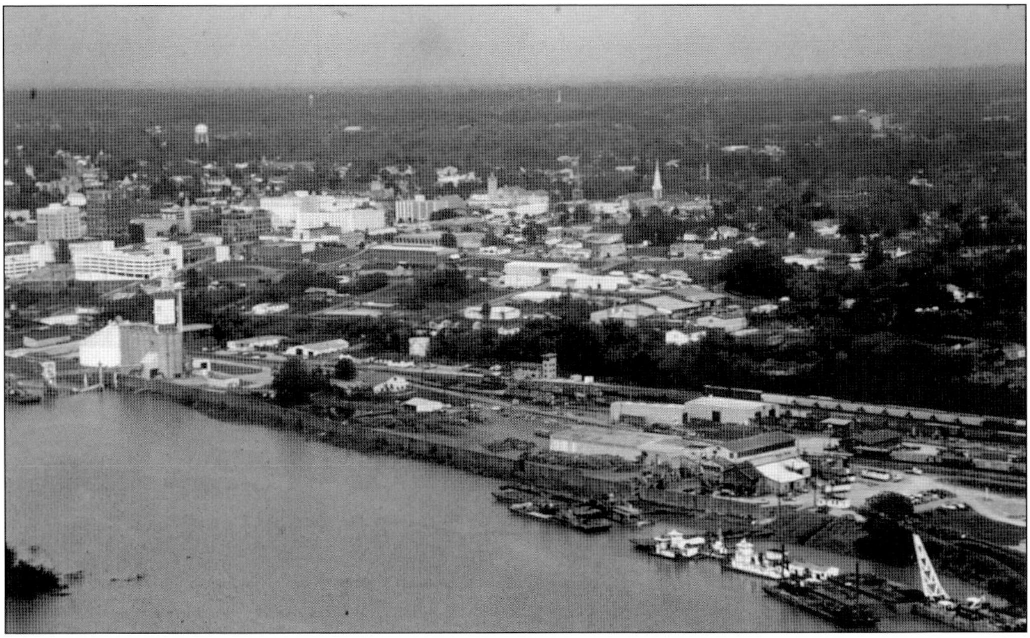

Here we see more of Vicksburg, with the camera moved to the right. Cannon from the Civil War are on display at strategic points on bluffs, overlooking the Mississippi as well as the battleground.

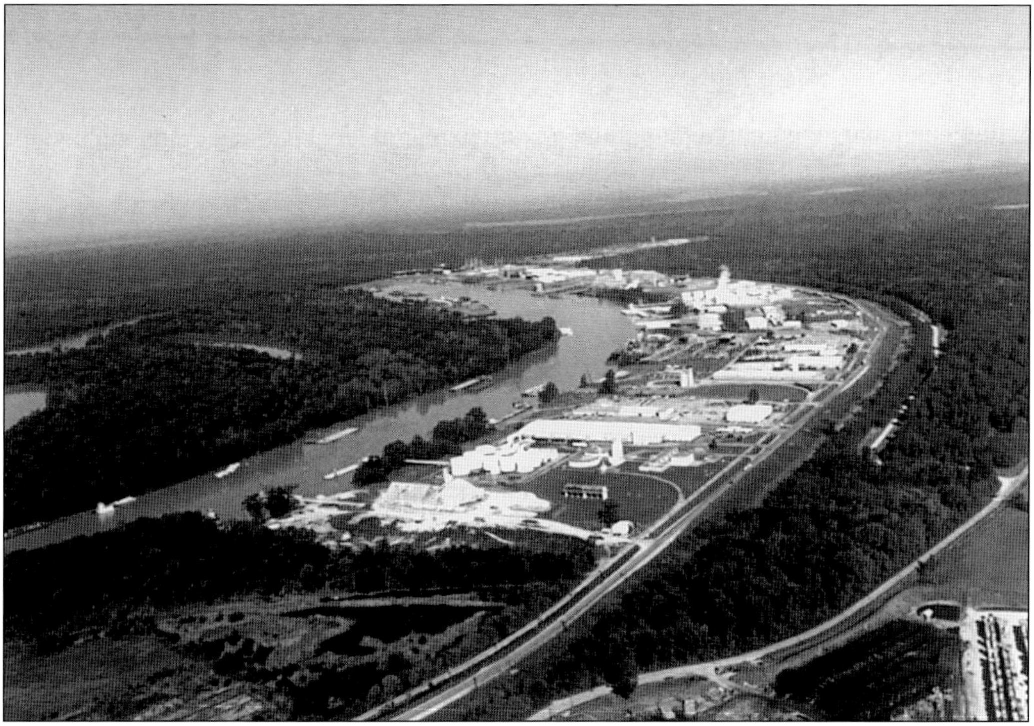

Here the reader sees an air view of the Port of Vicksburg, showing some of Vicksburg's industries.

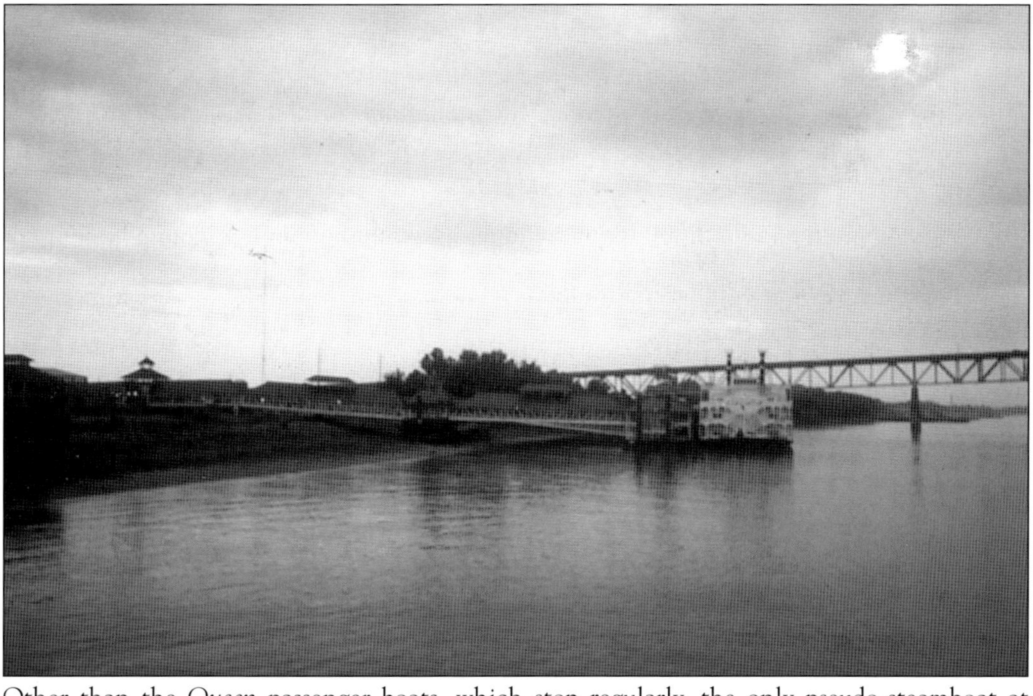

Other than the *Queen* passenger boats, which stop regularly, the only pseudo-steamboat at Vicksburg is a gambling boat, pictured here on the Yazoo Canal.

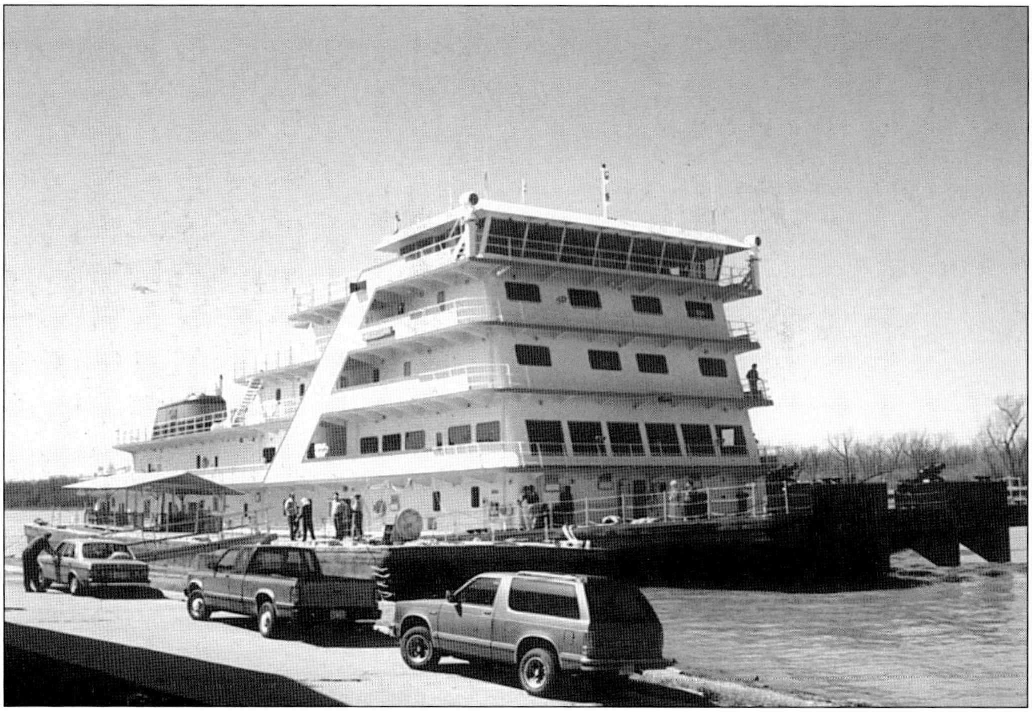

The MV *Mississippi* five-decker is the largest towboat on the river today. Here it is seen at Vicksburg's city port.

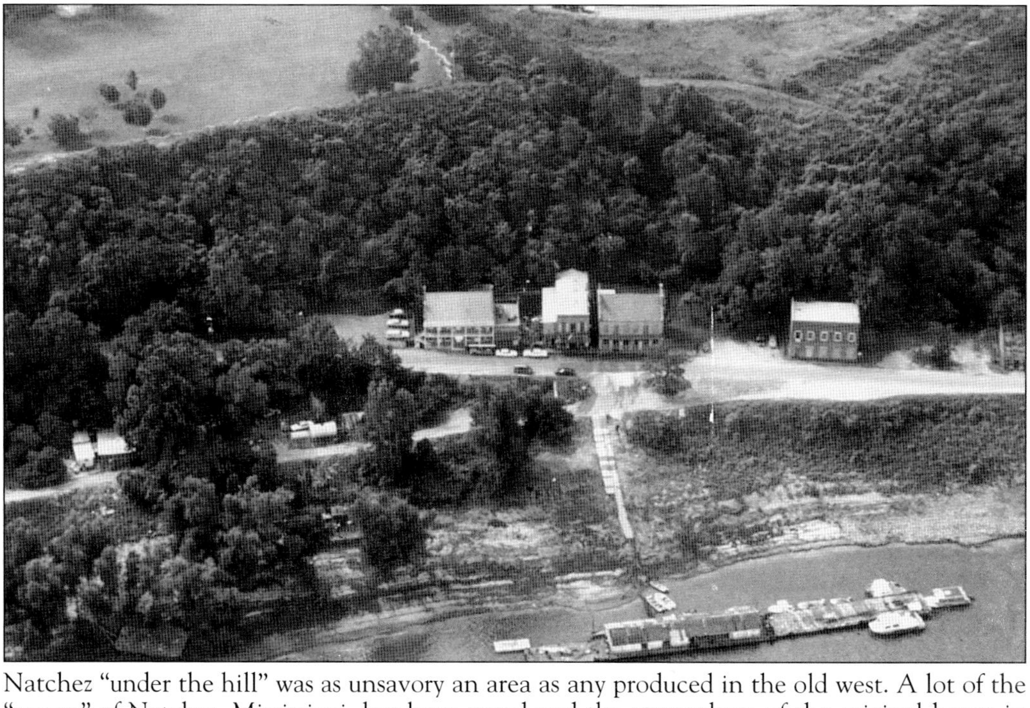

Natchez "under the hill" was as unsavory an area as any produced in the old west. A lot of the "annex" of Natchez, Mississippi, has been saved and the atmosphere of the original hangs in the air.

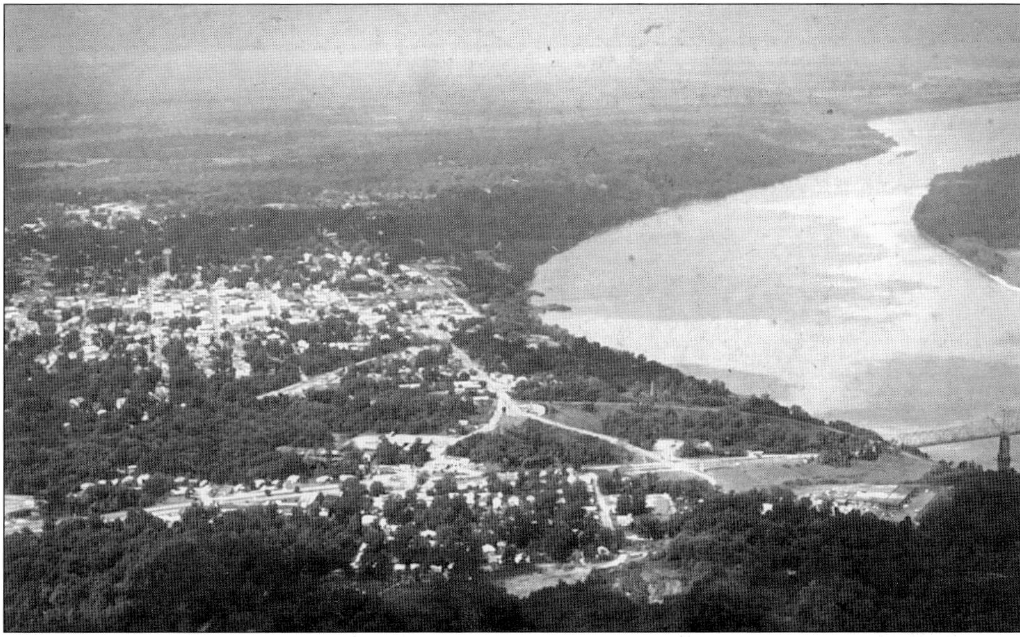

Above Natchez "under the hill" is the beautiful city of Natchez, Mississippi. Some preserved antebellum homes are open for tours.

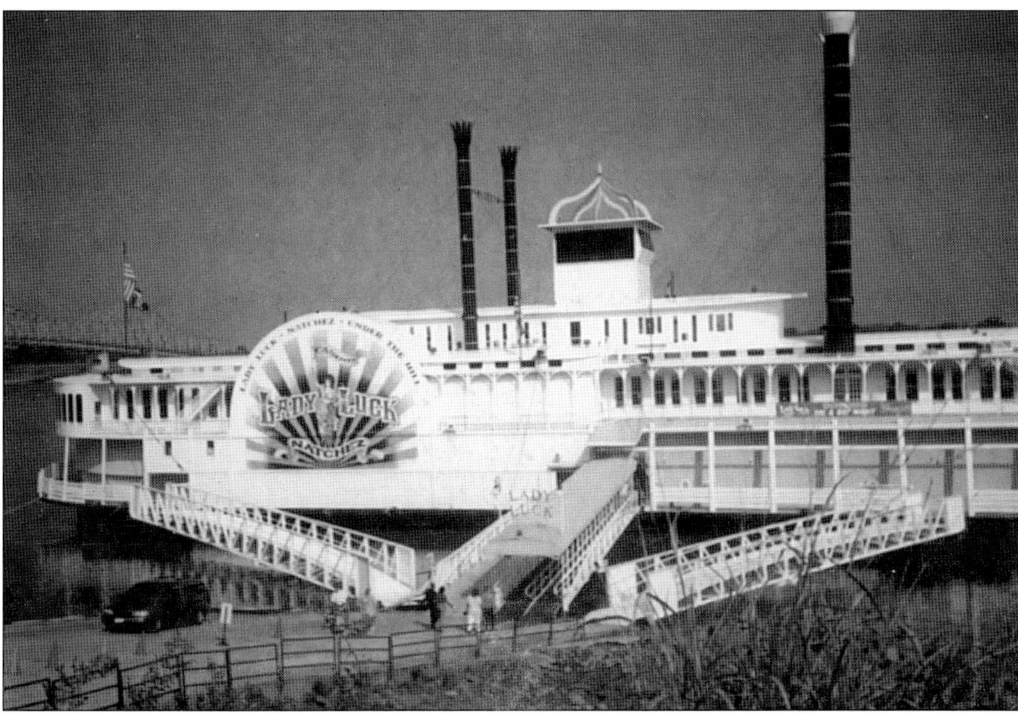

There are numerous gambling boats on the most navigable rivers today. Here the *Lady Luck, Natchez Under the Hill* is semi-permanently docked at the waterfront.

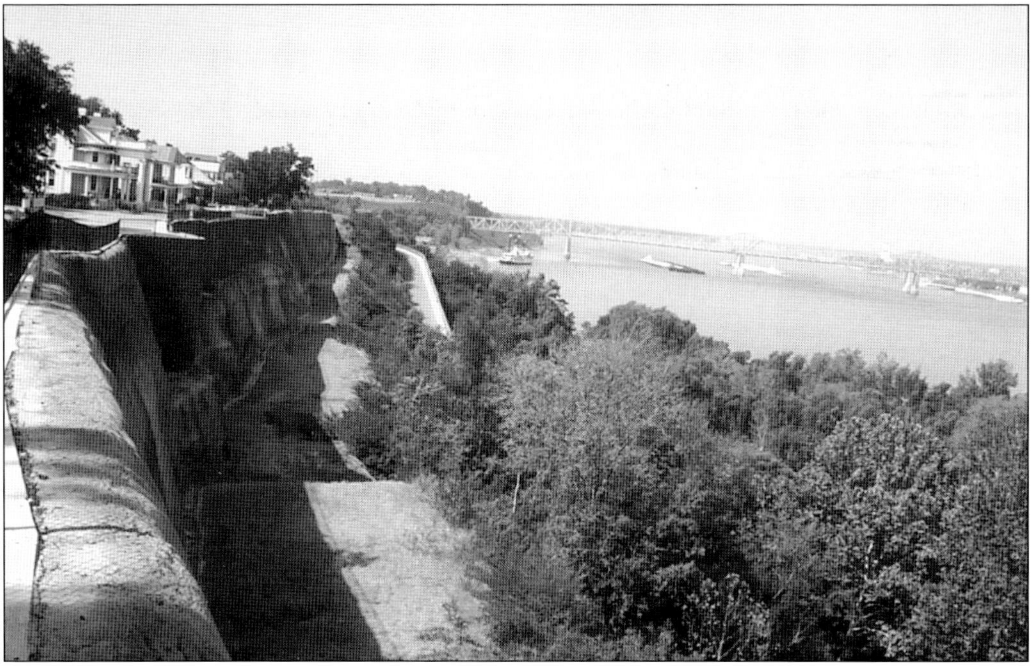

Here the reader can see a mix of architectural styles, sitting on a bluff overlooking the Mississippi River.

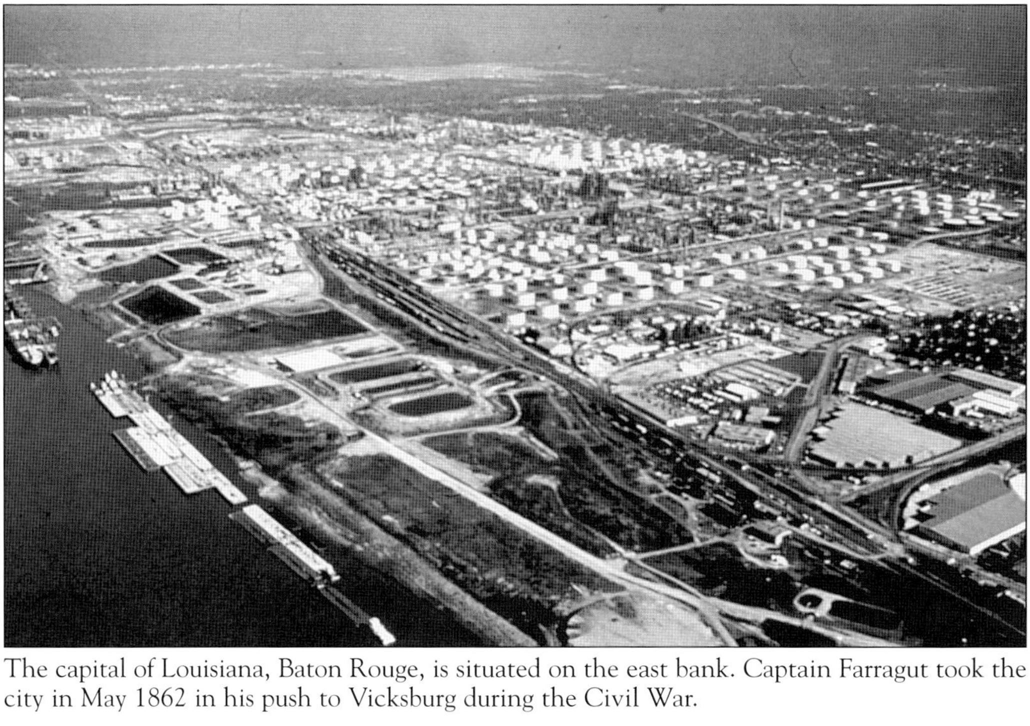

The capital of Louisiana, Baton Rouge, is situated on the east bank. Captain Farragut took the city in May 1862 in his push to Vicksburg during the Civil War.

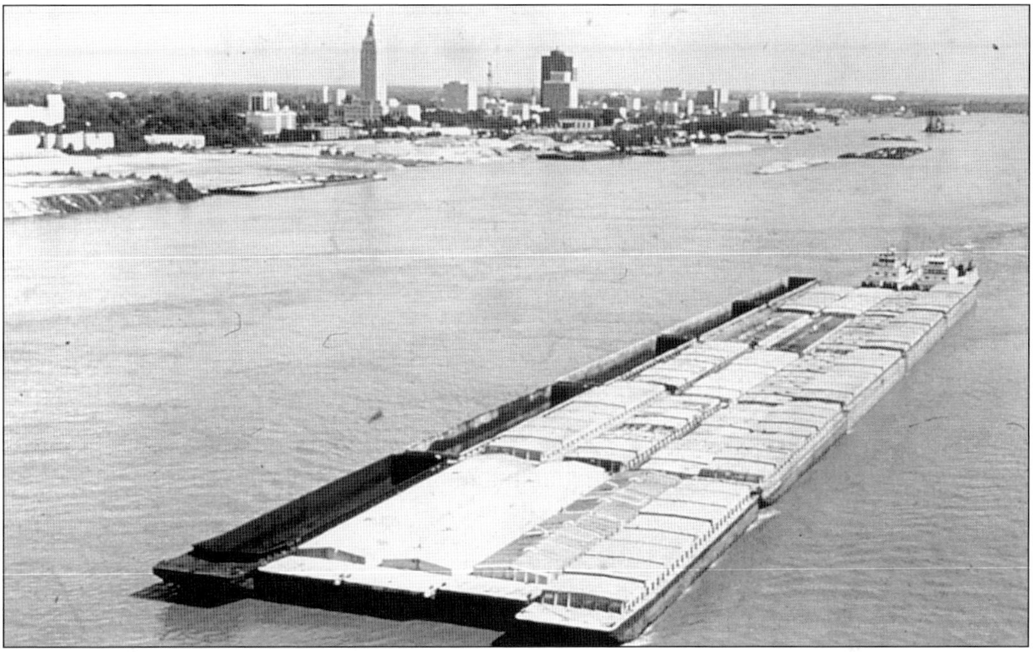

A tow of 25 covered barges is pushed through Baton Rouge, Louisiana, by two towboats. The Mississippi cuts the capital in half.

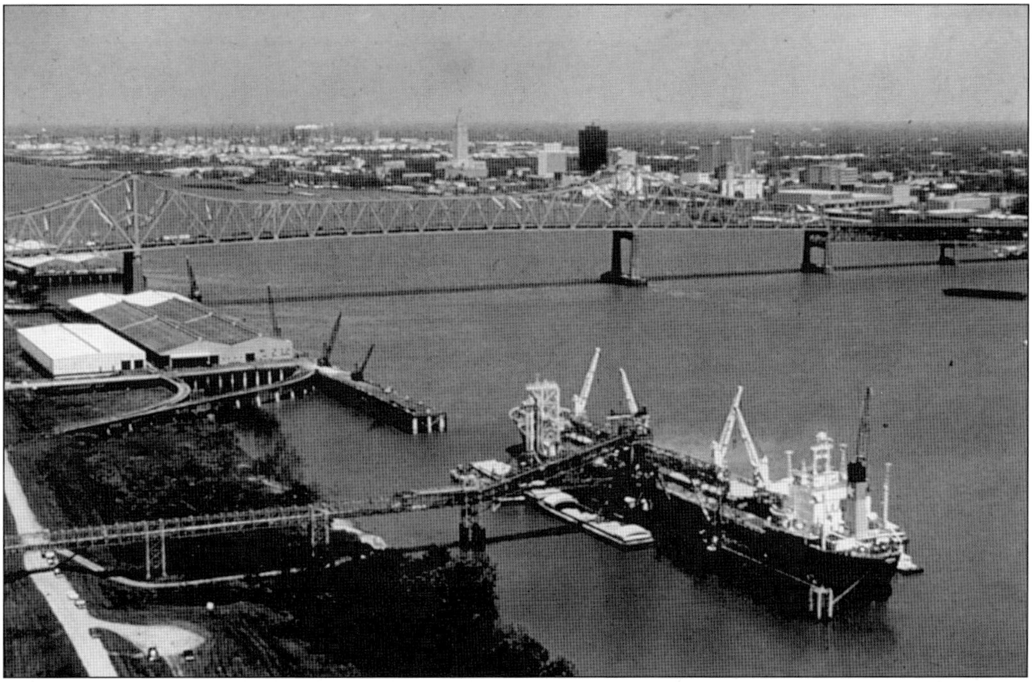

Sea-going vessels come upriver as far as Baton Rouge, to deliver imported products and take out finished material. Baton Rouge is French for "red stick."

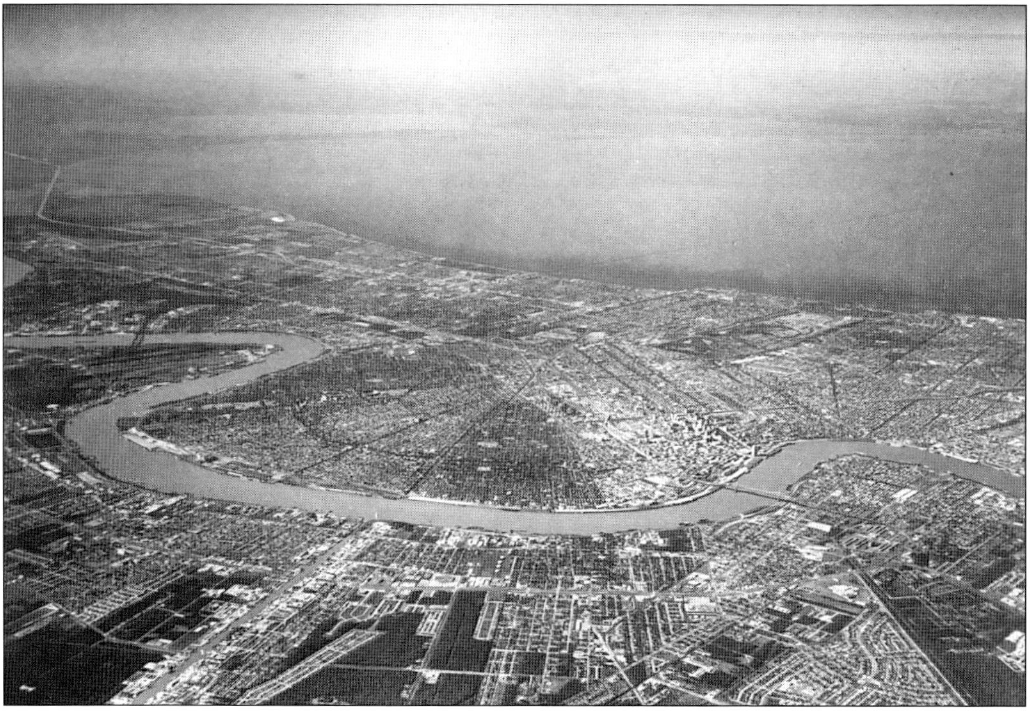

New Orleans is known as "The Big Easy" and "The Crescent City." The latter name is for a magnificent crescent shape the Mississippi River forms, snaking through the city.

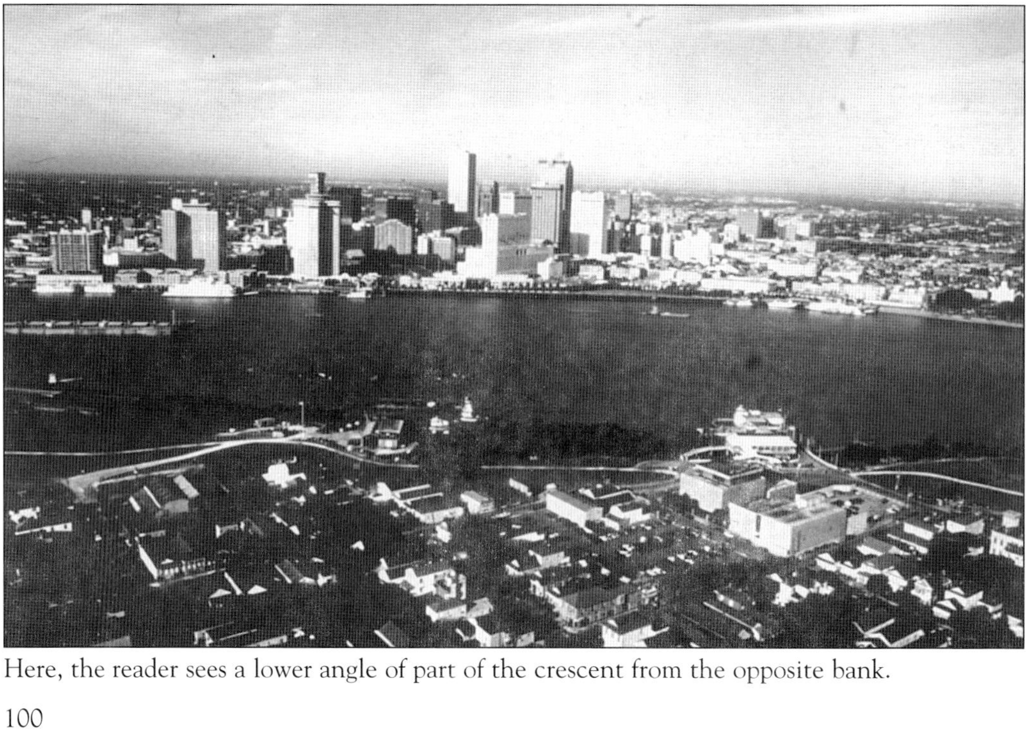

Here, the reader sees a lower angle of part of the crescent from the opposite bank.

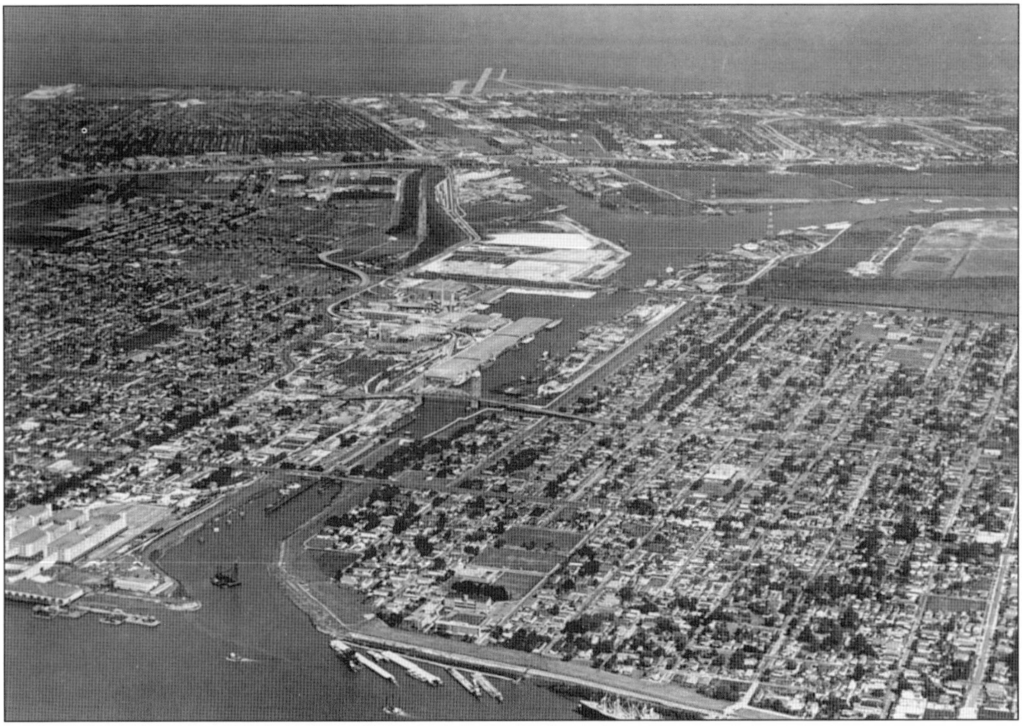

This photo shows the industrial land that links the Mississippi River with Lake Pontchartrain, north of New Orleans. Notice the ocean-going vessels in the foreground.

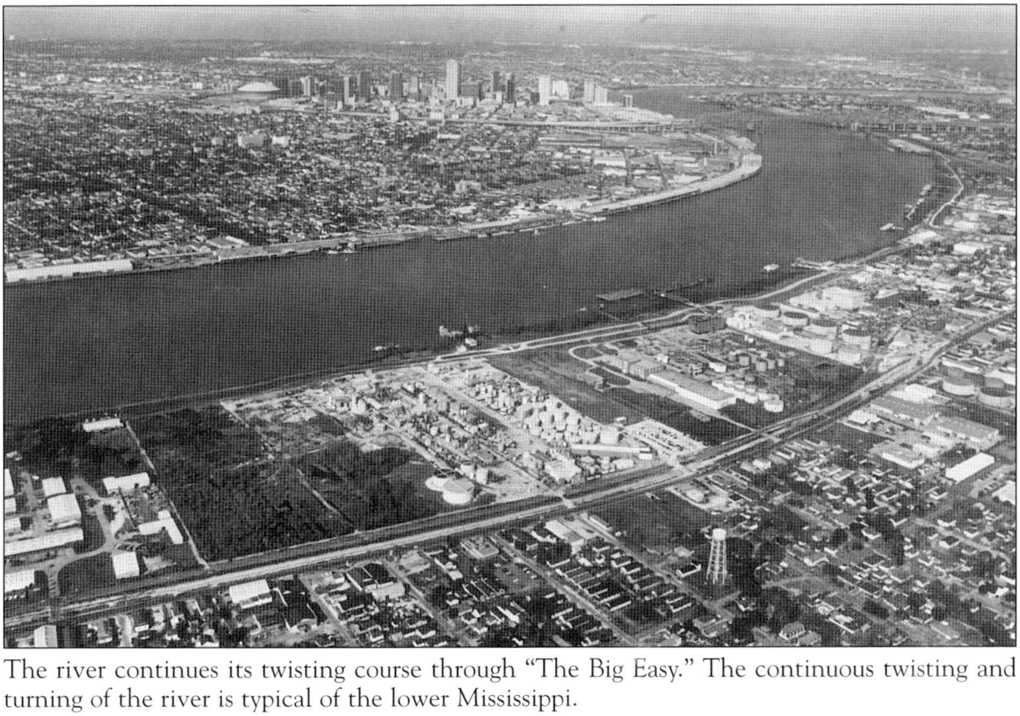

The river continues its twisting course through "The Big Easy." The continuous twisting and turning of the river is typical of the lower Mississippi.

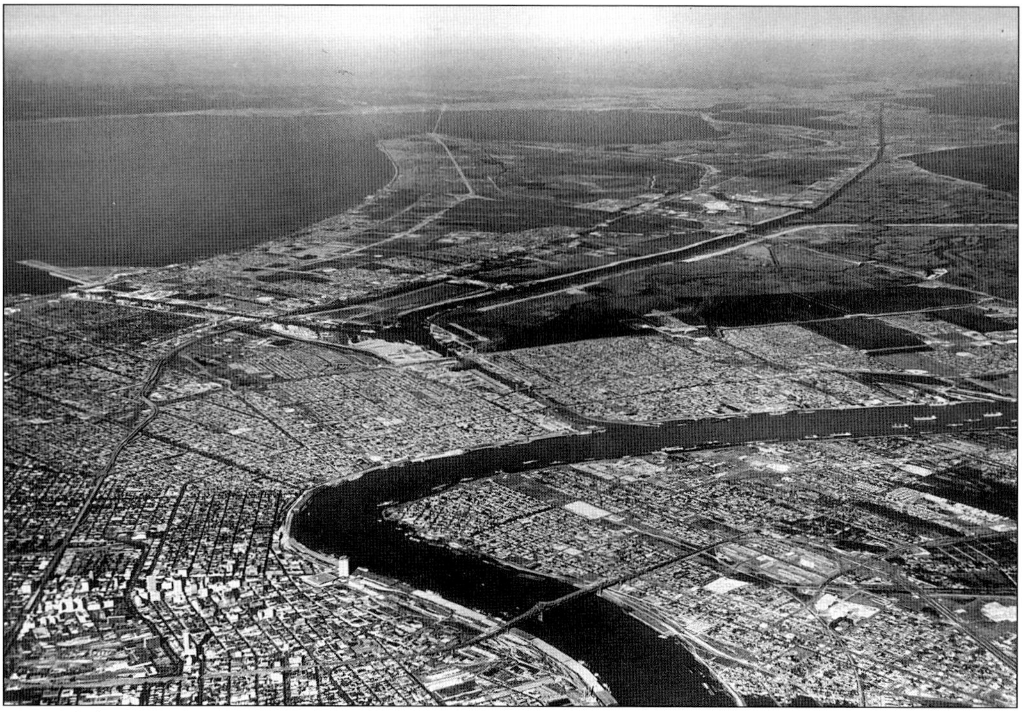

Part of the crescent passing through downtown New Orleans is pictured here. The Industrial Canal and the Inter-coastal veer to the east, upper center, and to the upper right, toward Lake Borge and the Mississippi Sound.

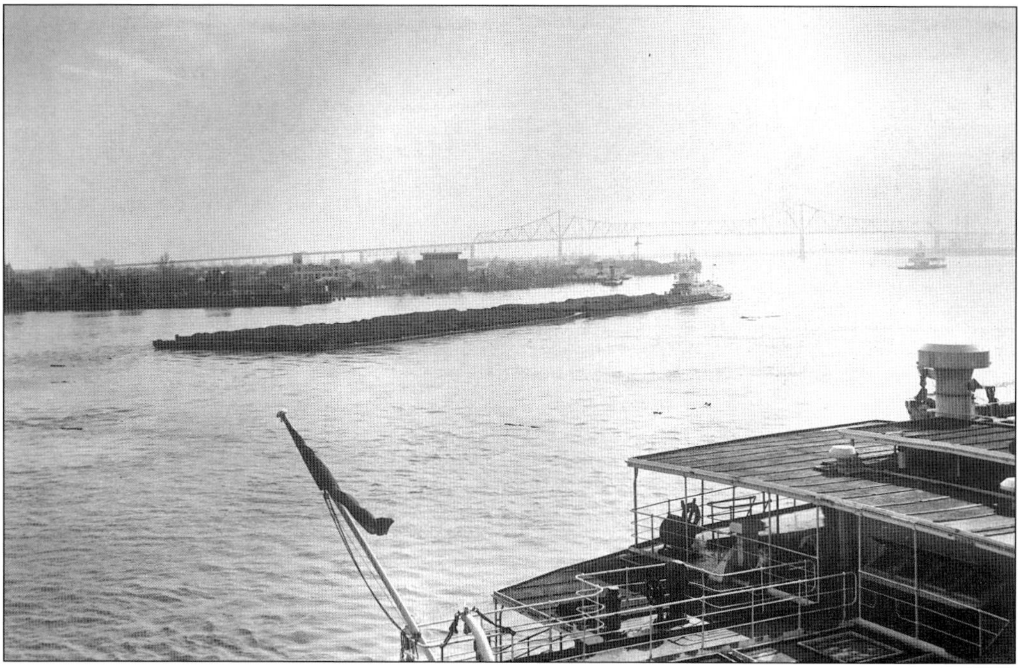

The curving river, especially at the crescent, makes for difficult maneuvering of large tows to the waterfront.

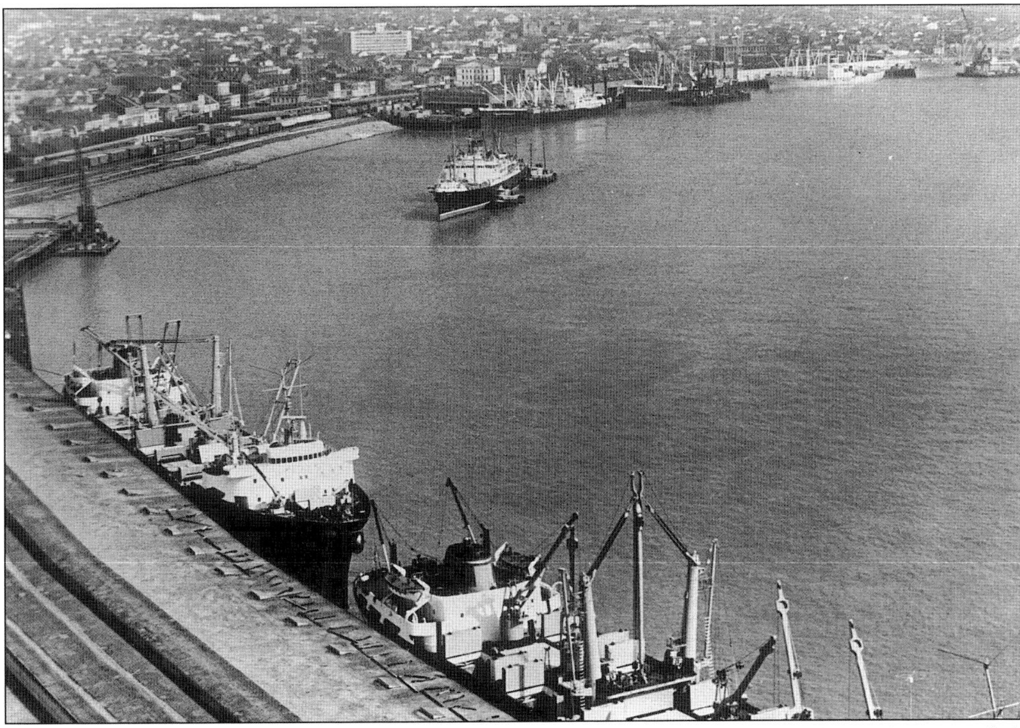

Ships of all sizes dock at the waterfront in New Orleans. Notice the rail yards, in the upper left, where freight cars will exchange commodities with the ocean vessels.

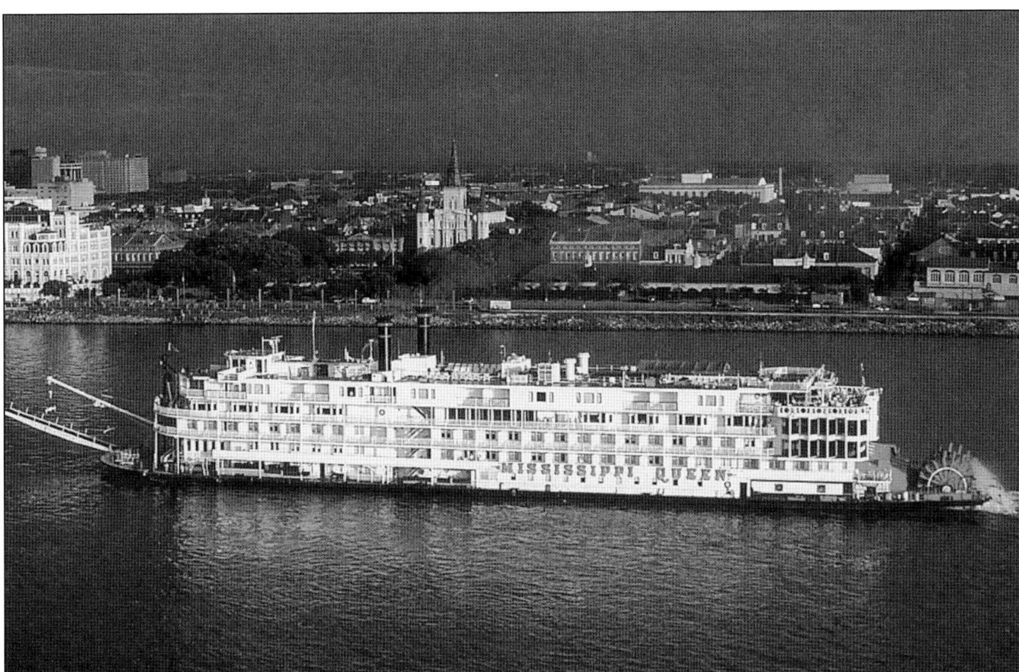

Here the reader views the *Mississippi Queen* steaming past the historic French Quarter in its colorful home port of New Orleans, Louisiana.

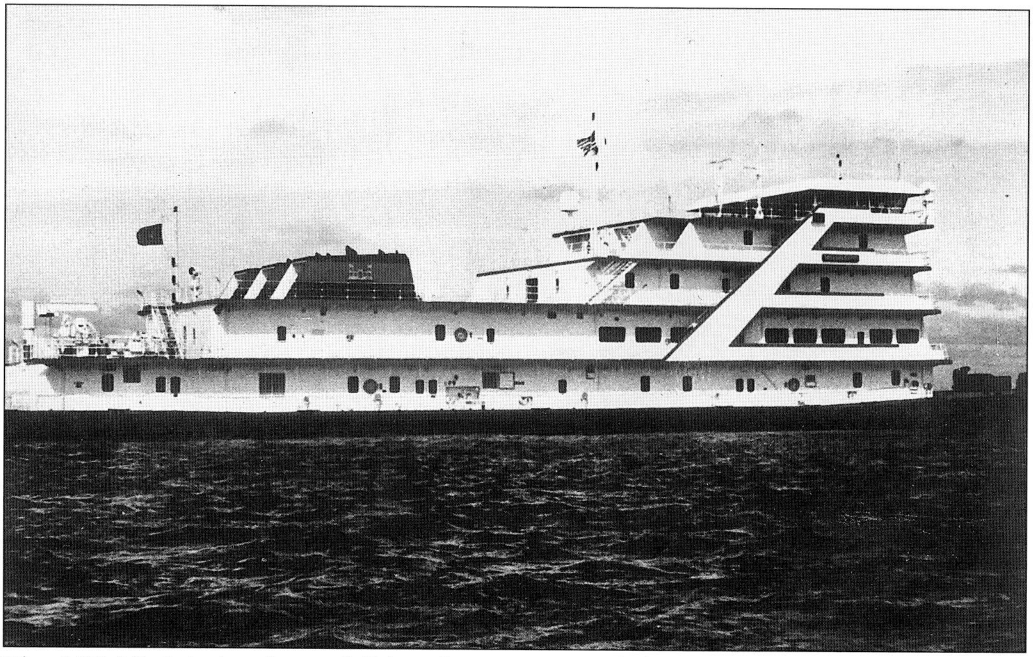

The MV *Mississippi* makes a full-length inspection of the Mississippi River, upriver and downriver, during low water each year.

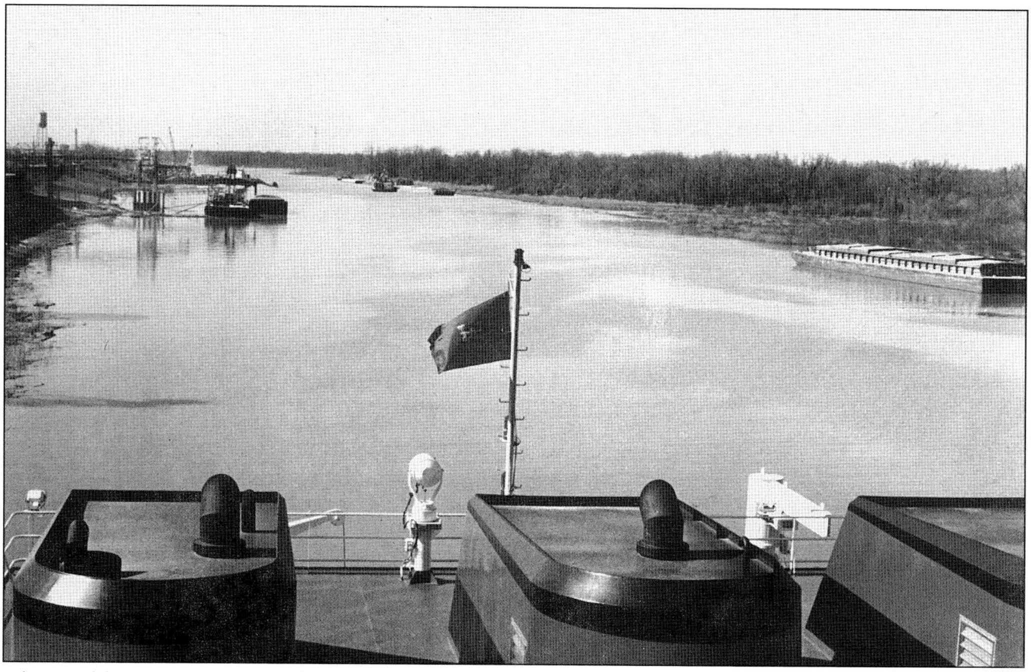

The visible portion of the *MV Mississippi*'s three diesel engines are seen here while she is docked in the Yazoo Canal at Vicksburg.

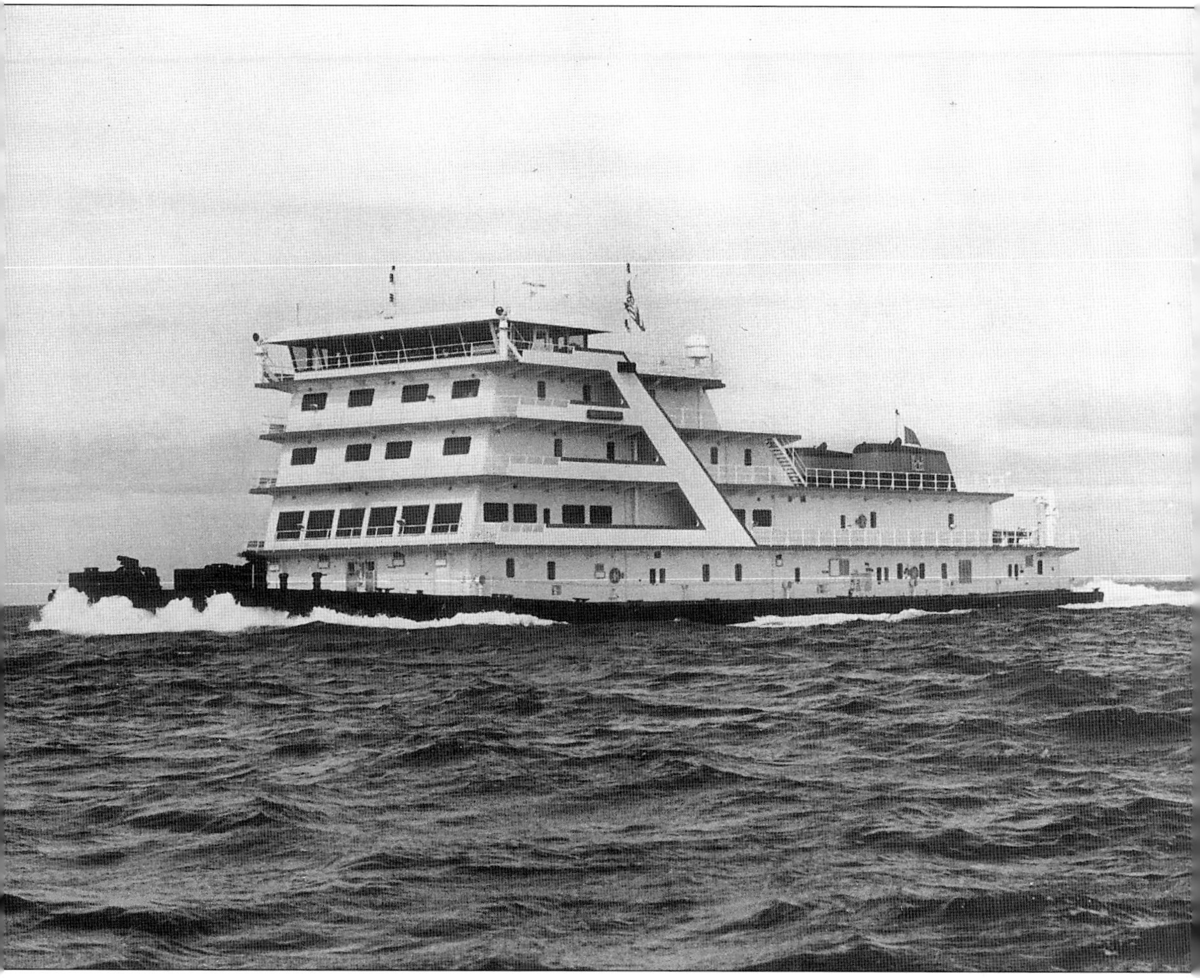

It is obvious to the reader that the MV *Mississippi* can handle large lakes or even the Gulf of Mexico, as shown in the picture above, as well as the Mississippi River. Notice the wake those three diesel engines are churning into a white froth.

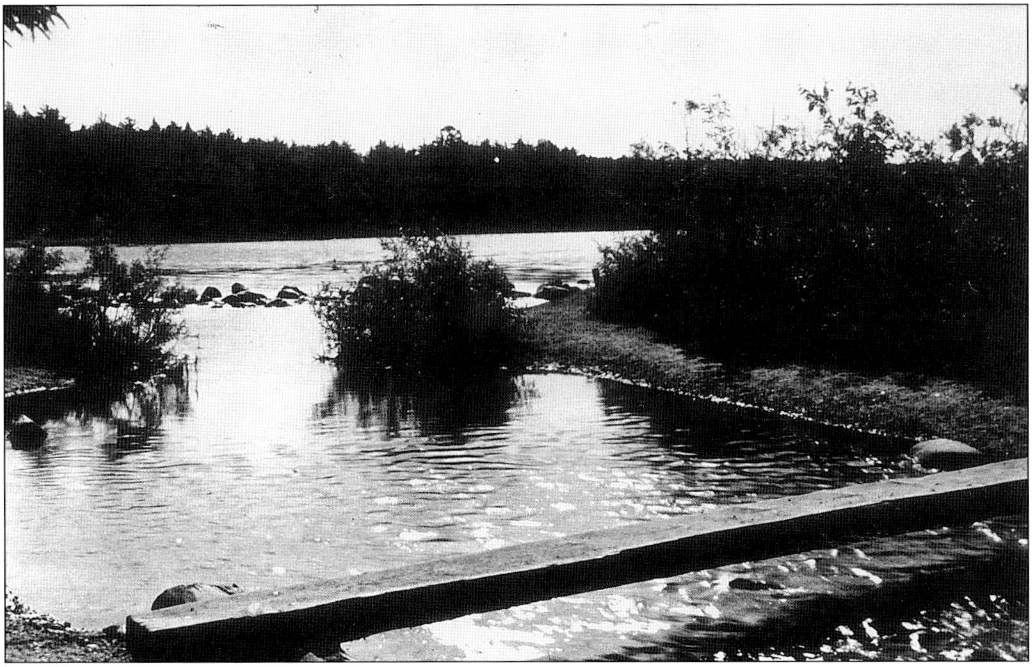

The accepted source of the Mississippi River is Lake Itasca in Minnesota. In recent years, some geologists have felt it could be located farther north. Until that is proven, the above photograph is that of the head waters of the Father of Waters.

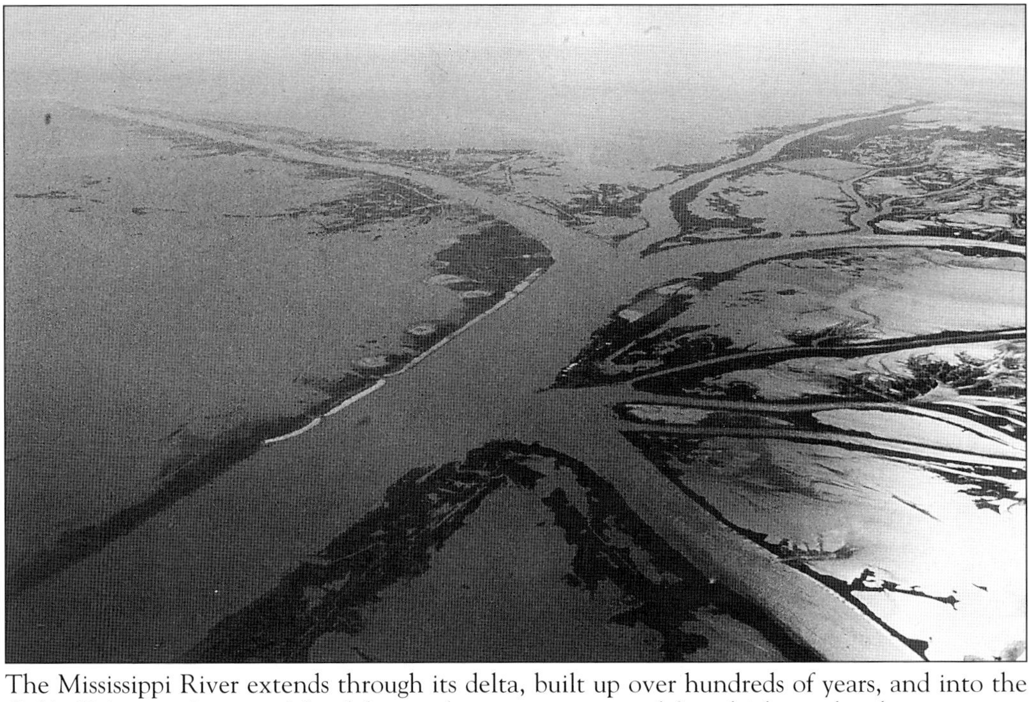

The Mississippi River extends through its delta, built up over hundreds of years, and into the Gulf of Mexico. A view of the delta can be most appreciated from high overhead.

The reader has traveled the 1,800-plus miles of the Mississippi that is navigable in pictures, and has seen the two waterfalls near the Twin Cities in Minnesota. Old steamboats and new diesel-powered towboats have been shown working on the river. In the picture below, a man relaxes watching a small craft pass by, while the sun sets over the Mississippi, Father of Waters.

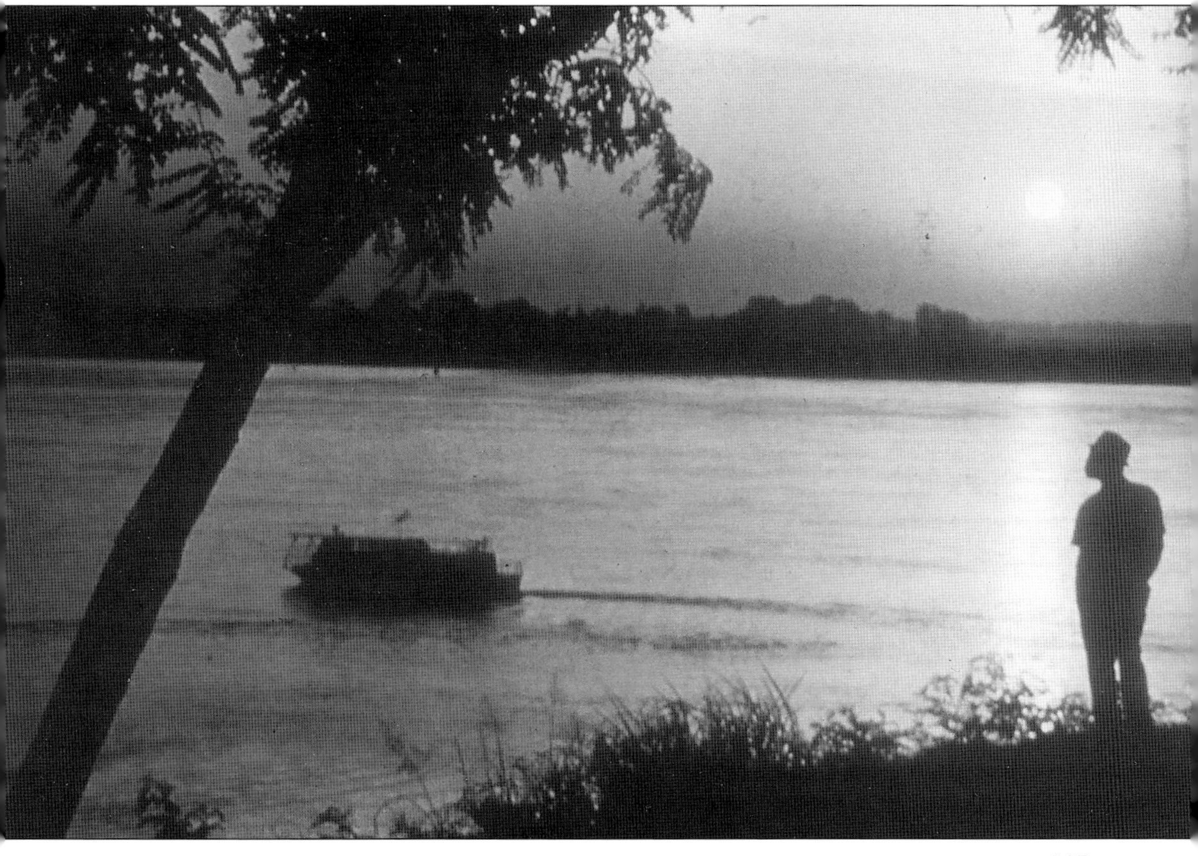

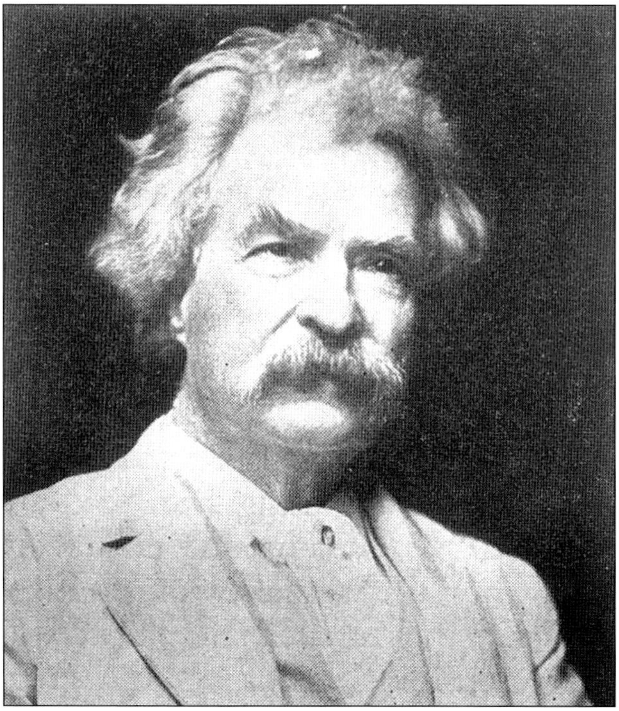

The final photographs in this chapter rightfully should be of Mark Twain (Samuel Langhorne Clemens), who single-handedly immortalized the Mississippi River with his stories of Tom Sawyer and Huckleberry Finn.

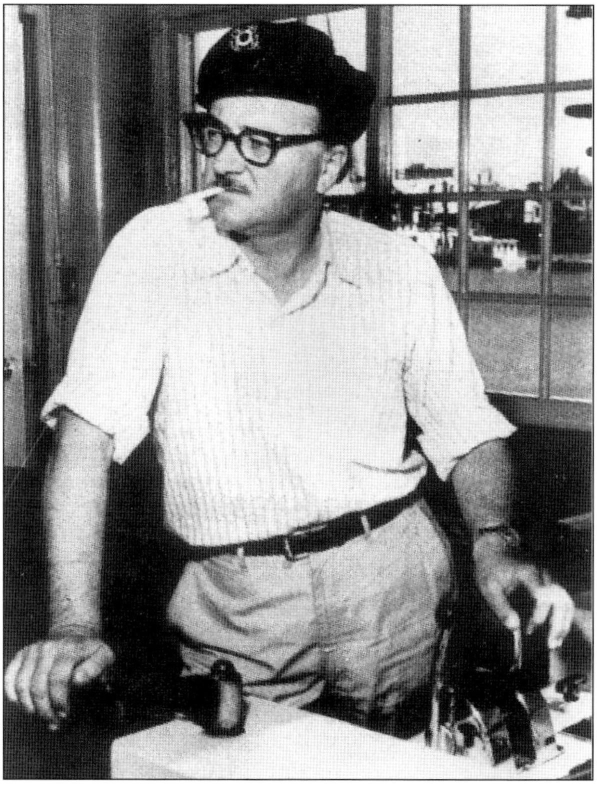

Richard Bissell, a native Dubuquer, who was also a pilot qualified for steamboats on the upper Mississippi, wrote several novels about life on the river. He was acclaimed as the new Mark Twain. Bissell had a successful career as a writer until 1977, when he passed away.

Five

FLOODS

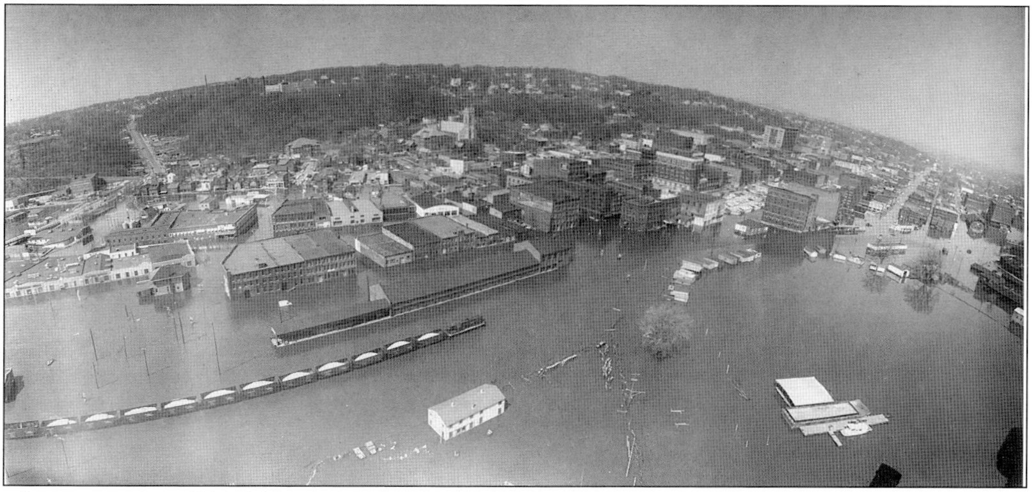

The curve of small buildings, at right center, is the western edge of the Ice Harbor. The bank of the Mississippi River is well out of the picture. The year is 1965, and the place is Dubuque, Iowa. The flood of that year convinced the Dubuque voters a flood wall was absolutely necessary.

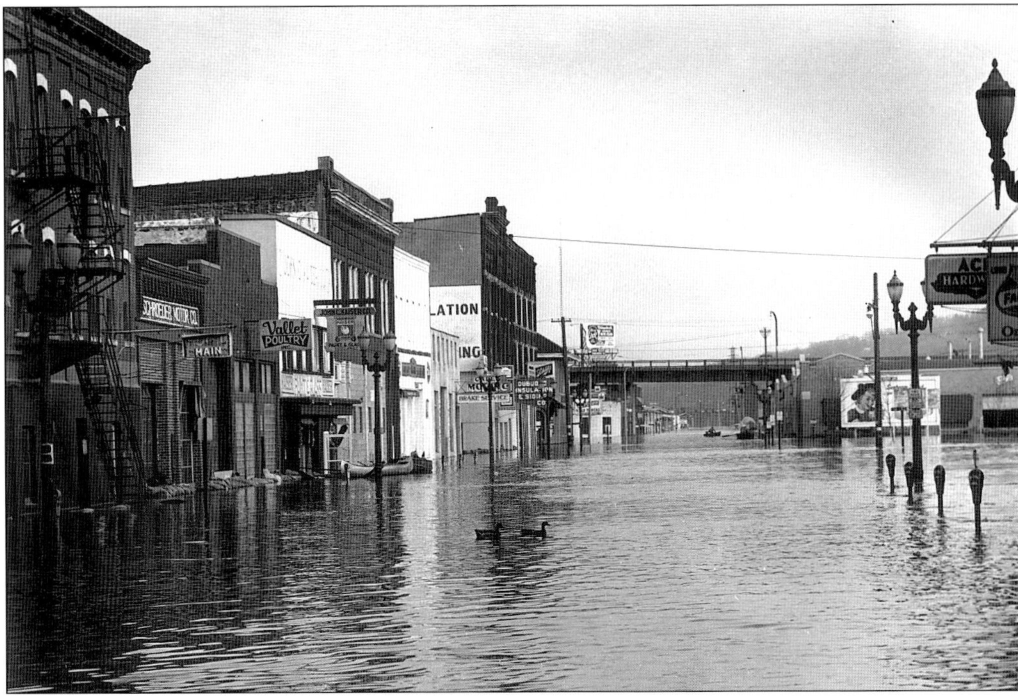

Venice, Italy, had nothing on Dubuque when it came to waterways instead of streets for the duration of the floods. The ducks thought it was fine.

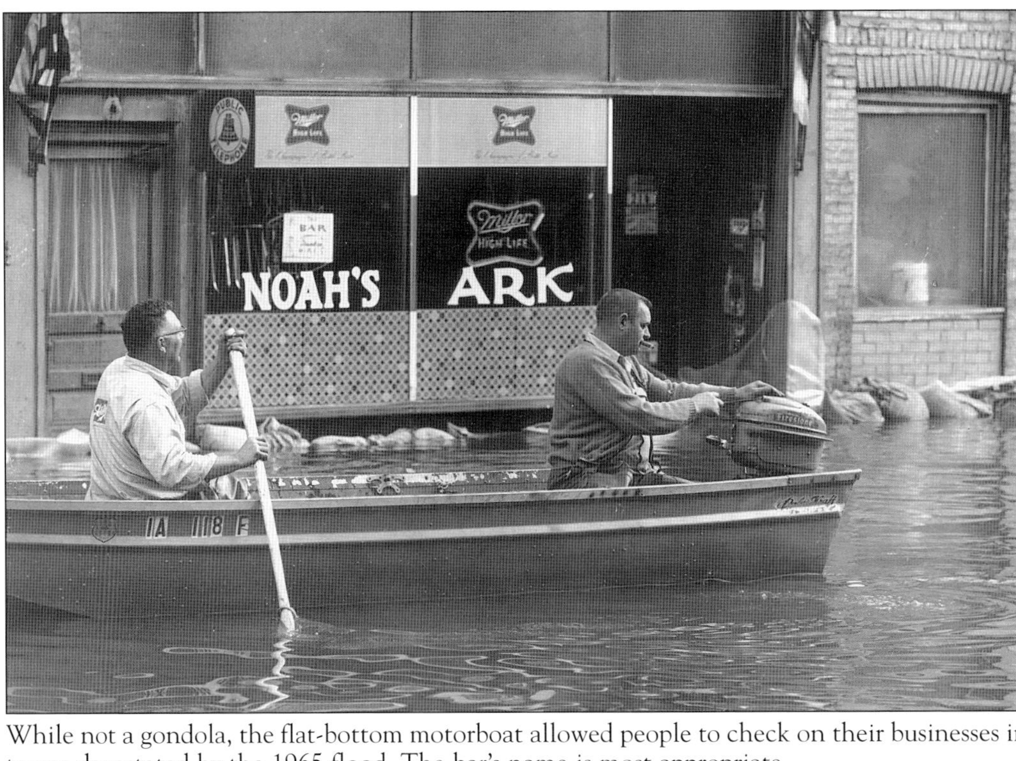

While not a gondola, the flat-bottom motorboat allowed people to check on their businesses in towns devastated by the 1965 flood. The bar's name is most appropriate.

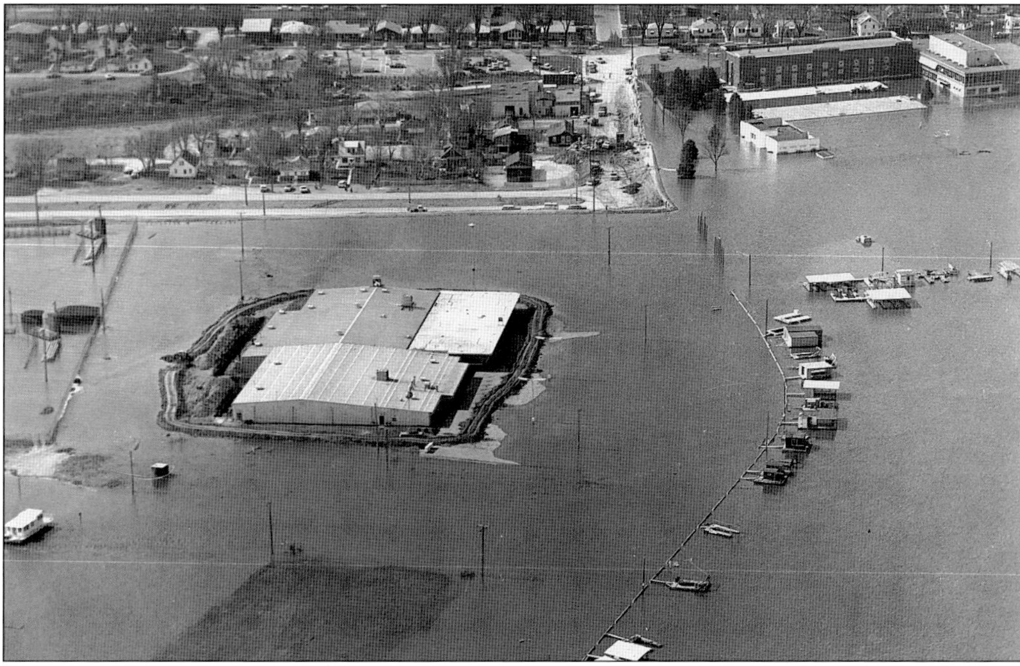

A few places of business managed to build their own flood walls of sandbags, such as the one above. The darker area is a rectangular lawn, and a city swimming pool is ironically under water in the upper right corner.

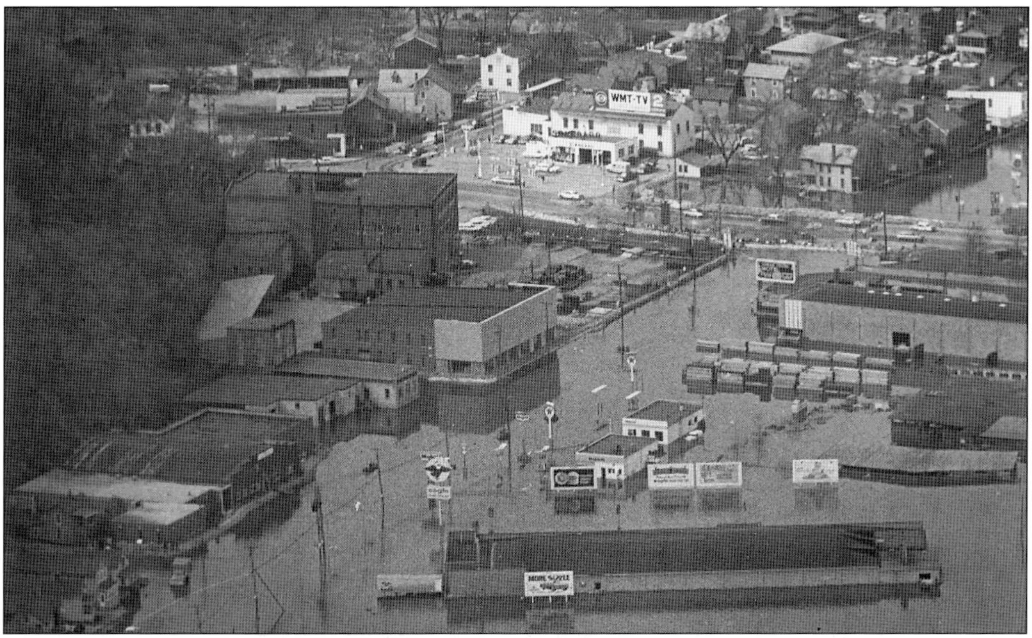

The city of Dubuque had volunteer college students, boy scouts, high school students, and anyone else who could lift a sandbag or fill them, attempting to keep Federal Highway 20 open. The parallel dikes of sandbags, above center on the right, were maintained around the clock and the people kept the only bridge open for almost two hundred miles up and down the mighty Mississippi.

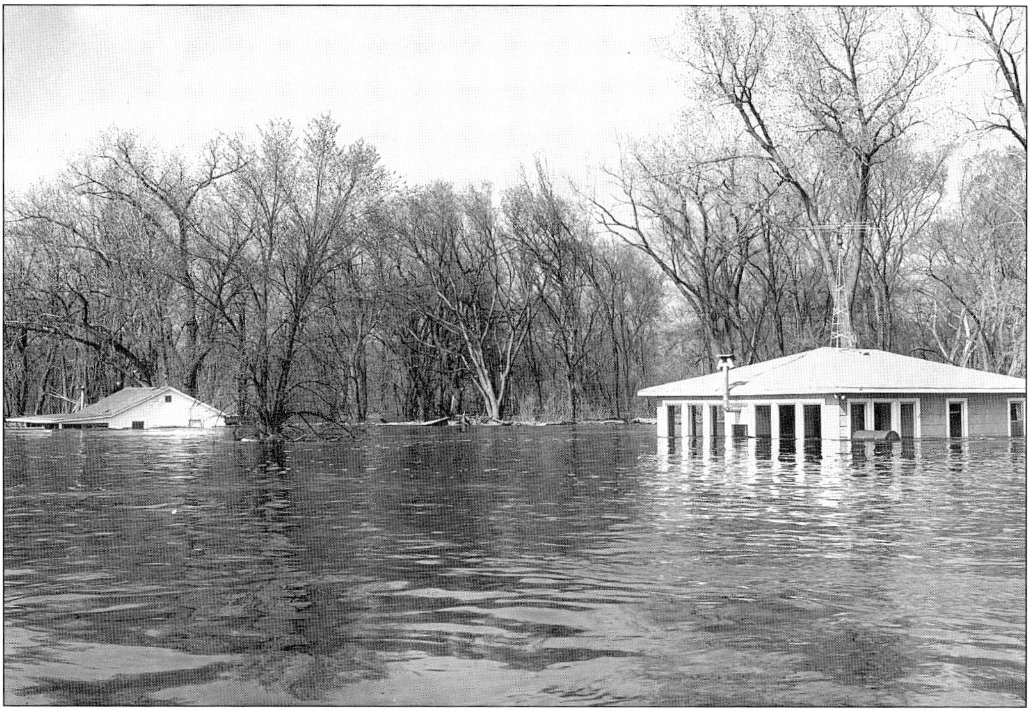

Wisconsin was equally inundated by the flood as evidenced by the two riverfront cottages in the photo.

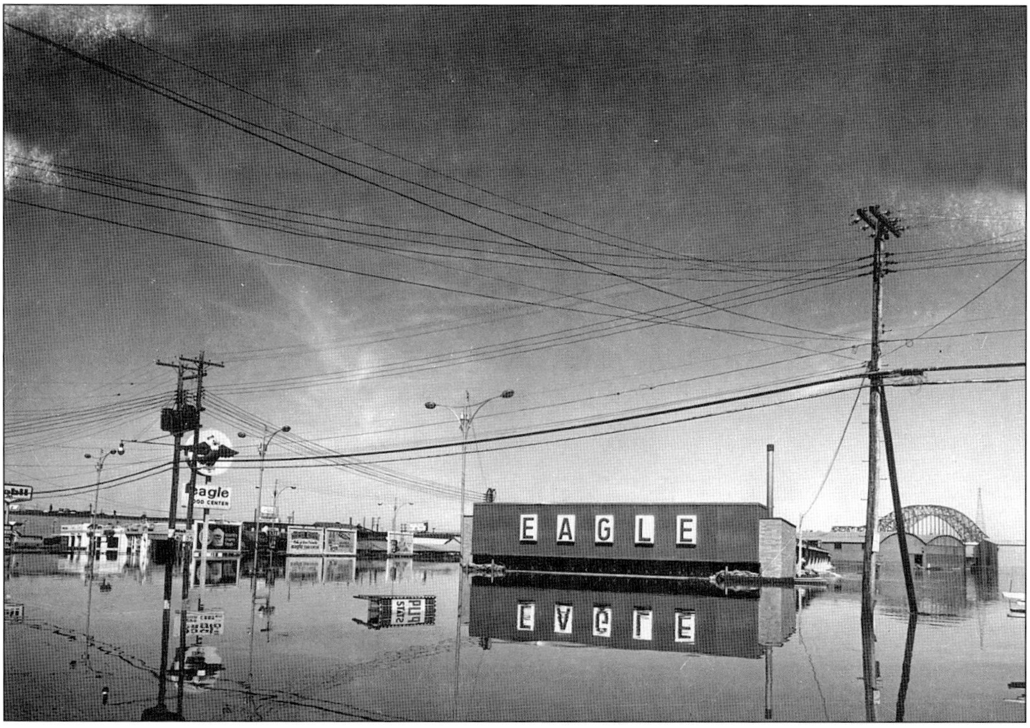

The Eagle Food Center in Dubuque's South End suffered much damage.

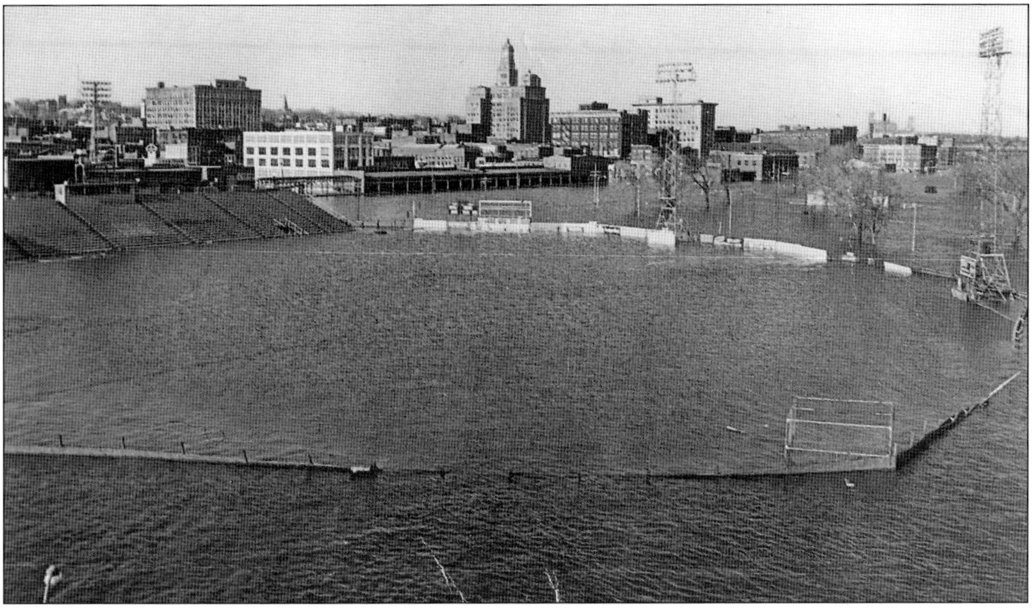

Davenport, Iowa was struck hard by the flood of '65. Pictured above is the city's athletic field. The bleachers are several blocks away from the banks of the Mississippi.

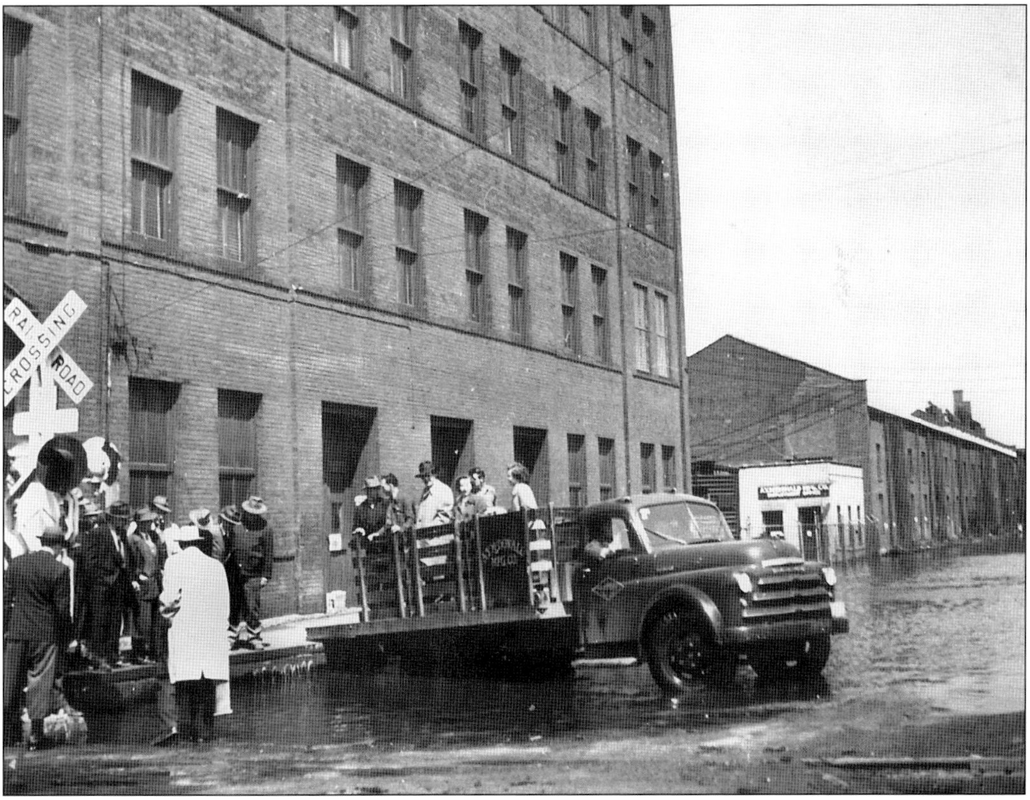

The A.Y. McDonald Company furnished transportation across flooded streets to its employees as long as it could.

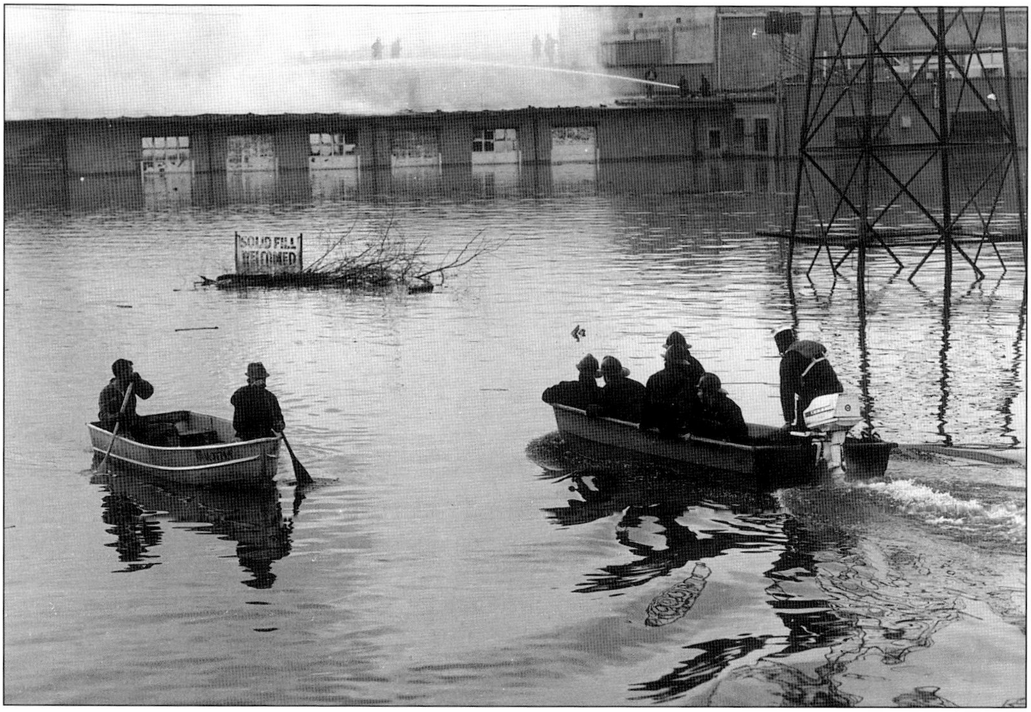

When the Fischer Cold Storage Facility broke into flames during the flood, Dubuque's finest, the fire fighters, responded by using motorboats. The sense of humor of Dubuque's citizens must be admired because of the sign: Solid Fill Welcomed.

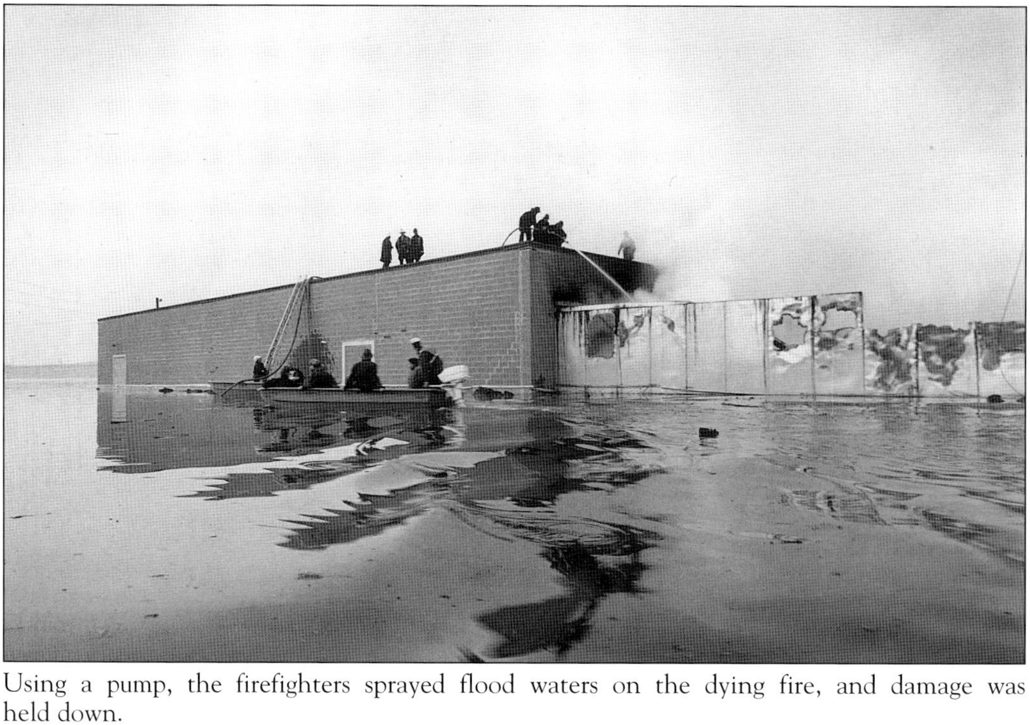

Using a pump, the firefighters sprayed flood waters on the dying fire, and damage was held down.

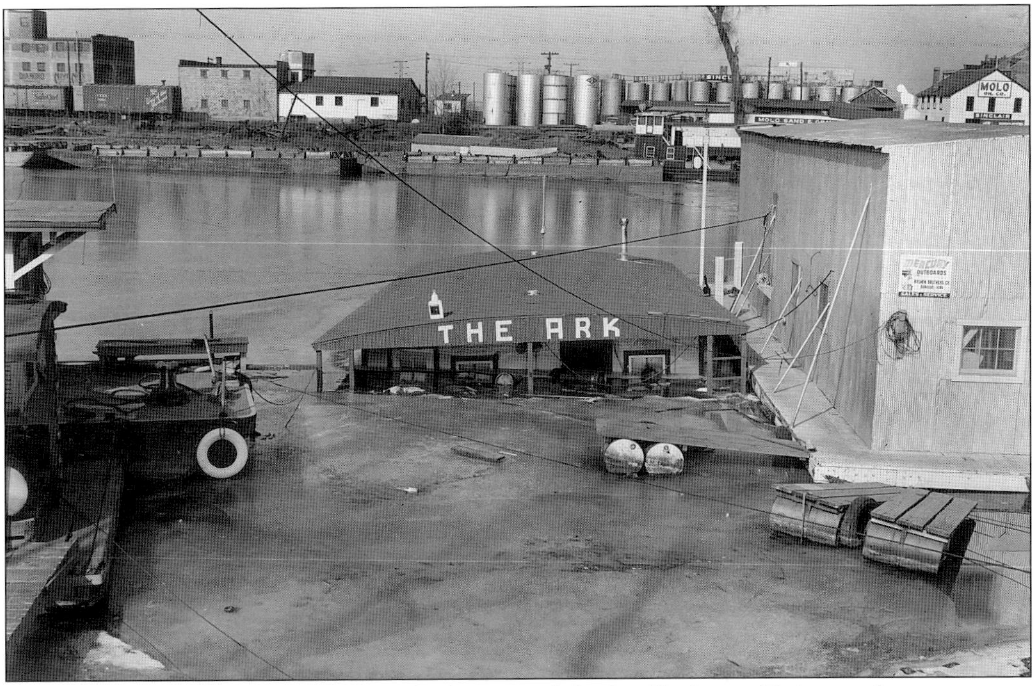

The Ark, a houseboat, sits askew on the bottom of the Ice Harbor in Dubuque, listing to port. *The Ark*, owned by Tom Roshek, was built from the hull of the *Aquila*, when Molo Sand and Gravel sold it.

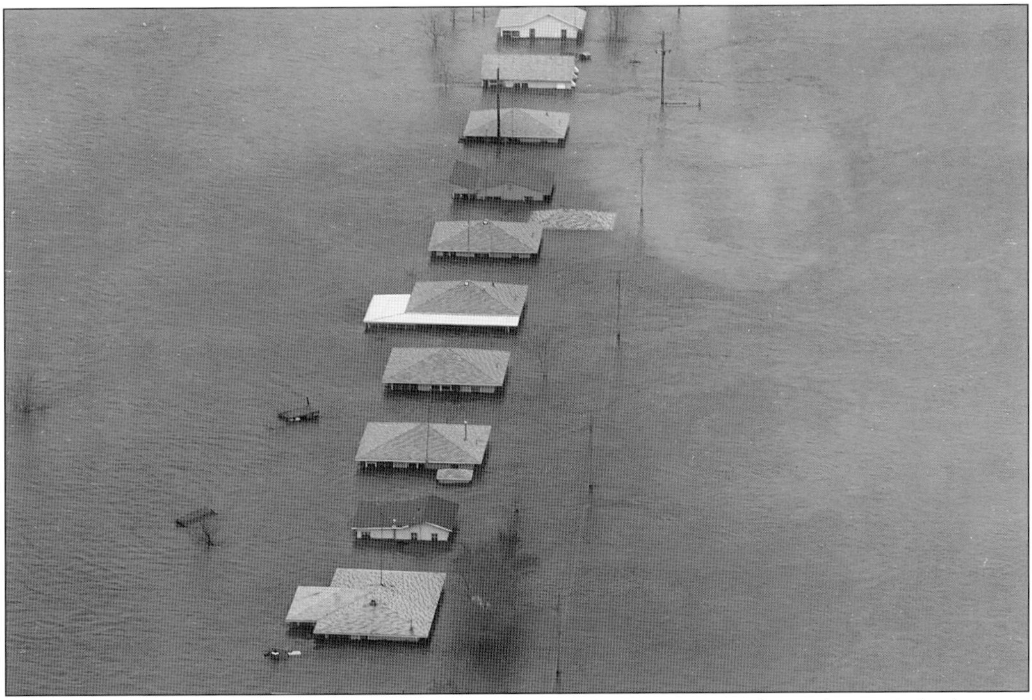

An unidentified housing development is pictured with the river to the right, and the houses' backyards to the left.

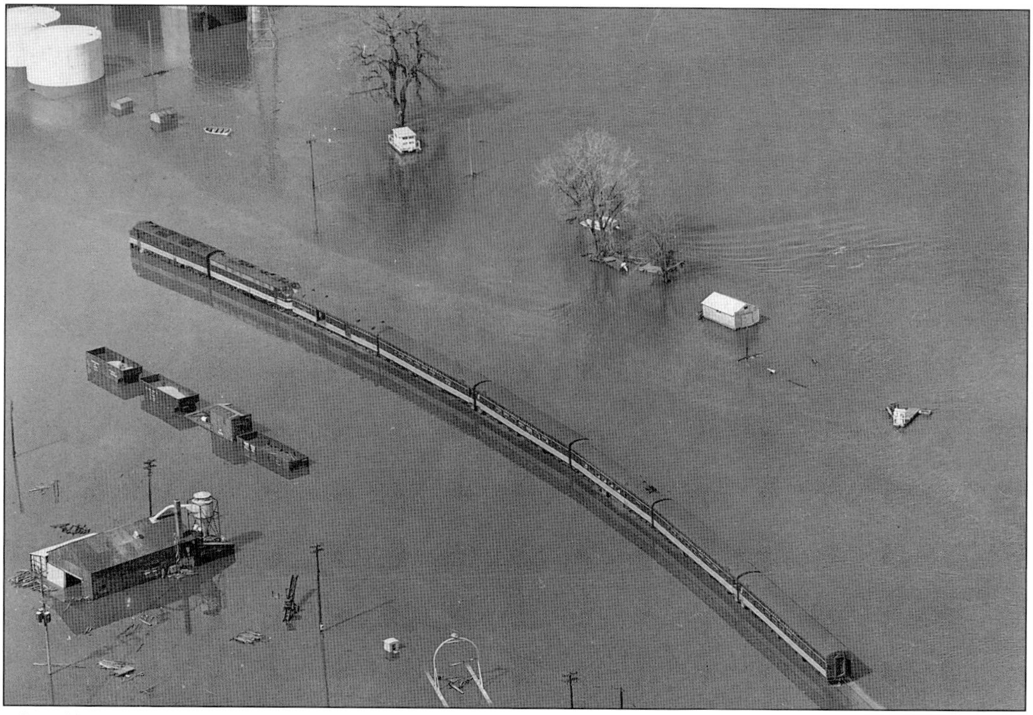

The Illinois Central's "Land of Corn" inches its way through two miles of water at two miles per hour, to keep the traction motors on the diesels' trucks dry.

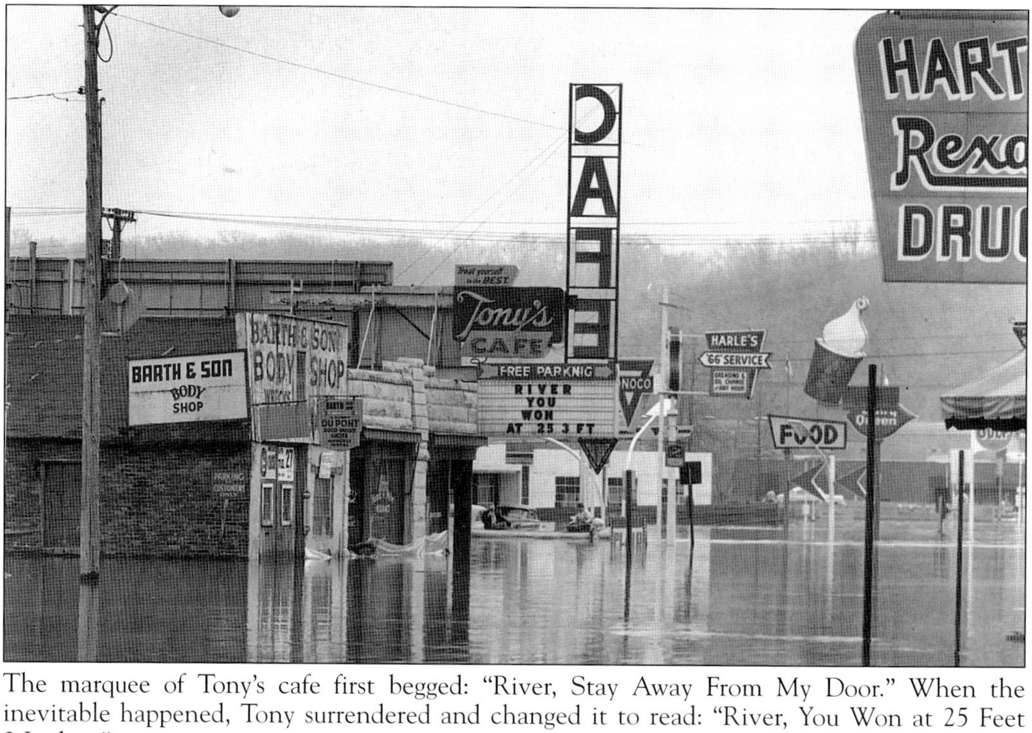

The marquee of Tony's cafe first begged: "River, Stay Away From My Door." When the inevitable happened, Tony surrendered and changed it to read: "River, You Won at 25 Feet 3 Inches."

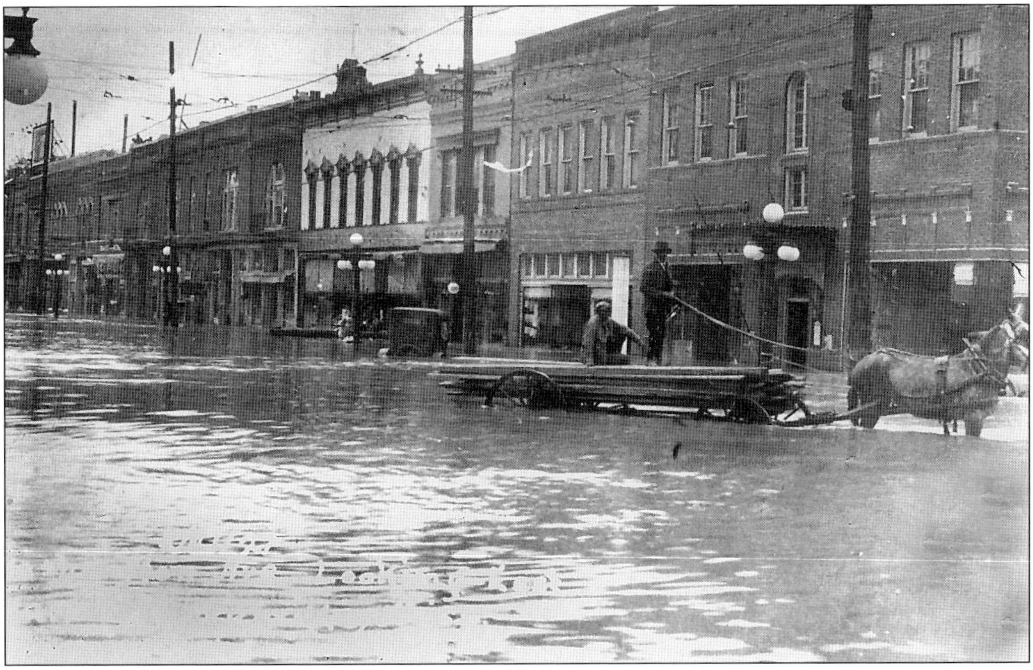

Floods can happen any year, but the flood of 1927 became a focal point, especially for the people of Greenville, Mississippi. People referred to events as " 'fore '27," and "ahfta '27." Above is downtown Greenville.

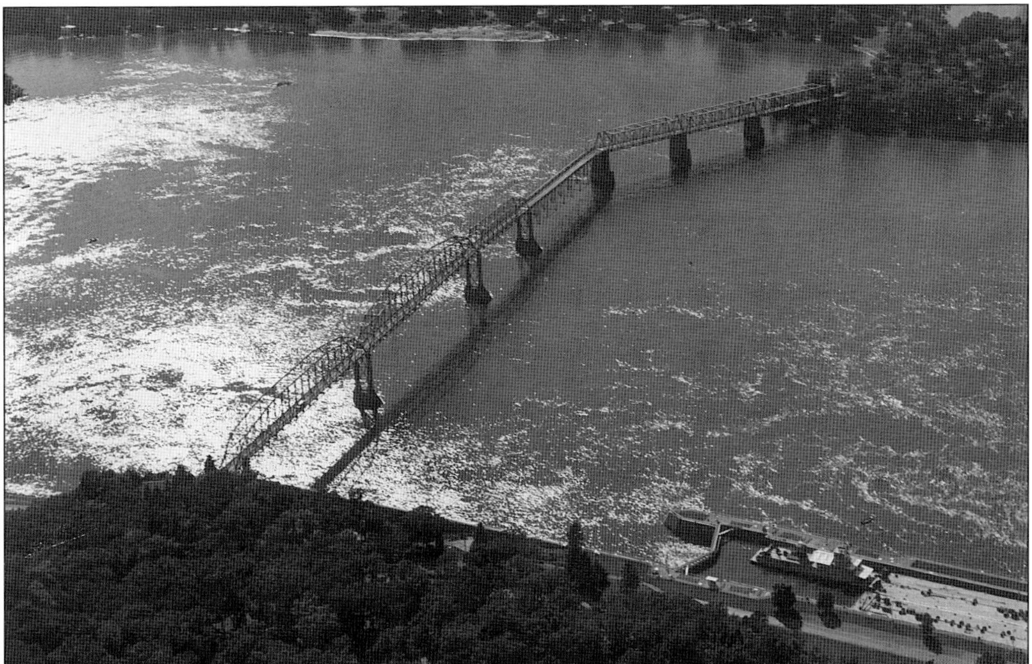

The reader will notice the Mississippi is out of its banks in Wisconsin, closing the bridge since the road is under water. However, the river is not rampaging enough to close Lock and Dam number 11 at the current time.

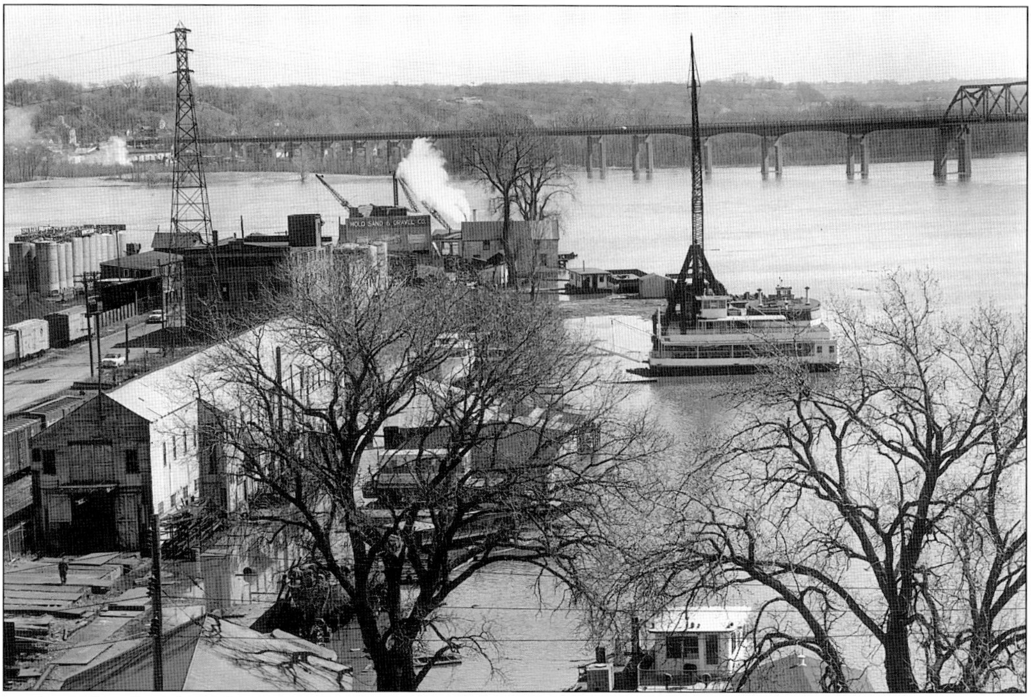

Before the flood wall was constructed to protect the city of Dubuque, the above scene was a common occurrence. To the right of the small boat, in the upper right center, the Ice Harbor flows out of its banks in 1961's flood.

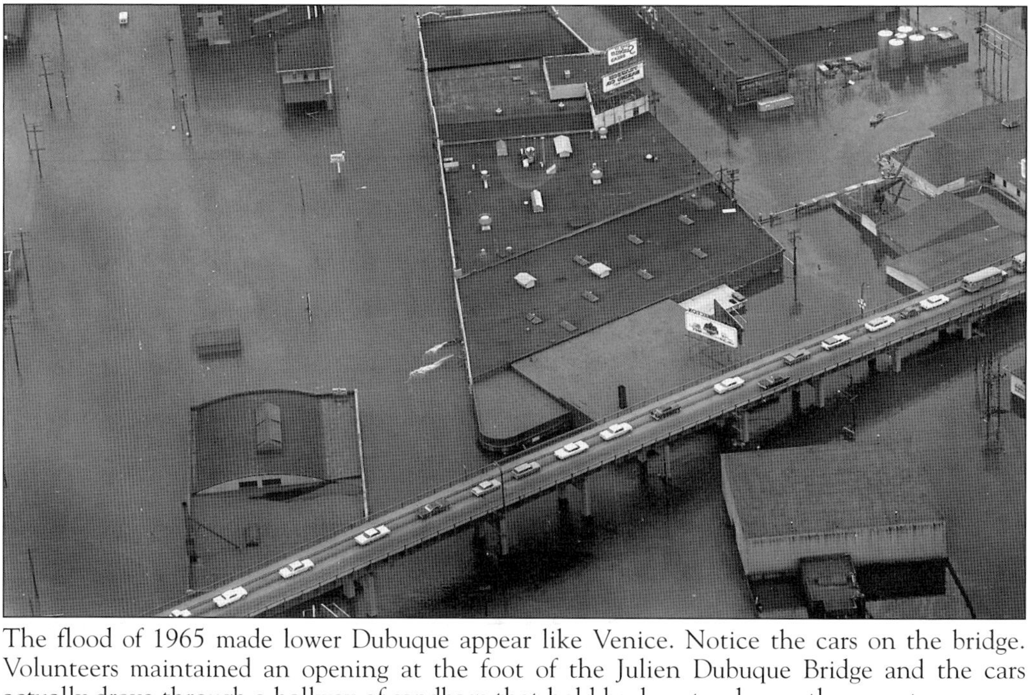

The flood of 1965 made lower Dubuque appear like Venice. Notice the cars on the bridge. Volunteers maintained an opening at the foot of the Julien Dubuque Bridge and the cars actually drove through a hallway of sandbags that held back water deeper than most cars were high. But Dubuque won the battle.

Six

Recreation on the Mississippi

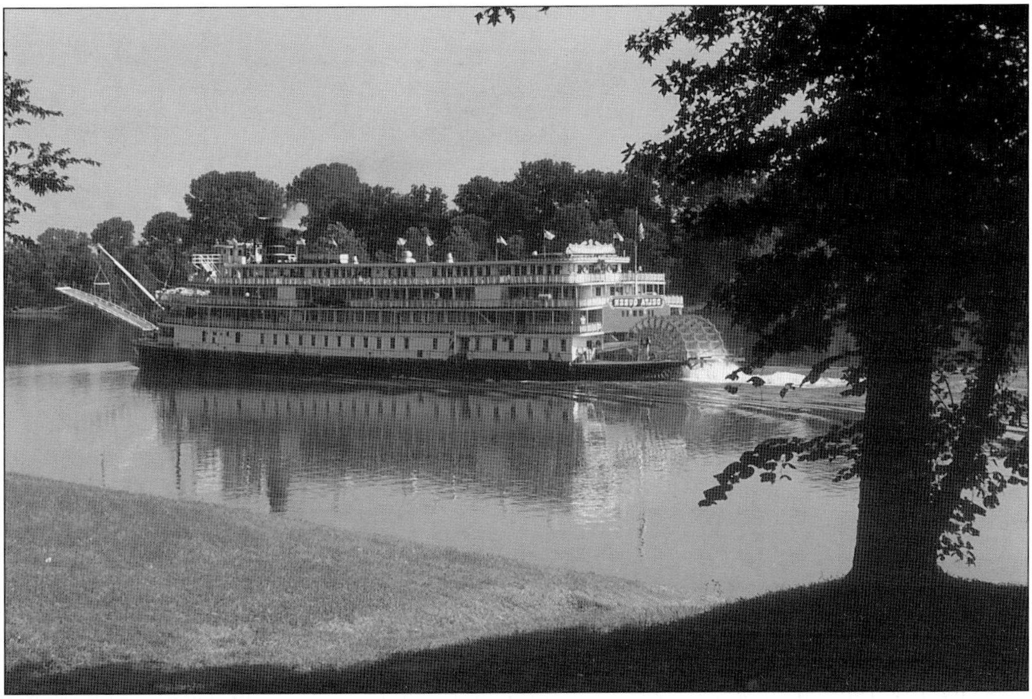

The *Delta Queen* is probably the crossover that links fun on the river in the past to today's recreation. A river trip of several days is a step back in time, especially on this one, the Queen Mother of passenger boats plying the Mississippi River and her tributaries in the 21st century.

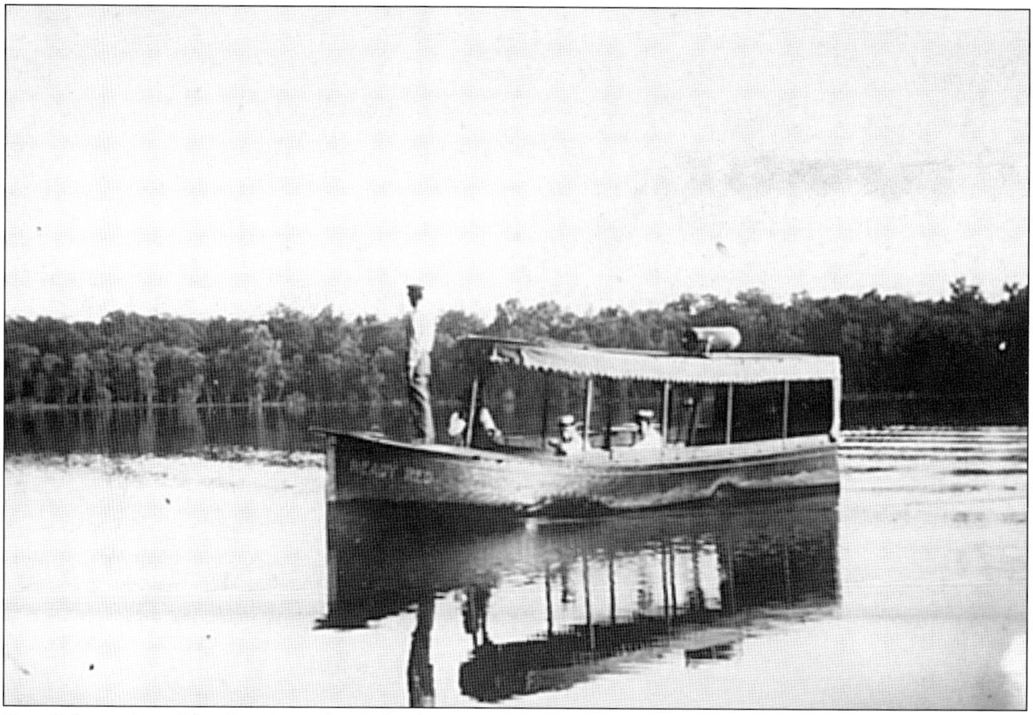

Small launches, like *Ready Red*, worked out of virtually every river town of consequence, taking passengers to picnic spots on islands or hiring out for a sojourn up or down the river.

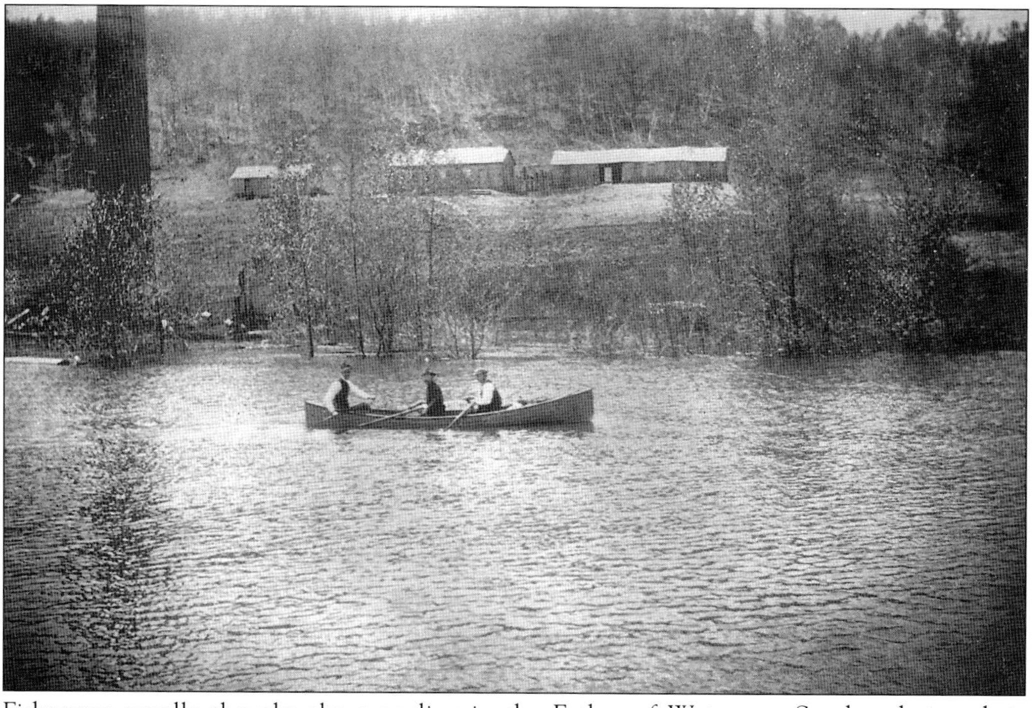

Fishermen usually thought about angling in the Father of Waters on Sunday, during their six-day work week. If they had a boat, so much the better.

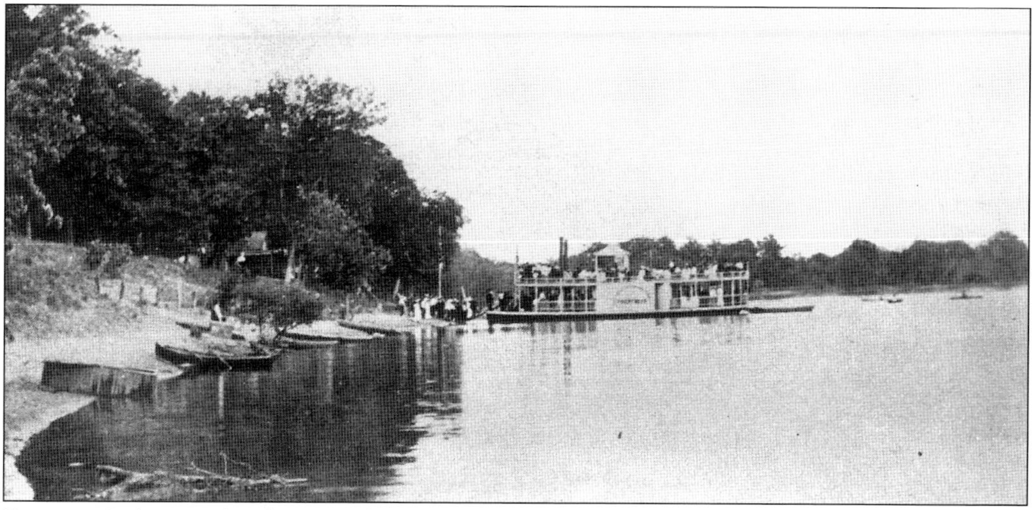

Frentress Lake, south of East Dubuque, Illinois, has always been an attraction to boaters for picnic spots, canoeing, and fishing. Now, in the 21st century, year-round homes line the shore, but the canoeing, fishing, and water skiing still flourish in the inland waterway of the Mississippi.

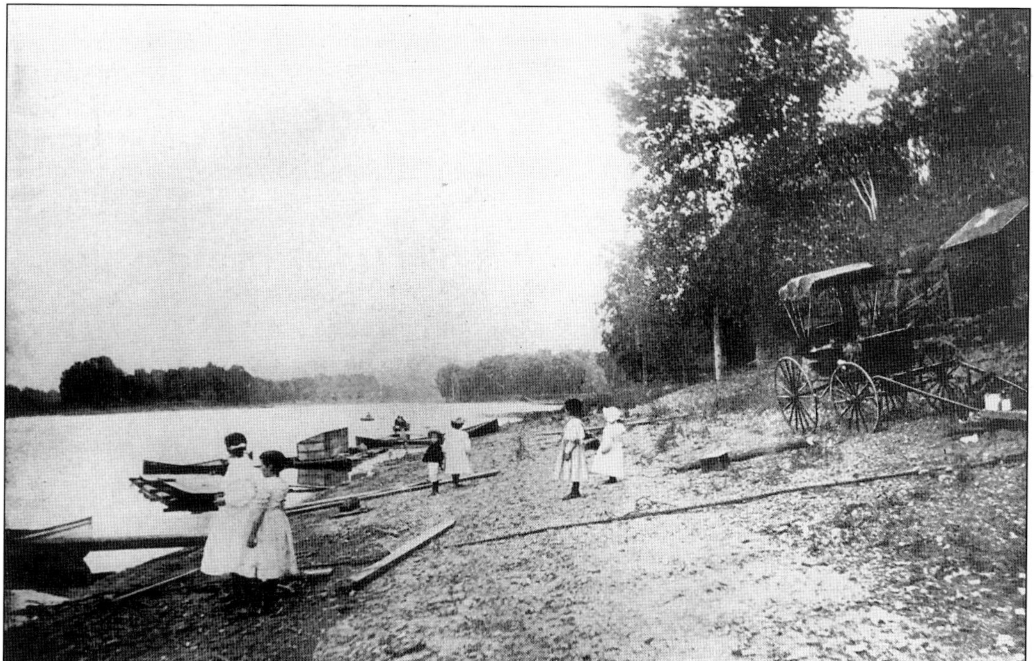

Shawondassee, on the Iowa bank, was an exclusive club at one time. Roads had been cut through the hills to reach the isolated beach, but the Milwaukee line stopped its passenger trains north and southbound to drop off or pick up members.

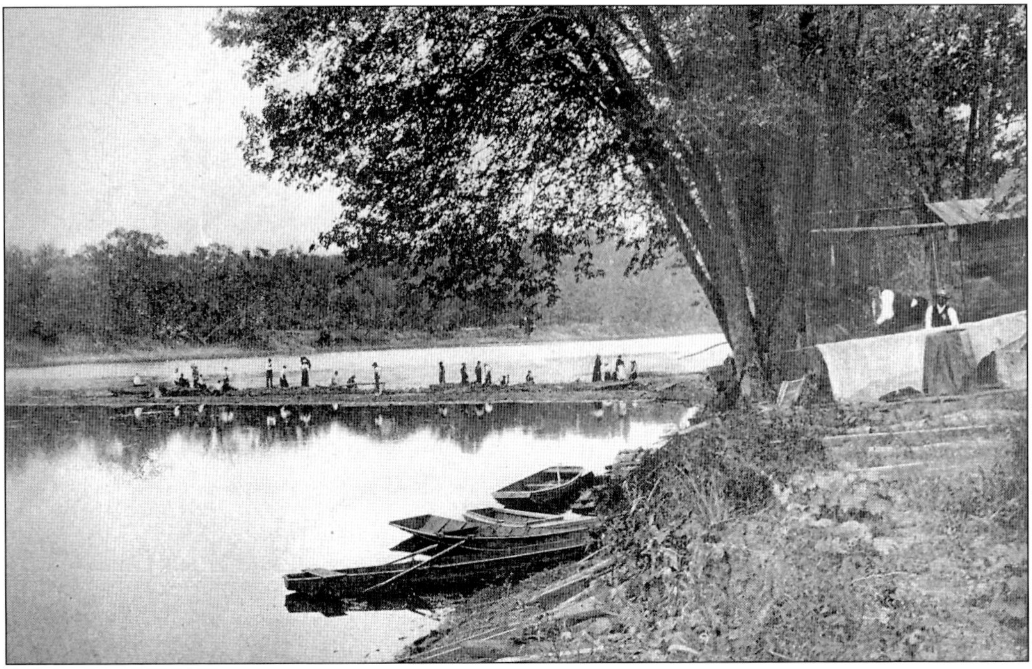

Sets of three wing dams, used to channel the water toward the middle of the river, were used by club members at Shawondassee to fish from, since fish liked to "rest" in the shade provided by the dams. Who needed a boat when a person could walk out that far to fish?

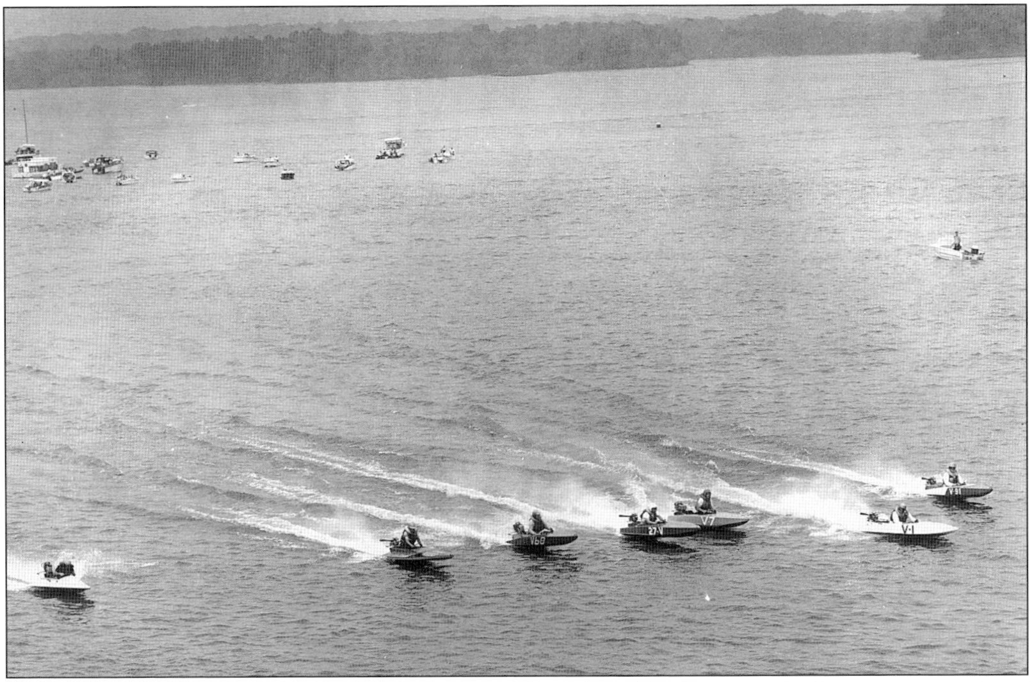

Since the internal combustion engine was perfected, it has been applied to every mode of transportation. Speedboat races have thrived on the Mississippi for years at many of the towns and cities holding festivals or celebrations.

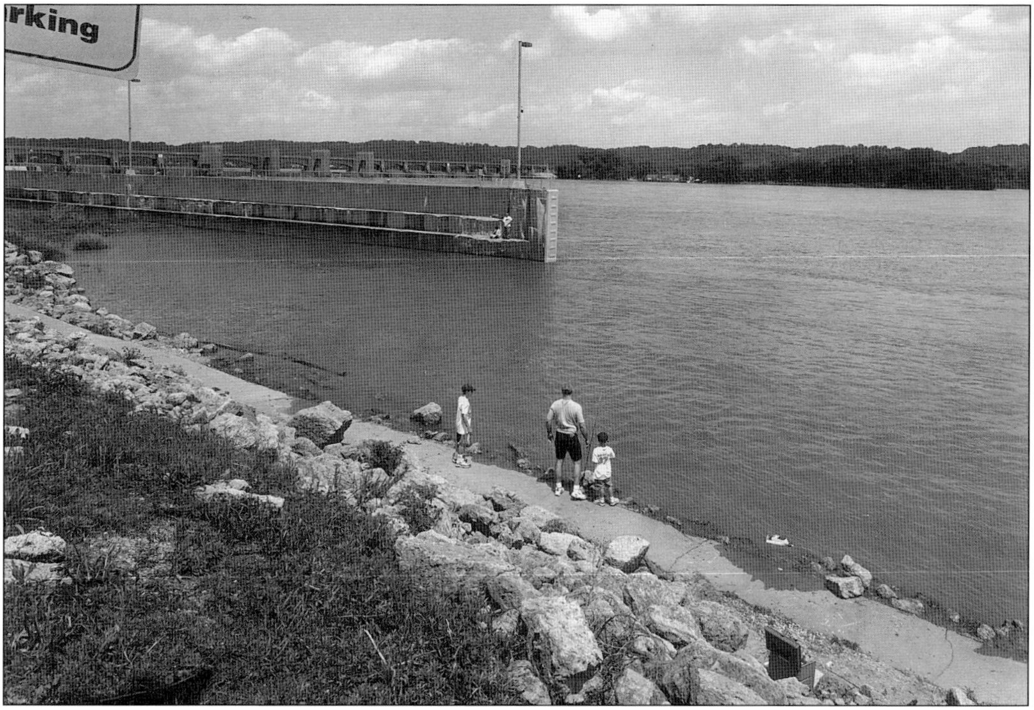

While the wing dams have been removed for the most part, fishing devotees have found the locks and dams on the Father of Waters great places to cast a line. Here, a father and his two boys have cast out, trying their luck.

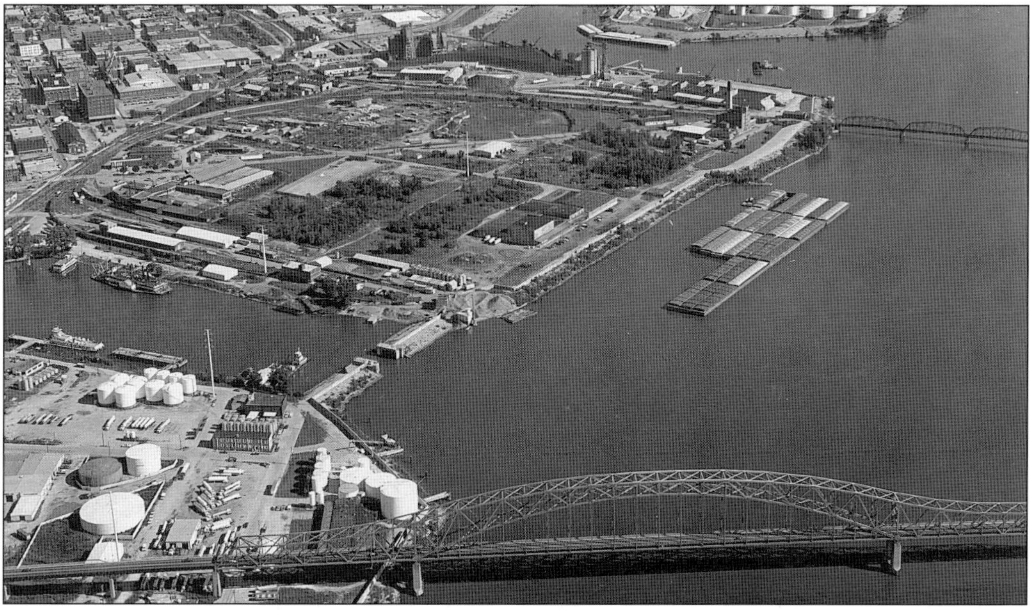

Dubuque, Iowa plans to enter the 21st century with a riverside hotel and shopping mall, and other shops to go along with the gambling boat and Welcome Center. The boat and Welcome Center did not yet exist when this photograph was taken in 1981. The flood gate is open to the Ice Harbor, and the new facilities will be right upriver from the flood gate.

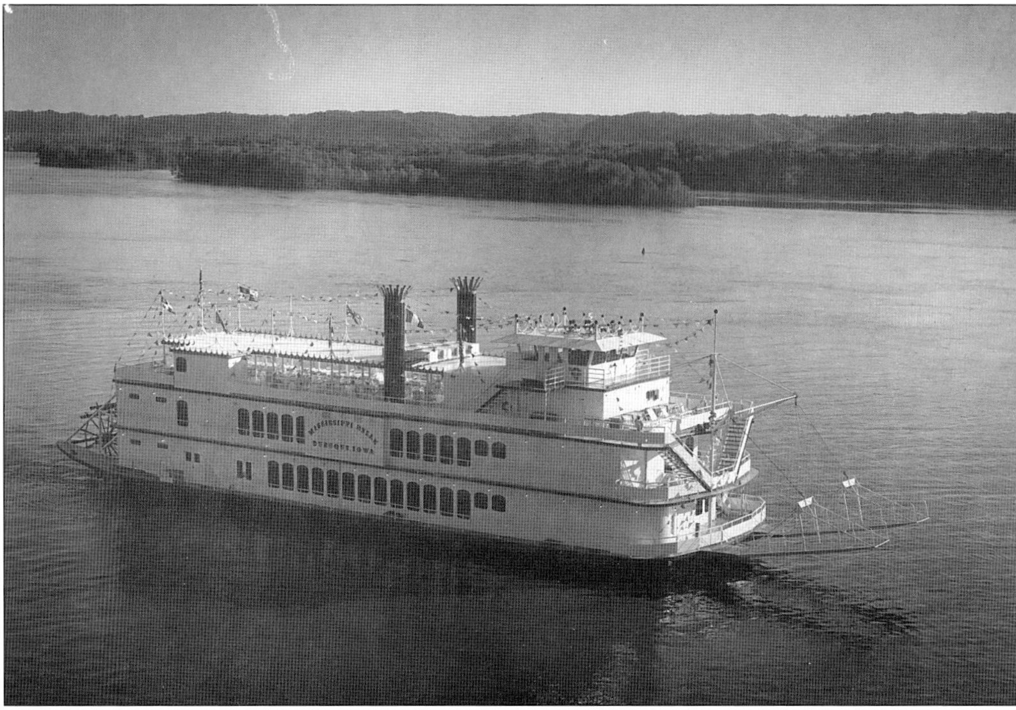

The stern-wheeler *Mississippi Belle*, out of Dubuque, Iowa, shows her starboard side to the photographer while she heads downriver, possibly on her shakedown cruise.

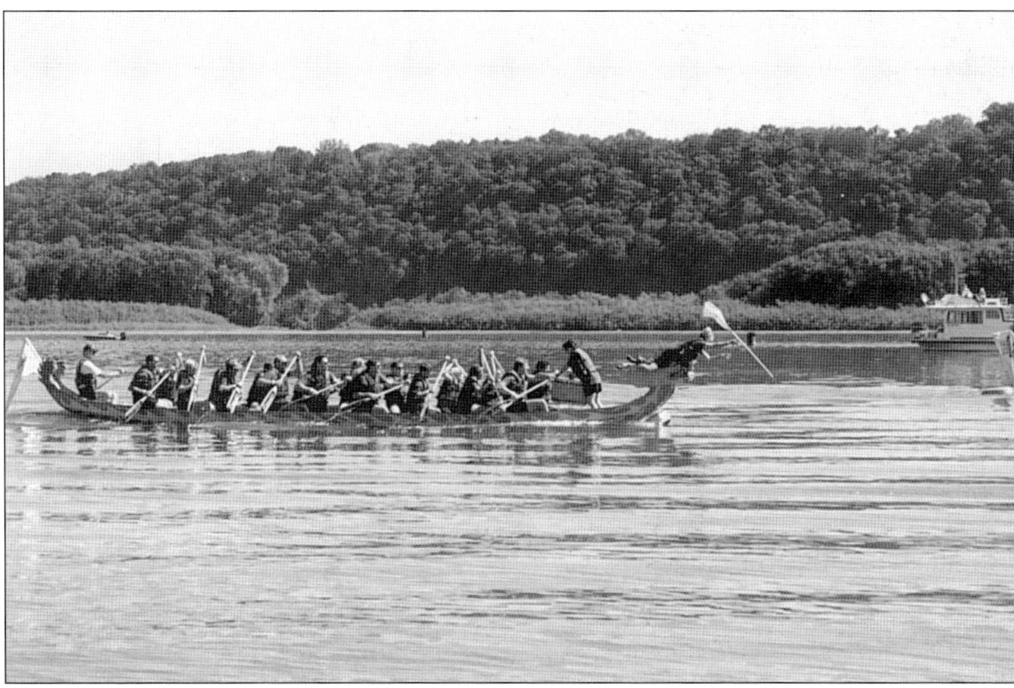

Every three years, the International Dragon Boat Championship Races are held in Dubuque, Iowa.

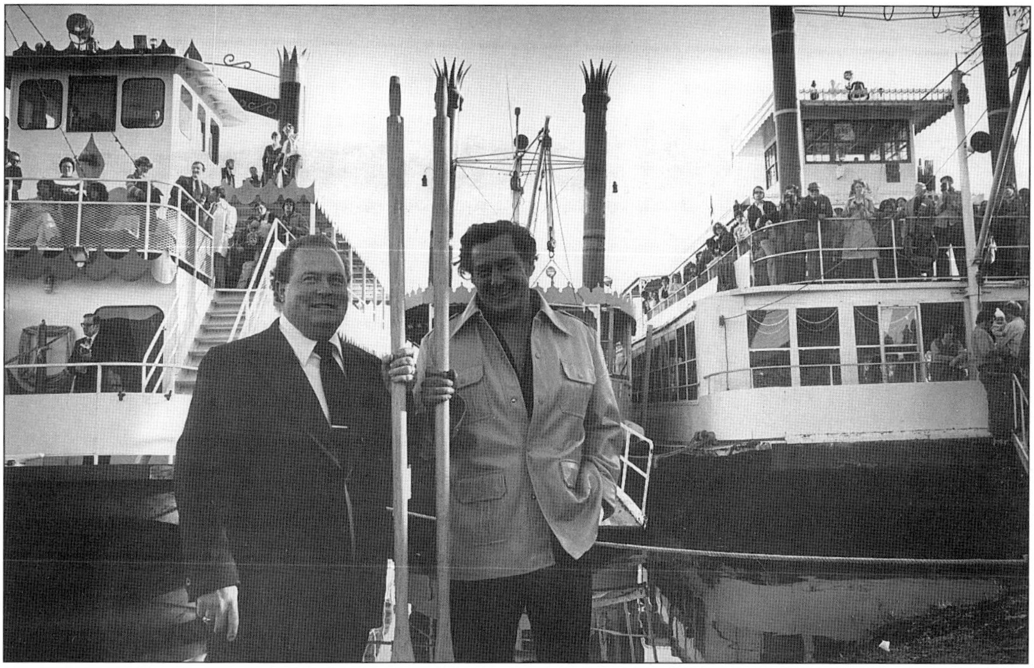

Rivalries were always a mainstay on the river. From the time before the *Robert E. Lee* and the *Natchez*, to today's 21st century boats, big boats have raced. Shown here, Bob Kehl, owner of several large boats, including at one time the three thousand-passenger *Dubuque Casino Belle*, prepares to race former Dubuquer Art Bull, owner of the *Julie N*.

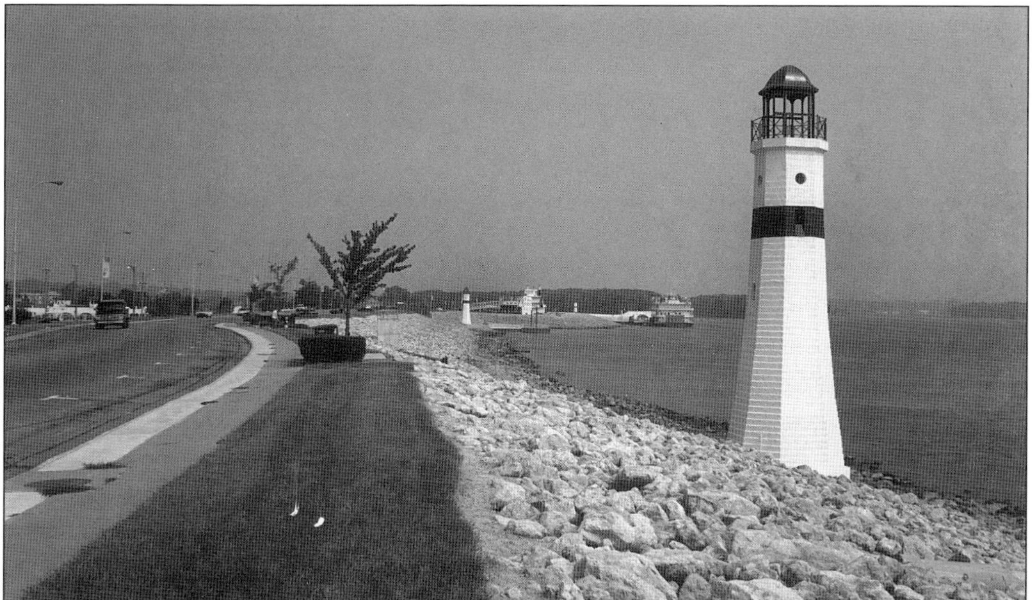

Clinton, Iowa's Riverfront Park offers a walkway, ample parking, and grass to lounge on near the river. Clinton's gambling boat, the *Mississippi Belle II*, can be seen on the left near the lighthouse.

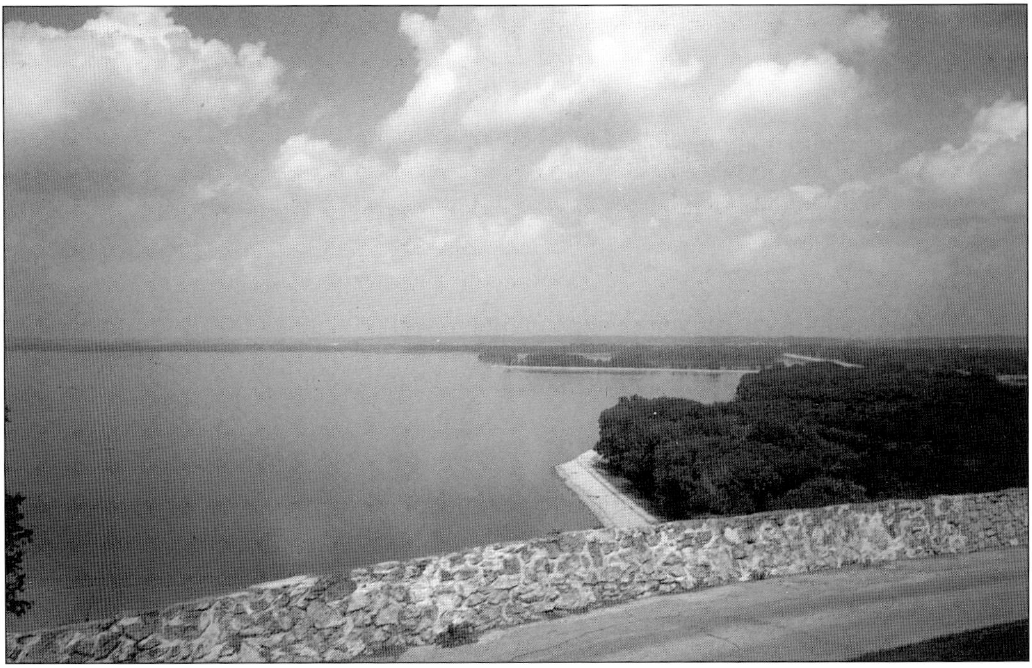

This is the view from the overlook at Clinton's Eagle Point Park. A series of lakes has been created behind the 29 locks and dams on the Mississippi, as indicated by the broad expanse of water below the park.

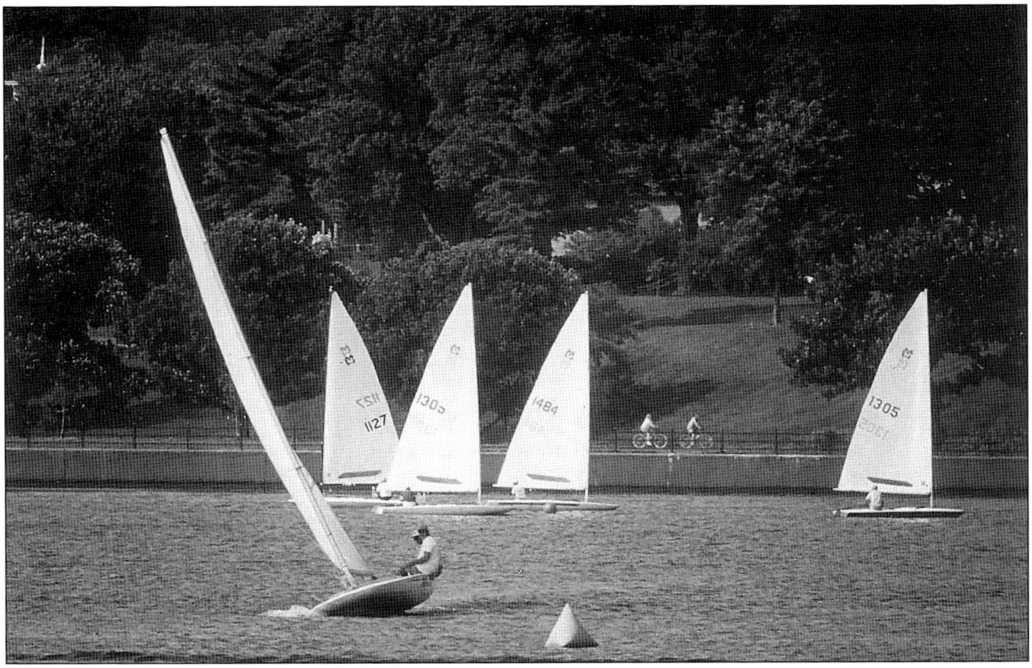

The lakes on the Mississippi allow sailboating, which has become a popular pastime. Here, five sailboats try for wind at Davenport, Iowa.

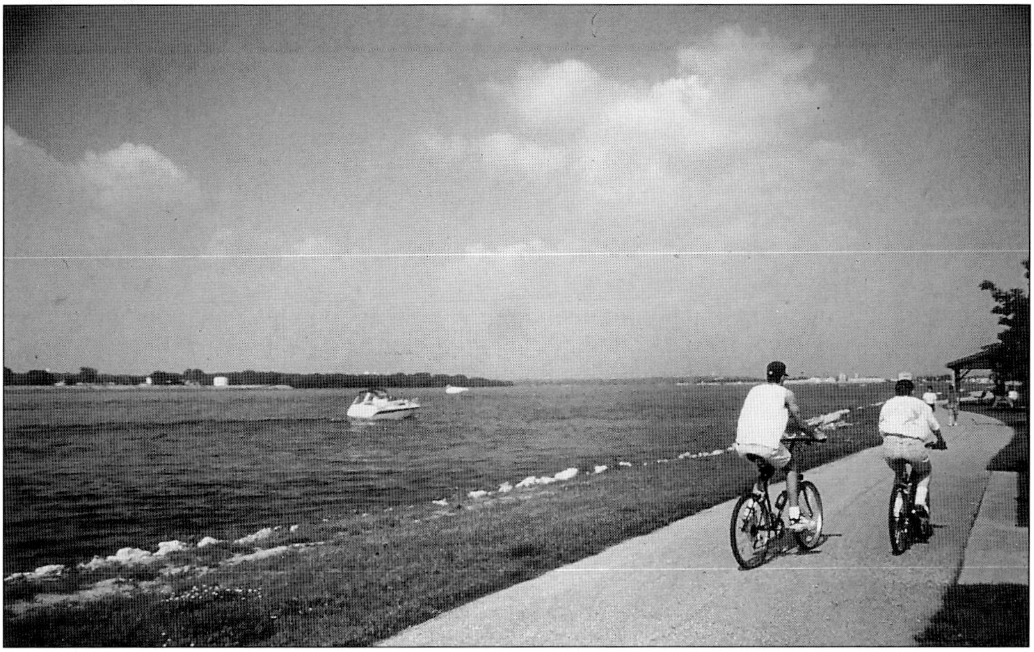

Bike paths and walkways have grown in popularity as shown at Davenport.

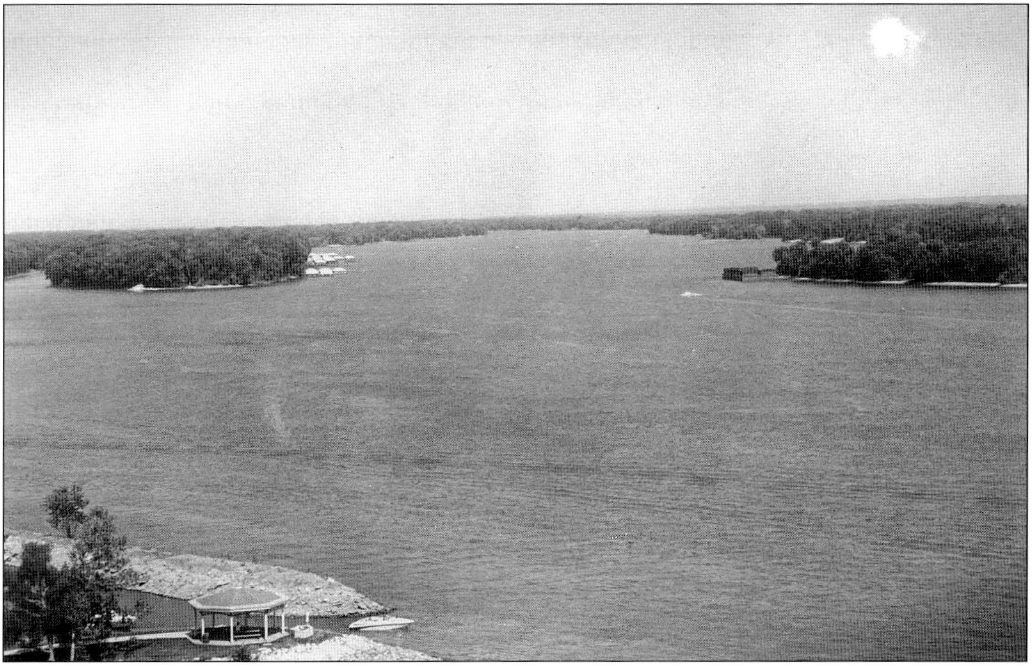

A park in the lower left-hand corner offers the people of Burlington, Iowa, an opportunity to relax at riverside.

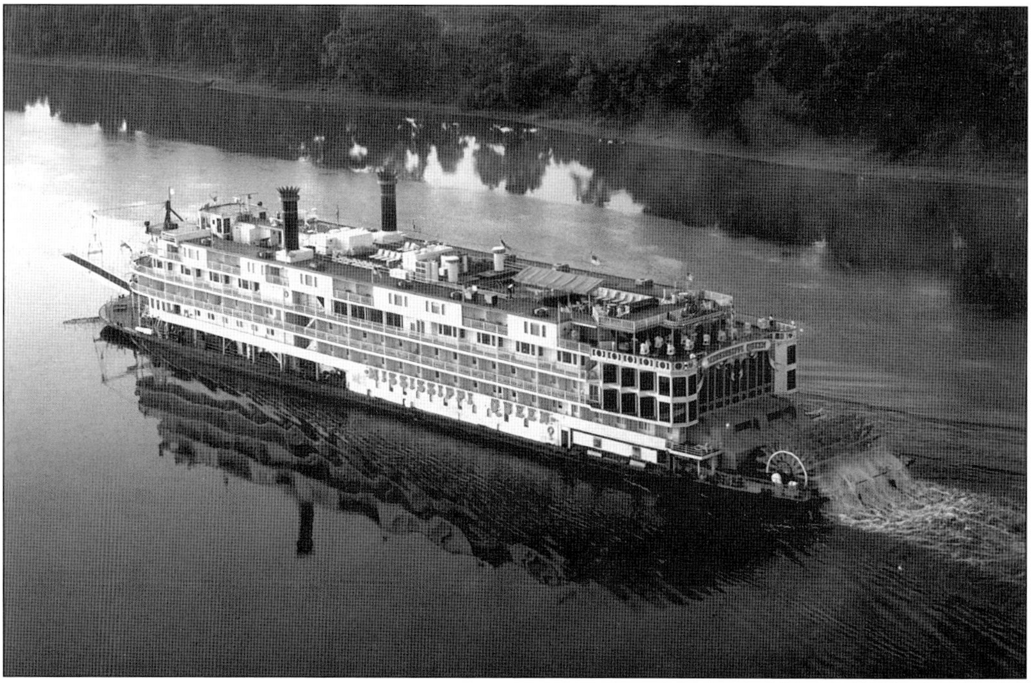

Built in 1976, the *Mississippi Queen* was inspired by Mark Twain's quote: "Someday, they'll build the biggest steamboat the world has ever known. . . And that one shall be the Queen of the Mississippi."

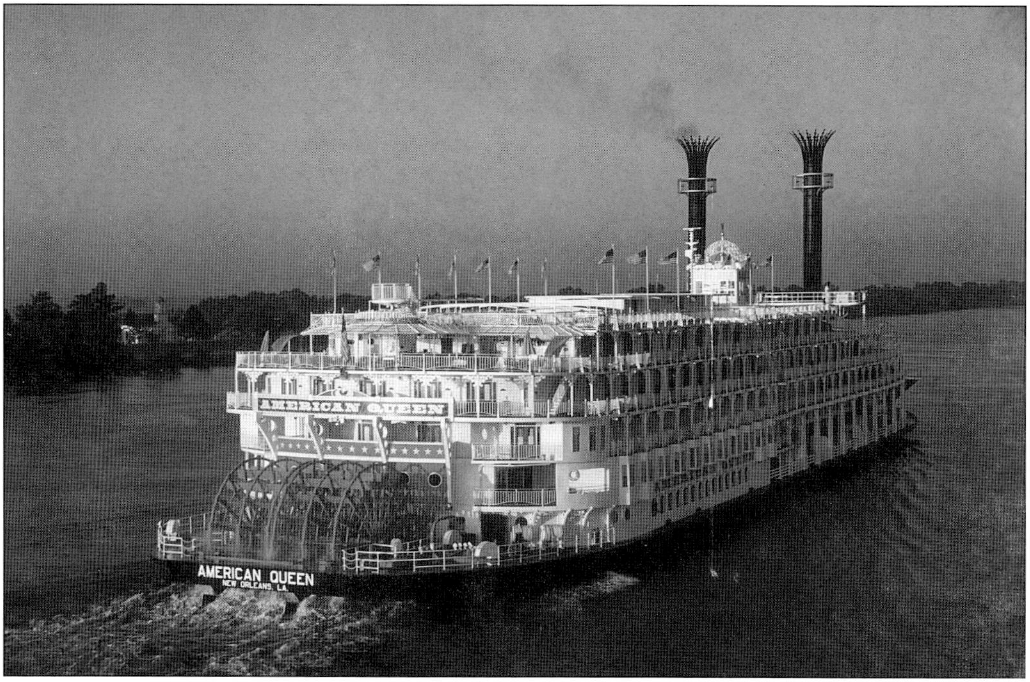

The *American Queen* is the combination of two centuries of steamboatin' design and tradition. Seldom does any of the three *Queens* leave port with less than a full passenger list.